ANIMAL MANAGEMENT AND WELFARE IN NATURAL DISASTERS

The devastating impacts of natural disasters not only directly affect humans and infrastructure, but also animals, which may be crucial to the livelihoods of many people. This book considers the needs of animals in the aftermath of disasters and explains the importance of looking to their welfare in extreme events.

The authors explore how animals are affected by specific disaster types, what their emergency and subsequent welfare needs are and the appropriate interventions. They describe the key benefits of management of animals to populations and discuss preventative measures that can be taken to reduce risk and build resilience. They also include a summary of recent debates and public policy advances on animals in disasters.

The book covers livestock, companion and wild animals, with case studies to show how the concepts can be put into practice. It provides a standalone text for students of disaster studies and management as well as professionals and NGOs who require an entry-level introduction to the subject.

James Sawyer currently works as Director of Programmes at CDP, formally the Carbon Disclosure Project. James was Global Director of Disaster Management for World Animal Protection for nine years, providing strategic direction for the organisation's liaison with national governments, UN agencies and the International Federation of the Red Cross and Red Crescent Societies. During his time at World Animal Protection he responded to many disasters including Cyclone Haiyan in the Philippines, Cyclone Pam in Vanuatu and the Mongolian Dzud of 2016. He has also worked as an international advisor for the British Animal Rescue and Trauma Association (BARTA) and holds an MSc in Emergency Planning and Disaster Management, is a Fellow of the Royal Geographical Society and a Chartered Geographer. James is a specialist in remote field team management with over 20 years of experience.

Gerardo Huertas currently works as Global Director of the Animals in Disasters Campaign for World Animal Protection. He has over 35 years of experience delivering disaster relief for animals across the world, including post-war operations in Nicaragua, Kosovo and Afghanistan, and other events such as the Haiti earthquake and the Indian Tsunami. His work has pioneered innovative solutions to climate change adaptation and disaster risk reduction for animals. His current role focuses on the most disaster vulnerabe countries in the world and campaigning for the integration of animals into national policy frameworks. He holds a MSc in Biology, Human Resources and advanced studies in Law and Project Management.

'The authors have created a critical first text offering accessible and useful reference on such a vital, emerging topic. Their wealth of experience gained in the field of strategic animal rescue is clear and this will no doubt, quite literally, become "the book" for rescue professionals, first responders, aid agencies, NGOs and hopefully governments across both the developing and developed world.'

Jeanette Allen, The Horse Trust, UK

'This book is a great primer for anyone who has work as a first responder or is interested in the importance of animals in disaster management. The survival of animals and their communities are intricately linked. This book is a must read for anyone in civil service, animal protection or disaster management fields.'

Dr Jackson Zee, Disaster Relief Unit,
FOUR PAWS International

'This book represents years of work and dedication to the welfare of animals and the environment. Additionally, it includes the experience and learnings captured and transformed into a reference volume contributing to the understanding of the importance of protecting animals during disaster situations. It explores the efforts made and direct relationships the topic has with various fields, including health, development and the economy, all within the sphere of risk management and human security.'

Dr Nancy Astorga M., School of Veterinary Medicine,
National University, Costa Rica

'The Central American Policy on Comprehensive Disaster Risk Management (PCGIR), alongside the Sendai Framework for Disaster Risk Reduction 2015–2030, establishes the importance and commitment to implement initiatives geared towards reducing the risk and vulnerability associated with livelihoods, including social services and goods related to agriculture and livestock. We consider this publication a must-read for further understanding the vital linkage between disaster risk reduction, resilience and animal protection, considering the cycle that unites human and animal life, from both a socioeconomic and a human and animal rights perspective.'

Roy Barboza Sequeira, Executive Secretary
CEPREDENAC, Guatemala

'In an increasingly anthropocene age we are still far too anthropogenic in our understanding and prioritization of problems. The theme of animal safety during hazard events is illustrative of this. Insufficient has been done to assure animal welfare during crisis, therefore protecting their fundamental "life" rights under hazardous conditions that many times are the result of human action, but which would also protect humans through maintenance of livelihoods based on animals that are critical for near to a billion persons worldwide. This book is key and critical for increasing awareness of this problem.'

Dr Allan Lavell, winner of the UNISDR Sasakawa DRR Award 2015
and former member of the IRDR Science Committee

'Without a doubt a much needed book that will contribute to the creation of resilience.'

Ricardo Mena, UNISDR, Switzerland

ANIMAL MANAGEMENT AND WELFARE IN NATURAL DISASTERS

James Sawyer and Gerardo Huertas

Routledge
Taylor & Francis Group

LONDON AND NEW YORK

from Routledge

First published 2018
by Routledge
2 Park Square, Milton Park, Abingdon, Oxon OX14 4RN

and by Routledge
711 Third Avenue, New York, NY 10017

Routledge is an imprint of the Taylor & Francis Group, an informa business

British Library Cataloguing-in-Publication Data
A catalogue record for this book is available from the British Library

Library of Congress Cataloging-in-Publication Data
Names: Sawyer, James, (Director of programmes), author. | Huertas, Gerardo,
author.
Title: Animal management and welfare in natural disasters / James Sawyer,
Gerardo Huertas.
Description: New York, NY : Routledge, 2018. | Includes bibliographical
references and index.
Identifiers: LCCN 2018003466| ISBN 9781138190665 (hardback) |
ISBN 9781138190696 (pbk.) | ISBN 9781315640907 (ebook)
Subjects: | MESH: Animal Welfare | Disasters | Disaster Planning | Animals
Classification: LCC HV4708 | NLM HV 4735 | DDC 636.08/32—dc23
LC record available at https://lccn.loc.gov/2018003466

ISBN: 978-1-138-19066-5 (hbk)
ISBN: 978-1-138-19069-6 (pbk)
ISBN: 978-1-315-64090-7 (ebk)

Typeset in Bembo and Stone Sans
by Florence Production Ltd, Stoodleigh, Devon, UK

Printed and bound in Great Britain by
TJ International Ltd, Padstow, Cornwall

For Samantha and Rose Marie, we stand on the shoulders of giants

CONTENTS

CONTENTS

PREFACE

In the past, the most common reaction when disaster management for animals was mentioned were looks of puzzlement, often followed by comments about rescuing cats from trees. Times are however changing, and although it still remains both an emerging and poorly understood discipline, more and more consensus is being reached about the importance of animals in disasters. This is one of the most unrealised issues in terms of its potential to help human welfare, and we were drawn to writing this book based on an experience James had when he first came to work within the topic:

> Upon starting in my new sector, my first reaction was to reach for a textbook that explained the principles and offered a guide on how to approach the topic and its management. Back in 2007 the textbook didn't exist and it still didn't over a decade later.

Articles exist, books on veterinary applications in disasters exist and some text exists on animal rescue; but there are no books that look at the overarching principles for those starting out in this field and their application across the range of areas that the topic spans. Critically, in addition to this need is the fact that animal disaster managers have to operate within two differing worlds and make them seamless. The first relates to the discipline as it relates directly to animals (welfare, veterinary science etc.) and the second is the discipline as it finds itself within the human backdrop of a disaster (humanitarianism, development etc.). No book has adequately brought these two worlds together.

This is the first book to attempt to develop a guide for those interested in understanding the place of animals within the risk and the disaster context, and from both the animal welfare and humanitarian perspectives. We explore the importance of animals to disasters and how aiding them and their owners helps the overall effort in disasters and secures better long-term outcomes for survivors. We explore how animals are affected and how the principles of emergency rescue move through disaster assessment and planning aid interventions. Critically we cover new thinking on how to prepare and reduce risk for animals and their owners.

This book is long overdue and badly needed. As population growth, climate change, political instability, displacement of people and natural disasters all collide, we see more marginalised people and more extreme events. Aid alone cannot solve such a complex problem as the longer-term outcomes on development, welfare and prosperity for human survivors are often intrinsically linked to the welfare of animals and yet, while the relationship is understood in principle, the prioritisation and deployment of measures to assist remain poorly resourced.

Collectively we try and distil over 50 years of experience, from large rescue operations in the jungles of Surinam in 1964 (Operation Gwamba), Kosovo in 1991 and Afghanistan in 2001, and the slow realisation that, while important, animal rescue wasn't enough. In the last ten years we have seen the issue emerge at the top tables of government agendas, United Nations resolutions and in the humanitarian sector. We have seen the emergence of a discipline and concurrently, a movement to ensure that animals receive the care they need. Parallel to this we have seen the development of an understanding that helping animals in disasters helps people, securing livelihoods and food security, preventing the degradation of economies and communities, providing companionship, peace of mind and psychological support during difficult times, and supporting health and nutrition.

Now is the time for a textbook to form a base study on the topic. Combining over 45 years of experience developing and delivering aid to millions of animals and representing the issue at the highest levels, the authors' experience and success in the area puts them in a unique position to provide a perspective of where the issue is and how it needs to develop in the future. The authors do not see this as the end point for study, merely a comprehensive overview of the principles of a discipline that requires further development. We very much hope both the whole book and individual chapters inspire readers to further study.

This book can be read as a whole text for use by veterinary students, emergency services, governments, humane groups, development and humanitarian workers or anyone in a role where animals come into their sphere in a disaster (which in truth is essentially everywhere). Additionally, the book has been written in a manner where chapters can be accessed in their own right, to allow individuals to access the overview they require on a topic. We hope it will form an important base text for academic and vocational study and reference.

Much of the book is drawn from the authors' experience and their perspectives on the required direction of the issue. In many areas of the book, there is little text or journal material to draw from but where it is available we have done so. The authors do however feel it important to acknowledge the support of key contributors. Key to the success of communicating the case studies that bring the depth to the book has been the involvement of NGOs such as Humane Society

International and World Animal Protection in the provision of imagery. Critical to the animal rescue element was world leading expertise of the British Animal Rescue and Trauma Association (BARTA) in finding the right level of the chapter which has the potential for so much detail. Many of our arguments on the imperative to protect animals are the result of discussions with many experts, but in terms of helping the authors drive change at national level, Economists at Large require a special mention for their unique ability to take complicated economic theory and make it accessible and impactful for decision makers.

Special acknowledgement needs to be offered to those who have worked with the authors. In the field, often under appalling conditions and with limited support and resources, these individuals have achieved the impossible. In the halls of the UN and the EU and in the government offices they have borne witness and given compelling arguments, using diplomacy to drive long-term action. These individuals are the founders of the discipline, often working against the odds to achieve their goals.

Animals touch every part of our lives, from the food on our plate, to the dog by the fireside and yet in disasters they often suffer and keep on suffering after the initial impact, in silence and as attention is drawn to the human plight of homelessness and short-term aid. Slowly people are understanding that not factoring in the animals into their response and plans can hinder evacuation, prolong PTSD (Post Traumatic Stress Syndrome) and stays in temporary shelters, and permanently damage economies.

But aside from the humanitarian imperative it is important to draw thinking back too to the individual animal need, something at the heart of the discipline of animal welfare. It is not acceptable for cattle to languish in water for weeks at a time with their feet slowly rotting or for livestock to consume grass covered in volcanic ash which grinds down their teeth and settles like concrete in their stomach, eyes and nostrils. Animals are sentient beings, they suffer in the same way as people and as civilised populations, it should be part of our responsibility to ensure the well-being of the creatures we so depend upon.

The next 50 years will see unprecedented challenges of population growth, climate change and urbanisation. Populations will move, often to more marginalised existences. Wherever people are, there will be animals and where these areas are disaster prone, the silent spectre of disasters will continue, sinking everyone into more and more vulnerability and despair.

This future need not be gloomy, however. No longer should you need to own a pet or be a farmer to care about the fate of animals in disasters.

1

WHY HELP ANIMALS IN DISASTERS?

Extreme events strike the world's populations on average 400 times a year. Wind storms, earthquakes, volcanos, tsunami, drought, snowfall and floods are all part of the natural rhythm of the planet we live upon. The phenomenon of disaster however is something a little more than that.

The United Nations International Strategy for Disaster Reduction (ISDR, 2009) defines a disaster as:

> A serious disruption of the functioning of a community or a society involving widespread human, material, economic or environmental losses and impacts, which exceeds the ability of the affected community or society to cope using its own resources.

What this tells us is that disasters have a specific geography and only occur when the impact of an extreme event exceeds the capacity of a population to cope with resources they have available at the time. Disasters happen at a localised, national, regional or global level and as populations grow so do losses.

Natural disasters, such as earthquakes, cyclones, floods and droughts continue to increase in number, scale and complexity. Increased population densities, rapid urbanisation, environmental degradation and climate change, poverty, movement of people and marginalised populations all contribute toward the worsening impacts of natural disasters. During the last decade impacts from disasters have shown increases in economic and social losses, creating displacement and suffering. This trend has led to an increasing reliance on humanitarian aid.

The direct damage costs of disasters alone have risen from US$ 75.5 billion in the 1960s to roughly a trillion dollars in the past decade. This rising trend has long-term social, economic and environmental cost to the people and communities affected by disasters. With the frequency of these events increasing and their associated economic costs spiralling, affected countries and the international community struggle to continue to provide the scale of assistance needed to help communities rebuild and recover.

It is estimated that over 40 million animals are affected every year, experiencing similar suffering and wide-scale loss of life. Many billions of animals are vulnerable to the risk of similar impacts annually.

Disasters don't discriminate between industrialised and developing countries or between rich and poor but the impact of disasters is often greater and longer term for poor communities as their limited resources make them less resilient and less able to recover. The International Strategy for Disaster Reduction (UNISDR, 2009) reports that in contrast to a trend of reduced human mortality in disasters, the 'value of lost assets is increasing exponentially'. When people depend on animal-based livelihoods for their survival, any losses resulting from disasters will be acutely felt. These animal losses have far ranging consequences for owners and communities who rely on them such as: food insecurity, loss of livelihoods, savings and insurance, and a decline in human health.

It is well established that where we find people, we find animals often in far greater numbers. While it is logical to assume that animals suffer in the same way as people, proportionately less is done to address this. This silent disaster that unfolds in the backdrop to the human story is one that is often unseen by those who have the power to make a difference.

While the role of animals in high income countries is possibly clearer, around the world poor people often rely on livestock for much broader purposes. Ironically, those who are closest to the individual animal are not blind to this, they experience it, but regularly are unable to access the support they require for their animals. Globally we see little consideration for animals in government legislation or policy. Hurricane Katrina was the first disaster to highlight to an international audience the plight of animals left behind and the challenges this can pose to people's safety and well-being. The impact of disasters on the welfare of animals and the simple solutions to reduce this are discussed later in this book. People, without a doubt, given the choice, will want to help animals in distress, but in terms of galvanising global understanding and action on the issue, a stronger justification is needed.

When one explores how closely animals' lives are interwoven with our existence, it is not a huge leap to assume therefore that impacts on animals conversely affect us too. The humanitarian imperative expands the principle of humanity to the right to give and receive humanitarian assistance, and animals ought to play a greater role in this. From a global perspective, one of the most pressing needs (in disaster relief) is to improve livestock programming with communities who rely heavily on livestock for their social and economic well-being (LEGS, 2015).

The key barriers to effective animal protection from disasters are:

- insufficient knowledge on animal needs in emergencies and a lack of skills in animal management;

- absence of resources for animal emergencies within the disaster cycle;
- lack of recognition to protect animals when the dependency between people and their animals is so high;
- responsibility for animal emergencies (nationally and internationally) is either unassigned or ineffective;
- absence of integration (people and animals) in emergency management;
- absence of organisation of subsistence livestock owners making emergency management of animals very difficult.

This chapter considers how animals have a huge role to play in this and how this creates powerful arguments for much greater attention of the plight of animals in disaster.

Economics

Disasters are economic events. They damage people, the things that people have accumulated or use to protect themselves and the items that they use to generate income. Mortality has shown a decline while asset loss an increase. The largest proportion of the world's animals are productive assets. Working animals and livestock keep the wheels turning and provide nutrition to billions. This was recently recognised in the Sendai Framework with the inclusion of language recognising the importance of productive assets: livestock, working animals, seeds and tools (UNISDR, 2015).

TABLE 1.1 Direct and indirect values of livestock

	Direct values	Indirect values
Animal sourced foods	Food for consumption Cash	Contribution to year round food security Nutrition – micronutrients that contribute to cognitive and physical development
Transport and draft power	Cash earned or expenses and labour avoided	Improved agricultural output Contribution to connectivity, links to more distant markets
Manure	Fertiliser Fuel	Improved soil fertility Improved agricultural output
Financial aspects	Cash income	Vehicle for saving Form of insurance
Social roles	Fulfilment of social and cultural obligations	Reinforcement of social support networks

Source: Campbell and Knowles (2011).

CASE STUDY: THE ECONOMIC BENEFIT OF EARLY INTERVENTION FOR LIVESTOCK IN DISASTERS

During the month of June in 2012, high levels of rainfall in the NE of India led to flooding in the state of Assam. Assessments highlighted that across the seven most affected districts, 1.7 million large animals and 378,000 small animals were impacted. While only 1,000 animals were estimated to have drowned due to the floods (Nema, 2012), the numbers left suffering were far higher.

The World Society for the Protection of Animals (WSPA) deployed a team to provide post disaster assistance to livestock and, working with regional and district government departments, delivered both acute phase interventions and recovery phase initiatives to address the flooding impacts on these animals. The team's focus was on the Demaji district which suffered some of the worst livestock impacts. The team's immediate response was to focus on the distribution of emergency feed and supportive medicine at the same time as providing veterinary care to injured and sick animals. This intervention was delivered to 56,206 animals owned by 4,265 households in the district.

In late 2013, Economists at Large undertook an assessment of the economic benefits of the intervention through the collection of quantitative and qualitative data on the economic value of the animals to the local economy (Economists at Large, 2014). This data was used to develop a cost–benefit model to estimate the economic importance of the intervention. The total cost of the acute intervention was USD 49,324 of which 78 per cent was for the distribution of rice bran and veterinary medicine with operational costs contributing a further 17 per cent. The benefits of the intervention consisted of the value of the animals assisted, using the net present value (NPV). As markets are volatile in the aftermath of disasters, animals were valued using the intrinsic value of the livestock based on the future benefits they would be likely to provide to their owners.

Knowles and Campbell (2014) found the intervention assisted $96 of livestock production for every $1 spent that supported the health and welfare of animals translating to worth of nearly USD 4.7m to the local economy. They also found that even if only 1 per cent of the treated animals survived the floods the operation would have broken even in terms of costs versus benefits. This study and similar studies are starting to show how powerful early intervention (reducing mortality and morbidity) for animal needs can be in securing existing economies and recovery phases as well as speeding up the overall economic recover post disaster. Aside from the maintenance of productive capacity, these initiatives help reduce de-stocking of herds which cannot be supported or maintained.

FIGURE 1.1 A small herder child helps to protect the flock during a Dzud in Mongolia in 2016

Source: James Sawyer for WAP.

In higher income countries, livestock are largely raised for food products and due to the value and nature of this market are generally well insured against losses. We do see inverse behaviour relating in places to a lack of focus on the well-being of the animal if it is to be replaced but the formal recognition of the value of the animal means that, on the whole, losses are protected against.

The situation in lower income countries, however, is somewhat different. The relationship with livestock is more complex and this is acknowledged by Campbell and Knowles (2011). We find that over 70 per cent of the world's poor rely on livestock for their livelihoods. Proportionately, a higher percentage of low level incomes are derived from livestock (Delgado *et al.*, 1999) and this can often be attributed to how resource poor these people are. In short, livestock allow them to access the resources available to them (forage, water etc.). Livestock are a highly productive use of labour and where formal labour markets don't allow access to women, the elderly and children, livestock greatly aid in providing wealth generation possibilities, food and income (Campbell and Knowles, 2011). These groups happen to be some of the most vulnerable to disasters in low income countries.

Food security

Livestock play a critical role in food security as both a direct and indirect influence and this is often highlighted when disasters strike. Livestock often provide an alternative source of food when crops fail or offer critical additions to limited food supplies. This can often be critical in the aftermath of certain disasters such as floods or storms where cropland may be inundated with seawater or crops destroyed by high winds. Animals often provide a critical fall-back for many communities living marginal existences (Figure 1.1). In the aftermath of Cyclone Haiyan in the Philippines in 2013, many fishing communities had lost their boats and nets, surviving purely on their secondary income breeding backyard animals. While their animals, prior to disaster, were an insurance policy of wealth generation for school fees, first communion and hospital bills, they very rapidly became the only source of both income and, critically, food. The lack of care offered to these animals led to a dramatically reduced level of breeding productivity and a higher rate of mortality, further exacerbating problems for the poorest.

With the trend of increasing urbanisation we are also seeing the rapid growth in peri-urban or 'backyard' animals in cities, even those as large as Mexico City. While these animals also play the role of a backbone of financial resilience to poorer families, in times of disasters they too are critical. The importance of the role of peri-urban livestock was demonstrated clearly in the 2010 Haiti earthquake where, despite widespread destruction, more than 70,000 animals were brought to mobile veterinary clinics for treatment post disaster. Indirectly we see huge inputs into the agricultural economy from draft power, specifically in lower income countries. Post disaster, often with cropping destroyed, the focus on recovering farmland quickly is paramount. Working animals are pushed much harder in the aftermath in roles clearing land and ploughing for new harvests. If these animals are sick, injured or suffering from lowered immune systems and stress from the harder work, then their productivity can drop rapidly, they can succumb to disease and often die (Pradhan *et al.*, 2008).

In Cuba in 2008 four hurricanes struck the island in the space of only six weeks and the authors experienced first-hand the plight of oxen working 8 acres a day when before they were only working a single acre. In Myanmar in the aftermath of Cyclone Nargis in 2008, many areas suffered over 50 per cent mortality of working animals (in some areas more than 95 per cent) which had a dramatic impact on subsequent rice harvests. Farmers battled contaminated land but they were unable to put all of their land into production as it couldn't be tilled without the input of draft animals. Subsequent introduction of new working buffalo into the region without adequate health checks and attention to welfare brought new diseases to existing (and highly stressed) populations of animals and increased levels of mortality. These factors had a huge impact on the rice production of the Ayerwaddy delta, known as the 'rice basket' of the country.

Livestock are therefore critical to not only maintain food production but also perform an important role in smoothing out cyclical differences in food availability for the world's poorest. Poor support for these animals, often worked harder in the aftermath of a disaster, or poorly planned restocking programmes can make a bad situation worsen very rapidly.

Nutrition

The role that animal products play in human nutrition is well known and the science well developed, and as such this section will aim not to cover the detail of this. It is therefore an easy extrapolation to start to draw logical conclusions about how the loss of animals or the decrease in their productive capacity due to injury, death, disease or stress will impact upon the ability of families to consume meat, milk and other products.

In both slow onset and rapid onset disaster there are often perverse reactions to the disaster which means that, initially, uptake of animal products can be higher than under normal conditions. This may be because a cow needs to be slaughtered because of injury or because of a need to de-stock animals rapidly due to the inability to care for them and feed them, or to try and recover some of the market value before their body condition drops too low. This is economically the equivalent of selling the family silverware but equally it can have a similar effect on nutrition when one considers laying hens, milking cows and goats, and any breeding animal. The ability to provide the relevant nutrition in the longer term can make populations more dependent on food aid for longer. If these populations cannot access food aid to fill this nutritional gap, then a deficit will occur in nutrients such as protein.

The easiest sources of certain key nutrients in low income countries is via animal products. Various studies have shown as an example that pastoralist communities derive between 20 and 50 per cent of their energy requirement from milk alone (Webb and Braun, 1994). It is well established that correct nutrition contributes to a higher chance of pregnancy success and maternal health, improved child development, increased immune systems and improved rates of schooling. Bearing in mind that these benefits are greatest in women, the elderly, the sick and children, who represent the most vulnerable groups in disasters, the imperative to better secure the productivity of animals should be seen as vital.

Sadler *et al.* (2012) described how for malnourished children in pastoralist communities who had lost access to milk, the supplementation of their diets with milk had the following effects:

- stabilised nutritional status over the course of the intervention;
- higher average nutritional status for children who consumed some milk during the intervention;
- significantly reduced cost of nutritional support through milk than traditional therapeutic feeding programmes.

Earlier intervention for livestock in the disaster cycle to maintain existing animal populations instead of the preference to replace (re-stocking) is seen as significantly beneficial to livelihoods but would also contribute to the maintenance of nutritional status in the aftermath of disasters with specific reference to vulnerable groups.

Social and cultural

Humankind has lived side by side with animals for millennia; they have guarded our homesteads, tilled the fields and produced for us. During the process of domestication, dependencies have developed in these animals and the responsibility of ensuring welfare has shifted from the animal to the person. Often surprising to those in the Western world is how culturally and socially important livestock can be in other parts of the world. The economic value of an animal itself leads it to be seen as quite significant in many countries. In the Indian subcontinent we see cattle used as dowries for weddings and in India itself the cow is considered sacred. In pastoralist communities in Africa we see significant social status attached to herd size and often different animals associated with different genders and ages depending on their perceived importance.

In Melanesian and Polynesian cultures, the pig is extremely important to the social structures that islanders live within (Figure 1.2). Often pigs are treated better than children and are used for very specific occasions. On the archipelago of Vanuatu certain pig breeds are of very significant value on the island and pig tusks are key for status level ceremonial wear. While often underplayed, the loss of key animals to certain cultures can lead to damage to social structures and sometimes a loss of pride or self-worth. Certainly this was evident in the aftermath of the 2010 Mongolia Dzud when many traditional herders found themselves the new urban dispossessed of Ulaan Batar; not merely a factor of economic loss but a social and cultural loss as well.

FIGURE 1.2 Vanuatu islander struggles to keep his pigs alive in the aftermath of Cyclone Pam in 2015

Source: James Sawyer for WAP.

Human–animal bond

It is often unrealised, but farmers do connect with their animals regardless of their end purpose. Events such as the mass culls in the aftermath of the foot and mouth outbreak in the UK in 2001 led to suicides of farmers regardless of the provision of compensation. After many years of meeting farmers I feel that I can debunk the myth that farmers see animals as merely commodities; they do really care and engage with animals as individuals. Bock *et al.* (2007) described prolonged, higher levels of daily interaction in dairy farming as providing stronger levels of attachment than beef farming, indicating differing levels of attachment with livestock. In terms of finding solutions to the issue, dehumanising farming and farmers in the animal welfare debate is both inappropriate and unproductive.

In the developing world the psychological link can be present with many working animals seen to be as close as family members. Spinsters will refer to water buffalo as their only friend and horses as being close companions, and breeding animals are treated with great affection. In the 2015 volcanic eruption of Fogo volcano in the Cape Verde islands an old lady presented my vet team with a mule, badly infested with mange parasites. When we asked of the history of the animal, she told us that the mule had worked for her for over 20 years but now he was too old to work 'he was just a friend'.

In other parts of the world, the connection with working animals is less tight and thus it is difficult to make generalisations about the human–animal bond with livestock due to it differing between production systems, species and development status. What can be extrapolated is that the loss of animals as productive assets does impact upon farmers psychologically either through worries about loss of income or through the bonds they may build with their animals.

When we look at pet animals, the bond is often stronger still. Many will remember the scenes in the aftermath of Hurricane Katrina in the United States and some will be aware of the problems emergency services had dealing with evacuating people from their homes or with abandoned animals (Irvine, 2009). Animals were a problem at the point of rescue but they were also an issue at the point of shelter where they were to be denied entry by municipal authorities to human shelters. This is a scenario we have seen played out time and time again – during the Bangkok floods of 2009, the Japanese Tsunami of 2011 and many other incidents. During the Haiti earthquake of 2010, people were often refused the ability to have animals in tented camps and many were returning to dangerous collapsed buildings to care for their dogs. Time and again people will brave exclusion zones and cordons to do so and anecdotal evidence shows repeatedly that pet owners can display unexpected, extreme or irrational behaviours due to their concern for their lost animals (Hothersall, 2012). Sadly, there are few statistically relevant studies to back up these anecdotal stories but Hesterberg *et al.* (2012) demonstrated in a study of three Latin American cities that almost three-quarters of pet owners stated that they would attempt to take their animals with them if they were evacuated. Nolen (2006) found similar intent within a survey of the American Kennel Club in 2006.

When we explore evacuation behaviour, Glassey (2010) found in New Zealand that the majority of pet owners either agreed or strongly agreed that they would ignore official warnings and return to the evacuation zone. This was a behaviour also reflected in the Yuba county flood where more than a quarter of pet owning residents who were unable to take their pets in an evacuation returned to the evacuation zone, almost all of them to get pets (Heath, 2000).

Certainly there seem to be practical constraints to the evacuation of animals (either pets or livestock/working animals) ranging from physical transport, handling by untrained rescue staff through to lack of consideration at points of shelter and the care required to maintain such animals. Hesterberg *et al.* (2012) estimate that the need for protection for animals in shelters is at least 20 per cent of the number of households in the area, but is likely to be much higher. When discussing these figures with municipal planners, puzzlement and confusion about what to do with this information is the most common response. If we were to consider a major incident in an affected city population of 100,000 people this would be a minimum sheltering need for 20,000 pets which would overwhelm existing capacity and immediately require temporary arrangements for animals. At its height, Rizzuto and Maloney (2008) reported 2,000 animals per day needing emergency sheltering in the aftermath of Hurricane Katrina.

When we consider the human–animal bond post disaster, it has been proven that animals often help people deal with the loss of life. Often animals are the only family member that a person may have left and thus a form of comfort, but also a trigger for memories to assist with the grieving process. Gerwolls and Labott (1994) found that pet loss can result in grieving or psychological distress and an increased prevalence of depression, and Lowe *et al.* (2009) detailed the significant negative impact that the loss of a pet animal had on psychological distress. This was compounded by an additional effect of age, with younger participants worst affected. Often studies and anecdotal reports detail how people experience the loss of a pet in the same manner as the loss of a close friend or relative.

Gender

The role that animals play in women's lives is now being increasingly recognised and it is emerging how the impact of the loss of their animals can negatively impact upon them. Two-thirds of the world's poorest livestock keepers are women, a factor that is often not well known or acknowledged; thus, the fate of some of the most marginalised animals is intertwined with some of the most marginalised people. Njuki and Sangiga (2013) detail how livestock are a rare source of wealth and asset holding that women in many parts of the world can own or manage. This wealth holding and generation can be assumed to flow more directly to the most vulnerable such as children, the elderly and the sick through this management.

Certainly the role of livestock in the lives of women in poor countries is more complex than merely offering a wealth holding. Working animals often play a critical role in the lives of women, providing draft power for the collection of firewood, water and other daily needs. The Brooke found that a donkey can save a Massai woman 25 hours of labour a week. The lack of care for these animals in the aftermath of a disaster and their potential loss can have profound impacts on women's lives. Baltenweck and MacMillan (2014) were clear to point out that development interventions that increase women's access and rights to livestock, and then safeguard them from theft or untimely death, could help women move their families along a pathway out of poverty. The risk of disasters retarding or altering that trajectory is profound. In terms of reducing risks and improving survival rates in harsh conditions, the Food and Agriculture Organization (FAO, 2012) found that women were more likely to prefer local breeds due to their ease of care. This approach is favoured by those in animal health as being a key decision factor in improving survival rates post disaster.

It remains problematic, however, for women to be able to access the correct measures to sustain their animals, especially during disasters. This is exacerbated by the fact that often these animals and their owners exist in harsh environments where they are at regular risk of drought and theft, and access to veterinary services remains expensive. Indeed it is argued that it could be beneficial to undertake joint aid missions targeting women and livestock in areas where female ownership is high. Baltenweck and MacMillan (2014) detail how a study of interventions of such a nature led to more children and women being vaccinated daily in joint human–livestock vaccination rounds than in campaigns targeting only people.

Engaging women in the protection of animals remains problematic but is critical to assure the survival of the animals under their care and thus their well-being and family livelihoods. Rota and Chakrabarti (2012) attribute this in pastoral communities to the fact that women are marginalised by their limited decision-making role and thus the lack of attention they receive within national development frameworks.

Certainly the role of women is not uniform in livestock keeping globally but in many of the poorest communities it is significant. Lack of attention to this key link in communities such as those involved in pastoralism in both risk reduction and disaster response work can only be detrimental to the well-being of animals and their owners. Equally, however, a better understanding and acknowledgement may in fact offer new, more impactful interventions in these regions with a greater chance of long-term success.

This chapter has shown the value of animals to people and why there should be an imperative to help animals within the humanitarian contexts. The UNISDR reports that in contrast to a trend of reduced human mortality in disasters, the 'value of lost assets is increasing exponentially'. The loss of animals as a key issue is starting to punctuate consciousness on a wider scale, but organisations and governments are struggling to take responsibility for this issue in a manner that sees animal protection as part of the solution. The United Nations recognises that disasters are key barriers to preventing economic growth and the achievement of globally recognised development goals. A lack of care of animals in these situations exacerbates this situation further.

Mortality of animals remains high during and after disaster events. Suffering of animals during and after disaster events is often acute and always prolonged. Decreased productivity of animals combined with the common response for people to push animals harder in food insecure situations exacerbates the suffering of animals. There is a clear and growing base of evidence linking the loss and suffering of animals to economic loss, retarded development, decreased human health, loss of livelihoods, decreased food security, and individual and community security and protection. In addition, the psychological impact of the loss of animals and the significant issues that inappropriate preparedness for animals causes highlight the need for action. In a changing world where issues of increasing loss from disasters, climate change adaptation, more marginalised populations, increased pressure on subsistence farming systems and increasing agricultural production we expect the negative impact to grow if people, communities and governments fail to plan for disasters. Without a focus on animal welfare in disasters, any gains made by the animal welfare sector in the medium term could be threatened by the onset of climate change. In the next chapter we will explore the humanitarian response to provide a guide to an emergency management for animals and to highlight the key touch points for collaboration and coordination.

Further reading

Economists at Large. (2014). *A benefit–cost analysis of WSPA's 2012 intervention in the Dhemaji district of Assam, India*. A report for The World Society for the Protection of Animals, prepared by Economists at Large, Melbourne, Australia. Available at: www.ecolarge.com/wp-content/uploads/2015/08/Economists-at-Large-2014-A-benefit-cost-analysis-of-WSPA's-2012-Intervention-in-the-Dhemaji-district-of-Assam-India.pdf

Heath, S. (1999). *Animal Management in Disasters*. St. Louis, MO: Mosby-Elsevier.

Irvine, L. (2009). *Filling the Ark: Animal welfare in disasters*. Philadelphia, PA: Temple University Press.

References

Baltenweck, G.D. and MacMillan, D. (2014). Livestock and women's livelihood: A review of the recent evidence. In Quisumbing, A., Meinzen-Dick, R., Raney, T., Croppenstedt, A., Behrman, J. and Peterman, A. (eds), *Gender in Agriculture: Closing the knowledge gap* (pp. 209–233). New York: Springer Science & Business.

Bock, B.B., van Huik, M.M., Prutzer, M., Kling Eveillard, F. and Dockes, A. (2007). Farmers' relationship with different animals: The importance of getting close to animals – case studies of French, Swedish and Dutch cattle, pig and poultry farmers. *International Journal of Sociology of Agriculture and Food* 15(3): 108–125.

Campbell, R. and Knowles, T. (2011). The economic impacts of losing livestock in a disaster: A report for the World Society for the Protection of Animals (WSPA), Melbourne, Australia: Economists at Large.

Delgado, C., Rosegrant, M., Steinfeld, H., Ehui, S. and Courbois, C. (1999). Livestock to 2020: The next food revolution. Discussion Paper for the International Food Policy Institute.

Economists at Large. (2014). *A benefit–cost analysis of WSPA's 2012 intervention in the Dhemaji district of Assam, India*. A report for The World Society for the Protection of Animals, Economists at Large, Melbourne, Australia. Available at: www.ecolarge.com/wp-content/uploads/2015/08/Economists-at-Large-2014-A-benefit-cost-analysis-of-WSPA's-2012-Intervention-in-the-Dhemaji-district-of-Assam-India.pdf

FAO. (2012). Invisible guardians: Women manage livestock diversity. FAO Animal Production and Health Paper No. 174. Rome: Food and Agriculture Organization.

Gerwolls, M.K. and Labott, S.M. (1994) Adjustment to the death of a companion animal. *Anthrozoös* 7: 172–176.

Glassey, S. (2010). *Pet owner emergency preparedness and perceptions survey report: Taranaki and Wellington regions*. Wellington: Mercalli Disaster Management Consulting. Available at: http://animalemergency.wikispaces.com/file/view/POEP+Report+Final+2010.pdf

Heath, S.E. (2000). A study of pet rescue in two disasters. *International Journal of Mass Emergencies and Disasters* 18: 361–381.

Hesterberg, U.W., Huertas, G. and Appleby, M.C. (2012). Perceptions of pet owners in urban Latin America on protection of their animals during disasters. *Disaster Prevention and Management* 21: 37–50.

Hothersall, B. (2012). *Perceptions and Practices of Emergency Preparedness amongst Animal Owners*. Bristol, UK: University of Bristol.

International Strategy for Disaster Reduction. (2009). *UNISDR terminology on disaster risk reduction*. Available at: www.unisdr.org/files/7817_.pdf

Irvine, L. (2009). *Filling the Ark: Animal welfare in disasters.* Philadelphia, PA: Temple University Press.

Knowles, T. and Campbell, R. (2014). *A Benefit–Cost Analysis of WSPA's 2012 Intervention in the Dhemaji District of Assam, India.* Melbourne: Economists at Large.

Livestock Emergency Guidelines and Standards. (2015). *Livestock Emergency Guidelines and Standards,* 2nd edn. Rugby, UK: Rugby Practical Action.

Lowe, S.R., Rhodes, J.E., Zwiebach, L. and Chan, C.S. (2009). The impact of pet loss on the perceived social support and psychological distress of hurricane survivors. *Journal of Traumatic Stress* 22: 244–247.

Nema, D.V. (2012). *WSPA Disaster Assessment and Needs Analysis: Assam flood.* Delhi, India: World Society for the Protection of Animals (WSPA).

Njuki, J. and Sangiga, P.C. (eds) (2013). *Women, Livestock Ownership and Markets: Bridging the gender gap in Eastern and Southern Africa.* London and New York: Routledge.

Nolen, R.S. (2006). Congress orders disaster planners to account for pets. *Journal of the American Veterinary Medical Association* 229: 1357.

Pradhan, K.S., Pratt, D., Pritchard, J. and Van Dijk, L. (2008). *Bearing a heavy burden: The importance of the welfare of working horses, donkeys and mules and their mutually dependent relationship with people.* FAO Open Forum on Capacity Building to Implement Good Animal Welfare Practices, Rome. Available at: www.fao.org/fileadmin/user_upload/animalwelfare/BROOKEReport.pdf

Rizzuto, T. and Maloney, L. (2008). Organising chaos: Crisis management in the wake of Hurricane Katrina. *Professional Psychology: Research and Practice* 39(1): 77–85.

Rota, A. and Chakrabarti, S. (2012). *Women and pastoralism.* Rome: IFAD. Available at: www.ifad.org/documents/10180/2a8e6b74-3ddc-4e1c-aa82-cbdf3390d348

Sadler, K., Michard, E., Abdi, A., Shiferaw, Y., Bekele, G., and Catley, A. (2012). *Milk matters: The impact of dry season livestock support on milk supply and child nutrition in Somali region, Ethiopia.* Feinstein International Center, Tufts University and Save the Children, Addis Ababa. Available at: www.savethechildren.net/sites/default/files/libraries/Milk-Matters%20Report%202012.pdf

United Nations Office for Disaster Risk Reduction (UNISDR). (2015). *Sendai Framework for Disaster Risk Reduction 2015–2030.* Available at: www.unisdr.org/files/43291_sendaiframeworkfordrren.pdf

Webb, P. and Braun, J. (1994). *Famine and food security in Ethiopia: Lessons for Africa.* Chichester, UK: John Wiley & Sons.

2

KEY PRINCIPLES AND MECHANISMS OF DISASTER MANAGEMENT

In the last chapter we explored the reasons to build an imperative to consider animals in disasters. Assuming one is convinced, then one must be able to understand animal need, plan accordingly and deliver the right measures to save and protect animal life. Within disaster response, intrinsic is aligning with existing efforts for people in disasters both for efficiency and efficacy. This chapter addresses the basic understanding a disaster responder should have of the principles and mechanisms of disaster management and how the animal issues are both perceived and currently managed.

Anyone involved in the discipline of disaster management as a responder, veterinarian or manager should first obtain a solid understanding of the principles, frameworks and structures that underpin disaster management. This is essential considering the scale of the infrastructure and resources involved in disaster management. A responder shouldn't operate without some coordination with this structure and in many cases wouldn't be able to effectively or safely do so without facing penalties. If engaged effectively, the consideration of government responses and humanitarian agency effort offers great benefits to effective working as a responder. For example, the Red Cross in Mongolia in 2016 carried animal feed supplies for the authors' response work offering access to a more sophisticated logistics pipeline and dramatically reduced costs for the operation, as well as allowing for aid to be accurately targeted to animals and people concurrently. In 2008 the authors worked with a quarter of the government veterinarians in Cuba to deliver aid to animals stricken after four hurricanes hit the island in succession, allowing enhanced access and a much greater footprint of activity. One should also remember that in many circumstances not engaging with these systems may prevent any kind of legal authorisation to operate. Understanding the legal framework for a response in a country is a critical first step. It is therefore a practical benefit, often a legal requirement and definitely best practice to engage with existing disaster management mechanisms. Understanding humanitarian practice fully is beyond the scope of this chapter; rather the aim of this section is to cover key terminology, functions and concepts that animal welfare actions need to interact with in order to assure maximum effectiveness. There are many books written on the issues of humanitarian work; this chapter aims to not cover the topic in great depth, but rather to offer the starting point for more reading and consideration.

The last 30 years have seen a continual evolution of the humanitarian approach, both at national and international levels, but two key factors relating to animal welfare should be considered when understanding this area. Historically animals haven't been included as a priority in disaster response and, with the exception of sub-Saharan Africa, not in emergency planning with any effectiveness or consistency. Chapter 1 demonstrated the importance of animals to post disaster recovery and the problems caused by not considering them within the response effort. Practically, the lack of focus on animal welfare continues to hinder humanitarian efforts. A lack of consideration within urban disaster management leads to increased risk for victims and rescuers alike, driving undesirable human activity in danger zones, unnecessary unrest at evacuation centres and further compounding emotional and physical recovery. In rural areas a lack of attention on the welfare of animals compromises the primary or secondary livelihoods of poor people, driving longer term stays in temporary accommodation and expensive restocking programmes. Consequently, restocking programmes do not adequately consider effective animal husbandry, with increased rates of mortality of restocked animals and reduced benefit to human victims. The authors estimate as little as 5 per cent of humanitarian aid focused is in this area despite emerging evidence showing how cost effective this approach is in helping people recover and rebuild their lives. In developing countries, the humanitarian system has struggled to work effectively in coordination with government emergency response and planning functions in the aftermath of major disasters whereas this partnership is generally more advanced and effective in developed countries. This means those delivering work for animal need in disasters may have to be able to reflect and work within two systems rather than one synchronous one in order to be effective; often acting as a bridge between the government and humanitarian systems. Positively, progress is now being made in recognising the vulnerability of animals and animal owners, leading to increased focus on protecting farm, working and pet animals. Moving toward a single synchronous system offers humans and animals far more efficient and effective response and recovery.

Finally, it is important to consider that conceptually, an animal responder faces a challenge when engaging with humanitarian entities as the concept of sentience and welfare are not well understood and this often leads to well-meaning programmes including animals failing. In its simplest sense the more the shift occurs from seeing animals as inanimate objects of aid or development, to understanding how meeting their welfare benefits the overall aims of a programme, the more effective animal focused aid will become. Progress has been made in this area with agencies such as the International Federation of the Red Cross and Red Crescent (IFRC), but a sector-wide shift away from this approach promises great benefits.

The history of disaster management

While the principles of humanitarianism go back many hundreds of years, the formation of a professionalised approach to disaster management really emerged on the international scene in the 1960s through the United Nations General Assembly resolutions relating to large natural disasters in Iran and the Caribbean (UNISDR, n.d.). However, disaster management was response focused until the 1970s when the conceptions of risk reduction began to emerge.

By the 1970s, the need for coordination of disaster response was recognised and this led to the creation of the United Nations Disaster Relief office (UNDRO). Still, however, the focus of effort was primarily on relief and the concept of management systems in disasters was at an early stage. During the 1980s, the relief initiatives and the systems relating to them became further formalised and the more rounded concept of disaster management formed. This led to a move toward a more holistic definition and approach to disaster management focusing on developing a cycle that included other elements than simple disaster response (Coetzee and van Niekirk, 2012).

In the aftermath of the Kobe earthquake in Japan, the disaster management community began to focus discussion on disaster risk reduction and preparedness and 1990–2000 was declared the International Decade for Natural Disaster Risk Reduction. This drew focus on early warning systems and reducing risk through building codes and planning. In 1994 the Yokohama Strategy and Plan of Action (UNISDR, 1994) was adopted while the phenomenon of El Niño was first given attention on the global stage. Natural disasters were declared a major threat to the socio-economic stability of nations and prevention was seen as the main solution to this. The first decade of the second millennium saw the birth of the International Strategy for Disaster Reduction (ISDR) which led to the formation of a new UN inter-agency task force and secretariat with clear sustainability objectives. At the same time, the international effort was designing models for better coordination of effort with 1993 seeing the launch of the United Nations Disaster Assessment and Coordination (UNDAC) system that included, for the first time, the concept of a cluster-based approach.

The Indian Ocean Tsunami of 2004 created an unprecedented challenge to the disaster community both in terms of its impact and geography. The resulting issues with coordination cemented UNDAC's role and the cluster system became consistently adopted. The aim was to improve information sharing and avoid the duplication of effort. While global clusters would run permanently, disaster specific clusters would be activated as necessary. The concept of the cluster coordination system is explained below. In 2005 a World Conference on Disaster Reduction was convened in Kobe, Japan, to review the past and to set the global Disaster Risk Reduction (DRR) agenda for the next decade. In the wake of the Indian

Ocean tsunami, this event saw the birth of the Hyogo Framework for Action, 2005–2015: building the resilience of Nations and communities to disasters (UNISDR, 2005).

The Hyogo Framework for Action (HFA) initiated a decade-long effort to reduce the toll disasters bore on human life, to adjust the concept of natural disasters to one that recognises the role of humans in exposure and vulnerability, and to introduce the concept of Disaster Risk Reduction as the most important centre of most efforts. Hyogo also marked the first documented instance of discussions relating to animals at risk and animal welfare during disasters. However, the small workshop titled 'Intersection of Animal and Human Issues in Disasters' sadly had little tangible influence on the final resolution. The lack of impact came from the lack of visibility of animal need and knowledge of how this provided positive and complementary benefits to humanitarian beneficiaries. These benefits and opportunities only became realised as the focus on the full disaster cycle developed.

During the first half of the 1990s, the struggle to develop a more comprehensive risk management approach was evident, and Civil Defence departments, humanitarians and development agencies around the globe slowly bought into the concept of risk management and disaster risk reduction, shifting their resources into the different stages of the disaster management cycle.

This global resolve served as a focus to the various UN agencies (led by the International Strategy for Disaster Reduction – UNISDR); while the focus of some member states and international organisations to favour the notion of the management of risk beyond the emergency response level toward a more resilient, sustainable development much earlier came more into focus at this point. The picture was not uniform however with many developed countries achieving frameworks while developing countries often lacked the resources to realise this (Coppola, 2015). In practice, approaches of risk reduction and disaster response are not as easy to combine as they would seem. Rescue and relief personnel are operationally structured to move at a fast pace, meeting immediate needs, while risk reduction needs time (years), patience, perseverance and belief in the method and in people.

It was the media frenzy related to Hurricane Katrina in 2005 that really brought the plight of animals in disasters into the public domain. Stories of people refusing to evacuate without pets and the mass sheltering of animals by American humane groups directly led to changes in federal legislation to include animals in emergency planning in the United States. The value of companion animals to people and the risky actions they were willing to take, drove action to consider these issues

The last few years of the first decade of the new century saw how financial stakeholders such as banks, insurance companies, ministries of finance and development started to plan for a safer, more resilient future through less vulnerable development models. This sparked the beginning of wiser investment in risk reduction and resilience.

As the HFA mandate came to an end in March 2015, a new world conference was convened in Sendai, Japan. This meeting, near to the site of the most recent tsunami and the Fukushima nuclear plant was attended by nearly 50,000 delegates and cemented the Sendai Framework for Disaster Risk Reduction as a 15-year plan (2015–2030) (UNISDR, 2015). Key to this event was the inclusion of core language in the document stating the need to protect 'Productive assets: Livestock, Working Animals, Tools and Seeds'. This inclusion of these animals formally acknowledges their productive importance for the first time in global disaster policy, critically influencing national approaches to how to focus their effort on the issue. Additionally, for the first time there will be global measures of national and non-state action relating to the protection of these animals. Both the acknowledgement of the benefit and the driver of being measured against action to protect these assets should create a powerful driver in the right direction.

The present day

As we head toward 2020 and a new decade, we see an increasing focus on disaster risk reduction and preparedness at state level with global frameworks and key documents penetrating the humanitarian sphere, helping to drive the animal welfare issue forward. In 2016 the OIE (World Organisation for Animal Health, 2017) ratified global guidelines for Chief Veterinary Officers on disaster management and, while take up from the OIE isn't mandatory, these broad, high-level guidelines, largely focused on capacity, risk reduction and preparedness, form useful advice to governments in readying themselves for their next major event. The Sendai Framework for Disaster Risk Reduction is a 15-year, non-binding agreement recognising that the State has the primary role in reducing disaster risk but that responsibility should be shared with other stakeholders including local government, the private sector and others. Published in 2015, but finalised in 2016, the follow-up global framework to the Hyogo Framework for Action contains guidance for governments to protect 'Productive assets: Livestock, Working Animals, Tools and Seeds'. This language is already influencing governments to think about the resilience of their livestock and how to better protect them from disaster. At the user level the Livestock Emergency Guidelines and Standards (LEGS, 2015) is well established and being deployed in the field, especially in sub-Saharan Africa, and has become a companion document to the SPHERE standards, a key humanitarian publication.

It is undoubted that two decades of focused humanitarian effort has contributed to a trend of decreasing mortality but it has done little to arrest the increase in the loss of assets. We have experienced some of the most severe disasters on human record concurrently with shifts in media coverage of disasters with great intensity. In the last 15 years we have seen significant disaster events causing massive destruction of assets and high mortality in the Indian Ocean Tsunami, Hurricane Katrina (New Orleans), Hurricane Sandy, Irma and Maria (Caribbean and US mainland), Earthquakes in Port-au-Prince (Haiti), Sichuan province (China), Tohoku (Japan) and Kathmandu (Nepal), and Cyclones in Bangladesh (Cyclone Sidr), Philippines (Cyclone Haiyan), Vanuatu (Cyclone Pam) and Myanmar

(Cyclone Nargis). Alongside these events were droughts, floods and other extreme weather events that led to significant animal losses. Often these events don't even make the news; in a single Dzud event in Mongolia in 2010 it is estimated 11 million head of livestock perished over a six month period, having a dramatic impact on both livelihoods and national economies. In an age of instant access to communication, disasters have become both immediate and increasingly visual. At the same time the humanitarian community continues to struggle with the impact of the scale of these. In 2015 there are more people displaced than at any time since the Second World War and the combined shadow of poverty, conflict and the emerging challenges of climate change continue to drive people (specifically the poor) into increasingly precarious and vulnerable situations. The United Nations High Commission for Refugees (UNHCR) found that by the end of 2016 more than 65 million people were forcibly displaced. Where people go, they take their animals.

Core principles

The disaster cycle

The disaster cycle is a concept embraced as a core principle within disaster management. While its phases can be broken into subgroups and don't 'start and finish' as visually depicted, it remains a useful overlay for management. In practice what we see when we overlay the disaster cycle on an event is not a perfect fit. For example, a homeowner will not wait for the end of the relief phase before he starts rebuilding his home; rather, this reconstruction phase may start as early as day one concurrent with acute needs. This considered, the cycle has far more use for disaster managers to provide a structure to plan activity and initiatives before and after a disaster event. It is important to note than there are regional and agency variations on the model, thus for ease of interpretation for animals the United States version is used here (Figure 2.1).

FIGURE 2.1 There are many variations of the disaster management cycle but, for the purposes of this book, this figure highlights the relevant components

Disaster response

Disaster response is the function of the disaster cycle focused on meeting immediate (acute) needs and is normally considered to contain elements of immediate rescue and then assessment and delivery of aid. The immediate rescue phase, which can be counted in days, is normally undertaken by local assets (both convergent and emergent) but in certain technical rescue environments, rapid response rescue teams may be activated nationally, regionally and internationally. Formal national rescue teams will adhere to the International Search and Rescue Guidelines (www.INSARAG.org) and can often be found in a compound where national teams will congregate to operate from. These teams often have early stage intelligence of the scale and nature of the animal problems and, critically, based upon their early stage surveys of urban areas and animal responders should familiarise themselves with the INSARAG building marking codes to assure their own safety and avoid duplication of effort.

After the immediate rescue period (and often during), effort is focused on needs-based assessment and the delivery of targeted aid, normally in the areas of food, water, shelter, evacuation and medical care. Animals experience the same needs as people and thus require similar responses. Sometimes these can be complementary and sometimes these need to be delivered by technical specialists. Realistically, while nominally seen to last for the first four weeks post disaster, acute needs can extend to three months (and beyond in a migration crisis or complex emergency). All work undertaken in this phase (except immediate rescue) should be based on a rapid Disaster Assessment and Needs Analysis (DANA). This ensures that personal opinions and organisational (and funder) agendas do not supersede the actual need of the beneficiaries. For animals, this assessment should be undertaken by specialists trained and experienced in understanding either livestock or companion animal need. More detail on how to conduct such an assessment for animals can be found in chapter 5 of this book. In terms of reducing mortality and suffering for animals to a minimum, action during this phase is critical.

Early recovery

Early recovery is a concept being used by some agencies and governments to acknowledge that people don't wait to start rebuilding their lives. Some models have defined phases (i.e. FEMA in the US) while others define recovery as a phase starting at the same time as response (UK government). This focuses on people rebuilding their lives and infrastructure either with or without external support. The authors' experience is that people immediately seek recovery for their animals either because they are seen as part of the family or because they are essential for their livelihoods. As such, for the purpose of this book, early recovery is discarded as a distinct phase as the entire recovery phase starts within hours of the event.

Disaster recovery

This is the process of rebuilding and rehabilitation. Often this merges in the medium term with development initiatives and principles but the earlier stages of a disaster will focus on getting people back on their feet. Key initiatives will include rebuilding or rehoming, restarting education and public health or securing and rebuilding livelihoods. This phase is longer term and often more costly. Depending on the initiative and agency (as well as the scale of the disaster) this can last between three months and several years. During the recovery phase we see critical need in supporting animal health and reducing stress from new conditions or increased work as well as the rebuilding of infrastructure to support animal shelter or health. As with the response phase, this approach should be needs based, as opposed to the often used approach in animal welfare of utilising donor funds given for the disaster to further or set up new streams of existing pre-disaster work (e.g. animal population control).

Disaster mitigation

Disaster mitigation measures are those that eliminate or reduce the impacts and risks of hazards through proactive measures taken before an emergency or disaster occurs. This is an area of the disaster cycle that is often integrated into preparedness or risk reduction but can stand alone as an important initiative. An example of this would be insurance against the loss of assets. This is often a difficult area to separate from preparedness and risk reduction and is often forgotten in the aftermath of disasters. Lessons learned, however, about risk and vulnerability are not yet fully integrated into insurance mechanisms as an example. Disaster mitigation is currently a difficult topic for animal welfare, especially on the issue of insurance. Experience from countries such as Argentina and Brazil highlight that insurance of livestock can drive behaviours where owners seek not to prepare for or reduce risks for their animals knowing that the insurance will pay out if they die. Until insurance companies work to include risk reduction and preparedness measures within policy stipulations to drive behaviour change, this situation is unlikely to change.

Disaster preparedness

This phase of the cycle is focused on the state of readiness to contain the effects of a disastrous event. This could be of personal capacity and resilience or service capacity that can provide rescue, relief or recovery. Preparedness is fundamentally focused on increasing capacity to cope, thus reducing the overwhelming nature of a disaster on persons, agencies and government functions. Preparedness is an issue that is sorely lacking for animal welfare. We find most government veterinary departments poorly equipped and trained to cope with the specific conditions of disasters and lacking mobility or unable to convert their normal activities to meet the needs of a post disaster landscape. Often emergency services also suffer the same lack of preparedness and most remain unprepared to deal with animal welfare situations as they are found. Integration into emergency coordination mechanisms continues to be an issue for animal focused agencies and there is a significant capacity gap in terms of resources overall compared to the scale of the issue. Preparedness requires long-term thinking, investment and focus on an event that hasn't yet happened or may never happen and this can drive decisions counter to the imperative.

Risk reduction

Disaster risk reduction (DRR) is a systematic approach to identifying, assessing and reducing the risks of disaster. A hazard is something that has the potential to cause damage or harm while a risk is the outcome of that hazard causing damage or harm; normally measured by assessing the impact of the severity and likelihood. DRR focuses on identifying hazards, assessing risk and then implementing measures to reduce either the severity or the likelihood of these hazards causing harm. Studies of the cost–benefit of risk reduction programs show that many multiples (up to 18 times) are more cost effective than disaster response. It must be noted, however, that they are more difficult to achieve success with, as they are longer term, often more expensive and require more buy-in from individuals, agencies and government structures.

Historically, risk reduction measures have been poor fundraisers for agencies working in the humanitarian sphere. Historically, most humanitarian organisations have been built around emergency fundraising and strong evidence shows that people need urgency to spur them to donate in numbers. The lack of urgency with risk reduction measures combined with the difficulty of asking people to make a donation for agencies to invest in a better future are much harder asks, often more the domain of development agencies, and thus these groups have struggled with wide-scale uptake. Within the development sector there has been a wider uptake of DRR largely due to vulnerabilities to disasters often finding their root cause in development issues. As an example, a root cause of a disease outbreak may be poor sanitation and public health prior to a disaster. For animals, risk reduction could involve risk mapping of community resources or the building of raised feed towers to protect fodder from the effects of flooding. Often the solutions are simple and highly replicable, meaning focus on these areas is highly cost effective. The issue remains, however, that again human nature dictates that thinking about these measures prior to a disaster is not common; rather, the issues (and the funds) are often considered only in the aftermath of a disaster.

Types of disaster

Natural disasters

While the term 'natural' disaster is still used widely in the media to describe natural events that cause a disaster, within the disaster management community this concept is debated. Within this debate, the anthropogenic view is that disasters such as extreme weather events, tectonic activity and asteroid strikes have occurred throughout the history of the planet and before the dawn of humankind; thus the term natural disaster should still be considered. However, some who take the United Nations definition of a disaster literally argue that disasters can only occur where a human population is involved, and thus their actions prior, during and after a disaster have some influence on the nature of its impact.

The authors would draw a perspective somewhere between these views. An extreme weather event in an area of the globe where humans aren't present can still devastate animal populations (wild or otherwise) and thus would still be a disaster within this context. This considered, human actions do have a large influence upon disaster impact and thus while the first blow can be caused by the event, the scale of the impact is determined at least in part by the nature of human actions. When we consider domesticated animals, the hands of people largely control animal fate in their placement, feeding, reproduction and health. Thus humans are responsible for animal vulnerability and their exposure to risk. For the purpose of this book, the authors will use the term to describe disasters caused by natural forces.

Technological disasters

This term refers to disasters caused by the use, misuse or malfunction of human designed technologies. Rarer in nature than natural disasters these can include biological, chemical or radiological agents and it is argued that war and post-conflict scenarios should be equally referred to as technological disasters. These disasters often create complexity in the rescue and recovery phases because of contamination, security or other after-effects and can occur in the aftermath of a natural disaster as a consequence of damage or evacuation caused by these events. An example of such a consequential technological disaster would be the Fukushima nuclear disaster caused by damage from an earthquake and tsunami in 2011. This event led to a large-scale evacuation and a lasting exclusion zone with many thousands of abandoned animals within. Another recent technological disaster of relevance to this book was the Ajkai Timföldgyár toxic spill in Hungary in 2010 in Veszprem county, where toxic sludge from an aluminium facility contaminated villages and the Danube river, causing death and chemical burns to people and animals.

Slow onset

This is a disaster caused by events creating a slow build-up of effects. Normally these have less immediate impact in terms of intensity but a longer-term impact, often on a larger scale. Often damage to infrastructure is limited while the impacts on livelihoods and well-being are often protracted and difficult to return to normality. If identified early, preparedness and risk reduction measures have the time to reduce impact but largely these events remain difficult to deal with, often because they 'creep up' rather than appear with sudden ferocious impacts, meaning agencies and governments struggle to recognise the early stages and thus fail to prioritise them. Largely environment focused, most progress has been made in drought early warning and response, specifically in the East African region with long-term forecasting helping greatly. This considered, recent droughts have shown the specific problems associated with dealing with the animal issue within these situations and the impact this has on people. The Kenyan droughts of 2014 and 2017 have shown some progress in early warning and support directly to people, but we still see significant impact for animals and further downstream for people's livelihoods. The nature of slow onset disasters means that pastoralists are faced with a slow decrease in the condition of their animals which leads to a decreasing price for their animals. This is at least partly due to the traditional practices of pastoralists who will increase herd sizes during good periods to offset losses during the bad periods. This discourages pastoralists from selling or destocking early, believing in the natural resilience of their herd numbers; but as the condition of all animals drops, they see the value of their herd drop and are not able to realise any release of this value to help with their situation. This behaviour becomes a negative feedback loop as body conditions of animals drop further and thus the price drops until the animals are in such poor condition they die or are sold in desperation, offering very little value to the owners. Much more focus is required on early phase intervention for livestock to bolster body condition, encouraging destocking of parts of herds to better allow key breeding stock to survive and thus better secure livelihoods. We see similar human behaviour in slow onset floods and cold weather events where the impact is so slow and creeping that animal owners cling on to try and ride out the event, rather than take more direct measures to secure their livelihood. Often slow onset disasters don't make it into the media until conditions are very dire for people. As the 2010 and 2016 Dzuds in Mongolia demonstrated, where these events have a huge impact on animals but limited mortality or immediate suffering for people, they may not even enter the public consciousness at all, compounding the inability of agencies to raise funds to provide support.

Rapid onset

These are disasters that arrive suddenly with very little or no warning. Intense in impact and leaving behind significant damage to infrastructure, loss of life and disruption. These disasters require a greater focus on disaster response with often more short-term acute need (Figure 2.2). Rapid onset disasters are regularly covered in the media and attention is increasingly drawn to the animal issue as the human drama story subsides. The intensity of the impact on human welfare often drives significant issues for welfare as humans struggle to meet even basic needs for themselves. Abandonment is common, leaving animals to suffer. Often facilities for commercial farming, such as generators and even structures cease to function

FIGURE 2.2 Vehicle travelling in newly laid ash in the aftermath of the Fogo Island
Volcanic Eruption in 2014

Source: James Sawyer for WAP.

and the abandonment by owners can mean large numbers of animals suffer and
die. In the aftermath of Cyclone Pam in Vanuatu, commercial chicken houses
were abandoned leaving hens to die from dehydration and heat stress. Animal
owners often simply lack the means to feed or shelter their animals, similarly
leading to long-term suffering and death for animals, but owners may also eat their
commercial stock out of desperation, which could be considered akin to selling
the family silverware in terms of its impact. We may also see animal owners in
desperate situations where they have loans secured against farms that they cannot
meet and as animals die they enter a spiral of debt or as they lose their working
animals they pull their children out of schools to help in the fields as a replacement.
The impacts of these events are covered in more detail elsewhere in this book but
the shock of fast onset events drives behaviours critical to consider when dealing
with animals.

Complex disasters

These events have complex root causes and have a historic nature. Often the
exacerbating factor is an armed conflict that leads to targeted destruction of civilian
lives, assets and capacities. They are usually long term, protracted and very difficult
to deal with. An example would be the Ethiopian famine of the 1980s which
contrary to common belief was less about food shortages and more to do with
access to food, agricultural policy and forced resettlement under the government

anti-insurgency programme. Animals may often find themselves in the middle of these events and their importance to livelihoods used against them as was seen in the Tana river conflict in Kenya in 2012 where animals were attacked rather than people due to their worth. Often in complex emergencies, people are displaced and the movement of people leads to the movement of animals. In a report to UNHCR on 12 displacement camps in Chad, Hulme *et al.* (2008) found livestock numbers in camps underestimated possibly by as much as 300 per cent and that potentially 300,000 head of livestock were posing problems that weren't being adequately managed. They found livestock competing for resources with local populations, leading to inter-ethnic conflict and causing environmental degradation, a risk of disease from the accumulation of herds and animals being grazed by children outside of the camp increasing their vulnerability. Other anecdotal evidence the authors have received from first-hand accounts of camp managers shows a risk to the security of the camp from criminal elements due to the value of the livestock, and cases in the Sudan where people registering in camps walk out and back into dangerous areas because of a lack of provision for their animals. There is no doubt that complex emergencies create significant challenges for agencies and beneficiaries alike and this remains an area lacking a coherent approach for the management of animals.

Management of disasters internationally

The United Nations plays a key role in the coordination and management of disasters under which most global response to these events occurs. During a disaster the UN activates and deploys assessment teams from the Office of Coordination of Humanitarian Affairs (UNOCHA). These UNDAC teams aim to ascertain the level of damage and then the need that has to be met. UN agencies with specific sector tasking (i.e. The UN FAO for agriculture) will launch their own assessment teams to focus on the detail of their specialist area. This leads to international appeals for funding and a joint reaction from UN agencies such as World Food Programme and the United National High Commission on Refugees as well as international non-governmental organisations (NGOs), such as IFRC or Oxfam (Inter-Agency Standing Committee, 2012).

Key agencies

UN Office for the Coordination of Humanitarian Affairs (UNOCHA)

The United Nations Office for the Coordination of Humanitarian Affairs is charged with strengthening the coordination of humanitarian assistance. UNOCHA chairs the Inter-Agency Standing Committee (IASC) charged with ensuring inter-agency decision making for emergencies, the delivery of needs assessments, consolidation of appeals, field coordination and development of humanitarian policy. In large or complex emergencies, OCHA will designate a humanitarian coordinator to oversee the UN response. OCHA also offers a 'surge' capacity to send experts to coordinate work such as an International Search & Rescue Advisory Group (INSARAG) for technical rescue, plus on-site coordination, and logistics. For animals, engagement with UNOCHA directly isn't necessary but they do form the umbrella of coordination for the event and also coordinate the delivery of funding appeals and the dissemination of this.

United Nations High Commission for Refugees (UNHCR)

The United Nations High Commission for Refugees is mandated to lead and coordinate international action for the worldwide protection of refugees and to work with the stateless and in certain circumstances, the internally displaced. UNHCR is often involved in the sheltering of people in temporary camps post disaster. Normally when people move to points of shelter, they will take animals and depending on the nature of the people, the disaster and the environment, this could be livestock or pets.

United Nations Development Programme (UNDP)

The United Nations Development Programme normally works with host governments on development programmes and is the UN representative of all UN agencies in a country. The head of UNDP in a country is normally the resident coordinator who may coordinate UN activities in a disaster if a humanitarian coordinator isn't appointed. UNDP will be heavily involved in post disaster recovery in the long term and will be a key agency to engage with in the development of risk reduction and preparedness plans.

World Food Programme (WFP)

The World Food Programme assesses food needs in many disasters and mobilises food aid. The WFP is the co-chair of the global food security cluster which oversees matters relating to agriculture. While WFP is not directly engaged in animal welfare, their influence on the food security cluster shouldn't be underestimated and it wouldn't be difficult to envisage a future where animal and human food aid might be delivered together in certain circumstances. WFP have taken the approach in recent years of agreeing aid in kind logistics support to some animal welfare agencies such as World Animal Protection (WAP).

United Nations Food and Agriculture Organisation (UN FAO)

The Food and Agriculture Organisation of the United Nations undertakes agricultural needs assessments post disaster and is the focal point for post disaster agricultural recovery work. The FAO has a critical role in coordinating emergency appeals through the UN system based on its needs analysis. The inclusion of livestock assessments in their work and the request for funds for the stabilisation, support and rebuilding of livestock related issues post disaster are critical.

International Federation of Red Cross and Red Crescent Societies (IFRC)

The International Federation of the Red Cross and Red Crescent Societies (IFRC) is the grouping of all national Red Cross and Red Crescent Societies. In disasters the Secretariat in Geneva will response through the national society based in the country concerned. The IFRC has a national society in virtually every country in the world and is critical in early response measures as well as long-term development programming. In 2012 the IFRC embarked on a long-term partnership with WAP to ensure its staff can assess animal welfare needs and address the issue in its programmes. They remain at the forefront of pushing animal welfare as a core component of humanitarian and development action.

The World Organisation for Animal Health (OIE)

The World Organisation for Animal Health (formerly Office International des Epizooties, but known as OIE) provides no disaster response or recovery capacity or action in disasters but has created guidelines for Chief Veterinary Officers of the affected country to work to.

Non-governmental organisation community

The NGO community is a broad spectrum of non-profit and for-profit agencies and organisations that are involved in disaster management. They vary in size from very large billion-dollar organisations to very local and focused in their geography and scope. They are found at all stages of the disaster cycle from immediate rescue through to preparedness and those involved in development rather than direct humanitarian activity. It is beyond the scope of this chapter to detail all of these NGOs, their sectors and how they operate but there are some to consider as an emergency manager involved in animal management.

- Cluster leads – the UN runs a coordination mechanism for disasters. Each of these clusters is appointed a lead or chair and some of these clusters are co-chaired by an NGO. Details of these NGO co-chairs can be found in Table 2.1.
- IFRC – the IFRC is the largest NGO and has national societies in most countries, is normally well integrated into government structures of emergency management and has resources useful to animal management. Since 2012 they have been committed to integrating better animal management into their programmes and are often highly supportive of joint programmes of aid for people and animals as was the case with their aid delivery in the aftermath of the Mongolian Dzud in 2016.

- Humanitarian NGOs with livestock related programmes – there are a number of NGOs including many mainstream organisations very active in livestock related programmes in Africa, especially the Sahel. Any operation in this area should take account of the work these agencies are already doing and the coordination mechanisms already in place.
- Humanitarian/Development NGOs focused on livestock programmes – there are several NGOs such HEFA international and ACF who focus a large proportion or all of their humanitarian work on the livestock sector.
- Animal welfare NGOs – these NGOs focus their work primarily on action to improve the welfare of animals. Some such as The Brooke and World Animal Protection (WAP) focus their work at the intersection between the benefits for animals and people as the most efficient space. Large international animal welfare NGOs such as the Humane Society International and the International Fund for Animal Welfare will be present in many large disasters.

Coordination during disasters (UN cluster coordination)

The United Nations Disaster Assessment and Coordination system (UNDAC) was established in 1993 as a mechanism to reduce duplication of effort, share information

TABLE 2.1 Detailing sector clusters and the cluster lead agencies for the UN cluster coordination system

The UN OCHA cluster system	
Cluster	*Cluster need*
Protection	United National High Commission for Refugees
Food security	Co-chaired – UN Food and Agriculture Organization and World Food Programme
Emergency communications	World Food Programme
Early recovery	United Nations Development Programme
Education	Co-chaired – UN International Children's Emergency Fund and Save the Children
Sanitation, water and hygiene	United Nations International Children's Emergency Fund
Logistics	World Food Programme
Nutrition	United Nations International Children's Emergency Fund
Emergency shelter	Co-chaired – UN High Commission for Refugees and International Federation of Red Cross
Camp management and coordination	Co-chaired – United Nations High Commission for Refugees and Institute of Migration
Health	World Health Organization

and to de-conflict operations to ensure that the disaster effort and the resources allocated were used in the most efficient manner possible. Its aim is to ensure predictability and accountability in international responses. It aims to do this through division of labour among organisations and defining roles and responsibility for sectors of the response. This is achieved through periodic forums that discuss sectoral issues, latest information and assessments and the intentions of all agencies involved in the 'cluster'. Thus cluster sectors for key areas of disaster response exist. Each of these sectors has a full-time global cluster that meets several times a year. During a disaster the national and local clusters are activated. Depending on the scale and geography of the disaster there may be one cluster or several at different levels, coordinating different agencies and interests. One of the key criticisms of the cluster system is how it is very NGO focused, often bypassing government coordination. It remains a challenge for the UN system to integrate government departments and actions into this key system as was the authors' experience in most major disasters in the last decade.

Management of disasters nationally

In developed countries, we find international assistance generally well integrated into a formal and organised framework for coordination and a good regulation of effort. This considered, balancing local effort and needs can be challenging when overlaid with national structures and this does differ significantly by governance system. As an example, the US operates under a federal system and we see agencies such as FEMA responsible for the overall disaster management picture but interlaced into this are state and county resources and coordination mechanisms. In other models of governance, power may sit less equally between national and local entities.

In developing countries we find a different situation. Often dislocated from the international humanitarian response is the specific nation's response to a disaster. Unless NGOs have staff already based in the country, the first 72 hours are typified by the utilisation of national response resources (both formal and informal) and local resources in affected areas. It is at this stage that the most can be done to preserve life of both people and animals and yet this is the stage where the resources and knowledge have often been traditionally the weakest in the response. Government and municipal departments are often under-resourced and lack the mobility and equipment (and often the training) to effectively undertake rescue and relief efforts and can find themselves cut off for days from any national level support. The conversion of day to day activities of an agriculture department to emergency relief or recovery is often not planned for, trained for and resourced. This means that often these departments find themselves needing to respond but often unable to do so, dealing with the challenges of staff attending to their own domestic crisis caused by the event concurrently with trying to perform their vocation. Information flow to national authorities that are often tasked with engaging with humanitarian structures is challenging and national entities often find their ability to receive accurate information from municipalities is challenged as either the mechanisms are not that strong, the technology weak or the interest lacking based on limited interaction during non–disaster periods. This is often the case in countries with fragmented landmass (such as archipelagos). Compounding this is the desire of NGOs active in the disaster to focus their effort locally to provide the most assistance, further complicating national coordination mechanisms, and thus the farther the disaster from the capital, the more challenging coordination can become.

Obviously local government, services, infrastructure and people will continue to be present long after the last humanitarian aid worker has left the area and thus local people and their governments ought to play a critical role in the coordination of disasters. Acknowledging that migration can occur in the aftermath of disasters, we still see large populations aiming to stay or return to their land and thus the needs of the population persist. The role of local government in recovery is critical in ensuring resources are used effectively and yet it is often heavily under-resourced and mistrusted. It is here we see the traditional weaknesses of the preparedness approach which is based less on risk assessment and more on historical experience. Thus we often find municipalities with high, present risk or regular disasters better prepared, resilient and resourced than those who may face a generational risk, albeit with potentially more serious consequences. This is not uniform across all disaster types either as we tend to find municipalities with high earthquake risk far better resourced than those with high risk of cyclones.

Perversely we often see humanitarian structures of governance in place running parallel but with little crossover to the government response, with government staff not being invited to key coordination meetings. Often government is involved at the highest level but those at a more local level who can actively change the outcomes on the ground find themselves working within a vacuum. This exact situation was experienced in Haiti in 2010 when it was commonly believed that a functioning government didn't exist as government buildings were destroyed. Often government staff were not invited to UN cluster meetings or even made aware of the mechanism and how it could be interacted with. This combined with the pervasive and inaccurate generalisation that Haiti was a corrupt country led to a preference away from working with local people and groups and toward a culture of a separate humanitarian effort.

Local response

In the immediate aftermath of a disaster, local people react first. They ensure that their families and animals are safe and those of their neighbours and communities. Often lacking the knowledge, equipment or skills to do this adequately they are dependent on local government to assist.

Local emergency services and functions of local government will be as active as they can be in the aftermath of a disaster (dependent on the impact on their own people and functions as well as their own family and property) and will be involved in rescue and relief efforts with the limited equipment and supplies they have. These agencies and functions have vital intelligence on the location of people, property and assets in the aftermath of the disaster. More often than not, and if not overwhelmed by the intensity of the event, the local government will move to reopen closed ways of access, repair utilities, clean waterways to avoid flooding, and reach isolated families in need. Often the formal mandated response organisations will experience activity from emergent resources. These such as local business, groupings of local organisations or even individuals with private means can often be critical in providing immediate relief, even though they will naturally not know what existing coordination mechanisms look like, and thus intervene directly with the need. Responders are less likely to have much direct control over their actions but should aim to include them into coordination mechanisms and rescue efforts where this benefits the effort, reduces risk for these groups and increases impact. The expectation should be however that these groups are likely to not be equipped or trained in the same manner, nor will they necessarily work to operating procedures or wish to. These factors all need to be considered when engaging emergent resources.

During this period and throughout the emergency, responders can expect to see individual volunteers and groups of volunteers. These can be local, national or international and will arrive with a range of skills, experience and equipment ranging from significant to very little. It is undoubted that lives are saved by the actions of unskilled individuals in the aftermath of disasters, whether it be digging through rubble in an earthquake or using a boat to rescue people in floods. These convergent resources often arrive unannounced and some will seek to coordinate but some will aim to act independent of this. The issue of convergent resources is challenging for responders. They may be able to act more quickly due to not needing to coordinate or not needing to follow operating procedures but they can also put themselves (and others) at greater risk and duplicate effort. An example would be multiple house searches because of a lack of knowledge of rescue marking or coordination.

Animal responding organisations are likely to receive offers of assistance from vets, vet nurses and untrained volunteers and this poses difficult decisions for them. These volunteers may be their only immediate resource but their actions may not be wholly manageable, they may offer resources but have differing views of how these should be deployed. It is the authors' view that engagement with these offers is better than ignorance of them as they are likely to be present regardless of agencies' viewpoints of whether they should be and there is an important role for professional responders in encouraging these assets to work within and for the established system rather than outside it. Consideration must be given to how different working as a vet in a practice in the developed world may be compared to working in a disaster zone and how techniques, approaches and equipment may change. The authors have seen many well-meaning volunteers suffering significant psychological and physical trauma from their attendance and actions in a disaster. A consideration may be to think of deploying such resource to help away from immediate danger, such as running rehoming, sheltering or transport of animals.

In an ideal world, the first levels of governance, e.g. municipalities, should be the best equipped and trained and the first to respond and help their people and constituency. These resources are often the only options for immediate aftermaths of disasters and their capability and resourcing, while weak for disaster response in the developing world, can be critical. In the developed world we see far better resourcing and training for local level resources for disasters. In developing countries equipment and supplies are often limited and related to daily activities. As an example, a veterinary department might struggle to resource drugs for daily outreach, and lack equipment and training to turn their operations over to disaster circumstances. Mobility is often a major issue in the immediate aftermath with provincial services unable to reach communities cut off from vehicle travel but lacking more flexible forms of transport. Often these staff will be balancing dealing with their own domestic strife from the incident at the same time as trying to fulfil their vocational duties.

Training for operating in volatile environments and working in a more self-sustaining manner do not often enter the equation of municipality budgets. Investment in preparing the most local level in advance of a disaster in developing countries is often severely lacking and is further hindered by the preference of development projects to build capacity and address vulnerability at the community level, often avoiding weaknesses in government systems. This lack of strength and resilience creates a vicious circle when local governments are side-lined or ignored by international donors in the decision-making process of where to assign funds, meaning even when money is available (post disaster) they cannot access it.

National response

National government will be involved in the marshalling of country level assets (such as the military or civil defence), international liaison and the collation of assessment information from regional and local administrative structures. When the intensity, size or impact of the event reaches levels beyond the capacity of these stakeholders and overwhelms their capacity, the country government may decide to ask the international community for assistance. In major disasters this can happen quickly but can also be delayed because of politics as was seen in Cyclone Nargis in Myanmar in 2008 where request for help and entry into the country for humanitarian groups was slow.

Government representatives should be present at coordination meetings with agencies and may expect registration of foreign aid agencies but both are rarely the case. National governments, if they remain a viable entity post disaster will be responsible for the long-term recovery of the country. Disasters such as the Haiti earthquake in 2010, Cyclone Hayan in 2013 and Cyclone Pam in 2015 all saw significant dislocation of government representation and coordination with the humanitarian effort.

Civil defence departments and armies can take control of command and coordinate evacuation or procurement and distribution of food, water, shelter, security and other essentials but this varies significantly by country. Often gaps are quick to emerge between national government and other agencies (humanitarian NGOs and the UN) and coordination can be problematic, especially under the stress of the response phase and with much information to gather. These gaps include differing views on command and control as well as differing assessments being undertaken that can lead to duplication of effort or ineffectiveness. Sometimes in very poor countries, suspicions of the effectiveness, trustworthiness or levels of corruption can create gaps in the coordination mechanisms. Equally some countries have an established mistrust of NGOs (examples include Ethiopia, Myanmar and Nepal) and may choose much tighter regulation or registration of all involved in the effort.

National governments often experience a lack of involvement in decisions taken by donating bodies and the humanitarian sector as was experienced in the aftermath of Cyclone Pam where disaster assessments and aid delivery were undertaken with limited involvement of decision makers in government. Often developing country governments find it difficult to assert their authority as they don't want to upset agencies who bring vital resources. At the same time NGOs and the UN often complain of issues of slow pace, corruption and government red tape. In the Haiti earthquake in 2010 this level of mistrust in both government workers and the hiring of Haitians due to corruption concerns significantly delayed and hindered aid delivery and was often contrary to the experience of other organisations (including those of the authors) who found working with government departments and proactively hiring local staff led to significant performance differences in the speed of aid delivery with little, if any, measurable corruption. These tensions on both sides do mean that there is a struggle to integrate national response with international response and to drive preferences, which leads to poor or superficial communication and, unless the government is willing to assert its authority, a piecemeal and superficial representation in UN and NGO coordination mechanisms. As an example, in the aftermath of cyclone Pam in 2015, government representatives were invited to co-chair cluster meetings but the reality was they were offered the opportunity to introduce the meeting and then it was run by the NGO leader with little reference to the opinion of the government representative. The NGO leader in this case had no experience in disaster management and was working within the country as a climate change consultant prior to the disaster but was presented as more knowledgeable than the government representative. This situation offers opportunities for the animal responding agency, especially in developing countries, as often departments of agriculture (or similar) will be keen to work with proactive agencies and will often have resources not yet deployed (either at all or effectively) and may be working in isolation.

Emergency management for animals

Emergency management of animals in disasters is then the systematic approach and management of the uncertainty in animal welfare and production, due to large negative events that may overwhelm the resources of their owners. It aims to reduce the potential catastrophic losses of animal owners who may depend on them financially or otherwise, as well as to prevent or reduce the suffering, harm and loss of animals. This is achieved through risk assessment/analysis, plus the implementation of actions and strategies to prevent, transfer, control, reduce or mitigate these risks for animals.

It is charged with creating the framework within which animal owners and the communities in which they and their animals live may reduce exposure and vulnerability to hazards for their animals, thus increasing their preparedness and resiliency to cope with disasters and save the relationships they have with those animals, all within the disaster cycle.

Emergency management of animals seeks to promote safer lives for animals and animal owners, through safer, resilient animal environs, steady production (and outputs) for farm and working animals and the mental wellness of pet owners, with the aim to build more resilient and sustainable communities dependent upon those animals, with the renewed and larger capacity to cope with hazards. The underlying, cross-cutting factors behind emergency management of animals are on one hand, the One Health concept (public health, which involves physical, mental and environmental health), human–animal relationships and animal welfare, and on the other, an accent on baseline animal welfare. Livelihood protection, food security and veterinary public health (epidemiology of zoonosis) are also among the foundations of these unique inter-species relationships.

Emergency management of animals protects them and the communities that own them or depend upon them by coordinating efforts and integrating all public health and veterinary-related health, animal welfare and husbandry activities necessary to build, sustain, and improve the capability to mitigate against animal risk to disasters, prepare for, respond to, and recover from actual natural disasters, acts of terrorism, or other man-made disasters. The principles, characteristics and distinctive features of disaster management for animals should follow the following principles:

- **Comprehensive** – risk management of animals considers and takes into account all hazards, all phases of the emergency management cycle involving animals, all stakeholders and all impacts relevant to the welfare of animals in disasters and of the humans that depend on them.
- **Progressive** – it anticipates future disasters to take preventive and preparatory measures to reduce animal risk or impact, and to build disaster-resistant and disaster-resilient animal husbandry, environs and populations. It also promotes the development and evolution of this skill in the context of risk management in general.
- **Risk-driven** – it uses rigorous analytical methods such as hazard vs. animal exposure/vulnerability identification, risk vs. impact analysis as well as strengths and opportunities in the setting up of preparedness plans, defining priorities and resources to reduce, mitigate or respond to the impact on animals and their owners.

FIGURE 2.3 A World Animal Protection veterinarian treats animals in the aftermath of Cyclone Haiyan in the Philippines in 2013

Source: James Sawyer for WAP.

- **Integrated** – it uses periodic drills and coordination mechanisms such as the Integrated Emergency Management System (IEMS) for approach and structure, and the Incident Command System (ICS) for on the ground work and as essential field tools.
- **Collaborative** – it creates a culture of cooperation and sustains broad relationships among public health and agriculture institutions, academia, the veterinary and farm animal sectors, animal owners and animal welfare organisations, to build consensus and to facilitate communication and coordination when in need.
- **Professional** – it uses a scientific and knowledge-based approach based on research, innovation, training, best practices, ethics, etc., to set standards for animal welfare, animal resiliency, one health, the protection of livelihoods and food security, all with risk in mind.

Current problems and challenges

When disaster strikes and animals may be affected, national governments reroute what's left of existing budgets to dedicate them to the perceived emergency needs. In the majority, where agriculture is a key sector, governments see this as a critical move merely to sustain both livelihoods and food security.

In regions such as Europe, North America and Australasia we see a growing focus on animal owners and authorities focusing on risk management. Outside of these regions, often local animal health authorities, the animal science profession and in general the farm animal industry are not experienced in risk management. In the aftermath of Cyclone Haiyan in 2013, the national government struggled to make contact with provincial animal health departments and a nationwide needs assessment for animals was not possible; this compromised the ability of the government to seek the correct funds for response and recovery and the deadlines for their report to be fed into the UN flash appeal did not match with the realities of their resources, meaning that the submission of an accurate report was missed as was the funding opportunity. At the local level, animal health teams were cut off in affected areas and lacked the resources, equipment and training, as well as any human surge capacity to get out into communities and help, at the same time as hindering the ability of the national government to build a true picture from an accurate disaster assessment (Figure 2.3). This led to a failure to access funding to secure life and reduce loss. The authors found both national and regional entities very keen to work as hard as possible to help animals and their owners but their lack of integration into the effort meant they had little ability to influence and access resources. It is the authors' opinion that the provision of immediate funds from the humanitarian effort to provincial teams for aid would have secured livelihoods in greater numbers. In this incident alone it was estimated that 4 million animals were lost in the immediate aftermath from injury or from consumption as farmers, unable to support them, slaughtered them to retain some value as food. In the aftermath it was estimated up to another 4 million animals were at risk of death from exposure to conditions of dehydration, heat and malnutrition. It is the second 4 million where swift action would have made an impact.

Often the lack of coordination with humanitarian structures, the lack of knowledge of humanitarian funding streams, and the inability to build a national needs assessment from local structures often leads to government ministries missing the opportunity to access funding from other governments via UN systems. On the other side a lack of engagement, coordination and regular lack of requests from governments to participate in these bidding processes means that the door is hardly open to facilitate this process.

To this point UN emergency appeals for funding have been customarily weak in animal needs assessment. The lack of livestock assessors in UNDAC teams often leads to a focus on cropping funding as a focus. In Cyclone Nargis in 2008 this approach was catastrophic. A focus on the provision of rice seed without consideration to support working animals that were responsible for the draft power required to plant the seed led to an unnecessary fall in rice production in following harvests. Surprisingly for such a key area there are very limited numbers of specialists able to undertake this kind of assessment. Where assessments do occur, they focus on 'damage assessment'. While this may be fine as a concept to assess the destruction of housing it in no way meets the needs of animals. A dead animal has no real productive or economic value and thus these assessments only serve to identify the loss. Meanwhile, often the surviving animals continue to die, thus increasing this loss. A focus on the needs of maintaining surviving animals would help the situation dramatically and reduce the financial cost of replacing animal populations further into the disaster. During the aftermath of Cyclone Pam in Vanuatu in 2015 the authors saw an entrenched focus on damage assessment of agriculture while surviving animals died from exposure to the sun and from starvation in their tens of thousands. An immediate operation to secure the surviving livestock of the Shepherd Islands would have cost $250,000 to help more than 50,000 animals and secure livelihoods, which would be many times more cost effective than restocking programs that weren't even practically possible. The local will was present, the food source was available but the understanding of the role animal welfare can play was missing.

In recent years, animal issues have been poorly represented in the cluster system. While the UN global food security cluster has embraced this concept, much work remains to be done to demonstrate that animal welfare can be a viable way of improving aid effectiveness, reducing losses and securing livelihoods and food. When we branch out from this sector, there remains work to be done to convince other sectors (such as sheltering) of the importance of considering animal welfare. At the same time we see a lack of priority from donating agencies toward the animal issue. The estimates of 5 per cent of international aid being spent on livestock related programming doesn't reflect the importance of this issue on the livelihoods of beneficiaries, especially in developing countries. This means that even when the money is asked for, often these appeals are critically underfunded.

If the money makes it out of the other end of the funding pipeline, we often see a complete lack of viable expertise and programme opportunity for the funding to fulfil. This is partly because the funding isn't at the scale to drive sustained activity and interest but is also due to the lack of involvement with government departments concerned with the animal issue. If government animal health functions were included in these assessments and appeals, a huge amount of capacity would come online to deal with the situation.

Finally the whole perception of dealing with animal aid dismisses the concept of sentience. While we wouldn't assume that we could treat a human like a piece of inanimate aid, we continue to do so with animals. Animal restocking, as an example, rarely includes welfare as a core component, preferring instead to deal with animals like a tent or water bucket. This approach is not consummate with achieving best value for donors to disasters. A focus on creating the best conditions for animals not only increases survivability, it reduces disease and increases productivity. It remains startling that this simple inclusion is so often not considered as a really easy way of dramatically increasing aid effectiveness. Thus the solution starts by creating capacity in the animal sciences profession, awareness at the animal owners level, and public policy at all levels of governance. While these perceived weaknesses are then resolved at the national and international level, at the local level, however, animal owners should invest in baseline welfare for their animals, in the form of proper identification and immunisation, preparedness planning for food and water, evacuation and first aid kits. Municipalities should invest in early warning systems for the animals in their communities, evacuation ramps and alternate routes for farm animals, temporary feedlots and corrals, plus periodic drills, as the foundation of a sustainable progress for their people. Provincial and state governments should finance the development of risk mapping and censuses, and promote investment in better and stronger infrastructure such as bridges, ways of access, buildings, and in the case of animals, alternative shelter in case of evacuation.

At all levels, but especially at the national level, swift coordination is needed between animal health authorities and stakeholders with civil defence departments and armies, to assure the protection of animals as essential assets for the protection of the livelihoods of their owners. State funds may be needed for large animal evacuation to source large amounts of trucks, fodder and temporary shelter and pastures. For companion animals, a solution needs to be found for the evacuation of people and animals to points of shelter. At the same national level, governments need to enact public policies for the protection of animals during disasters, including the protection of market prices for farm animals or their by-products (milk, eggs, meat) and essential fodder or grains to produce fodder or pet food, in the aftermath of disasters. At the international level there is a need to see the right people, undertaking the right assessments, in partnership with the affected government resources and then pushing harder for the recognition of animals as a key disaster management issue.

Finally the commercial sector has an important role to play. As opposed to rescuing and saving humans, the rescuing of different species of farm animals in different scenarios and commercial exploitations, versus the different types of emergencies merits special attention. Dairy farms and any type of animal farm under intensive production conditions need a different approach from free-range animals, if in need of evacuation, if only because the levels of stress should be managed differently during handling. Chicken farms require the mass movement and care of tens of thousands of birds at a time, which in turn includes safe handling and containment, distances to be travelled, alternative destination, and in the worst scenarios, mass euthanasia.

Overall, commercial facilities for mass animal production often include elements of resilience (back-up generators or strengthening against wind storms) but this isn't consistent and there is little consideration for the sharing of best practice. When we move to medium scale production however we see a different picture. Often these facilities are not resilient and suffer large animal losses. In the Caribbean as an example, the largest animal losses are found in medium size poultry producers due to the scale of the industry sector, the lack of available education for owners in risk management of their facilities and production and the resources needed to protect their assets. It is at this scale that we see farmers borrowing more, but mitigating much less, a trend the authors witnessed in Cyclone Haiyan in the Philippines. It is at this level that resilience concepts (such as easily removable roofing or emergency sheltering of animals) are critical and the sharing of best practice on resilient structures and systems can have the most benefit.

When we explore the concept of animal insurance we see a high level of global variation. In Argentina we see a system of insurance that doesn't work for animals. The lack of key risk-reduction based policy criteria in insurance policies sees farmers not moving to save their animals, simply knowing they will be compensated.

This is an example of a commercial system driving an utterly inhumane practice. As the cost benefit analysis in Chapter 1 demonstrates, however, this is short-termism at its worst as this approach barely takes into account the loss of productivity or the wider economic impact of the loss. It would seem a win–win for insurers and re-insurers to insist that, in order to gain insurance for livestock, simple risk reduction and preparedness measures have to be in place at the farm level to trigger pay-outs. Farmers would decrease loss and secure productive capacity and insurance companies would have to compensate to a much lesser degree in the aftermath of a disaster. Pet insurers insisting on similar measures would reduce chaos in certain urban disasters scenarios quite dramatically. The development of the disaster management discipline in recent years has generated much talk of a more active engagement of the private sector. Interestingly, in the animal sector there are huge benefits for the private sector being more actively involved in reducing risk and securing economies through more resilient animal management. Additionally, the wary dance that the private sector locally has to undertake to ensure that aid doesn't damage local markets and economies is one that needs to be resolved.

It would seem therefore there is still far to go to achieve the right conditions for animals, but progress is being made. We see the Sendai Framework galvanising governments into action and we see forward thinking NGOs such as the IFRC including animal welfare into their training for national societies. In addition we see many actors taking more active interest in animal welfare as a new frontier in humanitarian aid. In 2015 Margareta Wahlstrom (Special Representative of the UN Secretary-General for Disaster Risk Reduction) declared that animals should be 'considered in a societal response to disasters'. This single phrase crystallises how animals can no longer sit peripherally to the issue, being dealt with through different systems to mainstream disaster management; rather they need to be fully integrated both into thinking, delivery and coordination. Animal owners would expect nothing less.

In the next chapter we will explore how disasters affect animal well-being, exploring different scenarios and conditions and suggesting basic guidance on management.

Further reading

Coetzee, C. and van Niekerk, D. (2012). Tracking the evolution of the disaster management cycle: A general system theory approach. *Jàmbá: Journal of Disaster Risk Studies* 4(1): 1–9.

Coppola, D. (2015). *Introduction to International Disaster Management*. Oxford: Butterworth-Heinemann.

UNISDR. (2015). *Global Assessment Report on Disaster Risk Reduction 2015*. Available at: www.preventionweb.net/english/hyogo/gar/2015/en/home/documents.html

Lewis, J., O'Keefe, P. and Westgate, K.N. (1976). *A Philosophy of Planning*. Bradford, UK: University of Bradford, Disaster Research Unit.

Lopez-Carresi, A. Fordham, M., Wisner, B., Kelman, I. and Gaillard, J.C. (eds) (2013). *Disaster Management: International Lessons in Risk Reduction, Response and Recovery*. London and New York: Routledge.

McEntire, D. (2014). *Disaster Response & Recovery: Strategies and Tactics for Resilience*. Hoboken, NJ: John Wiley & Sons.

Quarantelli, E.L. (2006). *Catastrophes are Different from Disasters: Some implications for Crisis Planning and Managing Drawn from Katrina*. Available at: http://understandingkatrina.ssrc. org/Quarantelli

The Sphere Project. (2011). *The Sphere Project*. Rugby, UK: Practical Action.

United Nations Office for Disaster Risk Reduction (UNISDR). (2015). *Sendai Framework for Disaster Risk Reduction 2015–2030*. Available at: www.unisdr.org/files/43291_sendaiframeworkfordrren.pdf

Wachtendorf, T., Brown, B., Holguin-Veras, J. and Ukusuri, S. (2013). Catastrophe characteristics and their impact on critical supply chains: Problematizing material convergence and management following hurricane Katrina. *Journal of Homeland Security and Emergency Management* 10(2): 497–520.

References

Coetzee, C. and van Niekerk, D. (2012). Tracking the evolution of the disaster management cycle: A general system theory approach. *Jàmbá: Journal of Disaster Risk Studies* 4(1): 1–9.

Coppola, D. (2015). *Introduction to International Disaster Management*. Oxford, UK: Butterworth-Heinemann.

Hulme, J., Pope, S., Smith, D. and Wilsmore, T. (2008). Report to UNHCR Chad on Proposals for Livestock and Animal Owners in Eastern Chad. SPANA report.

Inter-Agency Standing Committee (IASC). (2012). *Consolidated Appeals Process (CAP)*. Available at: https://interagencystandingcommittee.org/consolidated-appeals-process-cap

Livestock Emergency Guidelines and Standards. (2015). *Livestock Emergency Guidelines and Standards*, 2nd edn. Rugby, UK: Practical Action.

World Organisation for Animal Health (OIE). (2017). Available at: www.oie.int

The Sphere Project. (2011). *The Sphere Project*. Rugby, UK: Practical Action.

United Nations Office for Disaster Risk Reduction (UNISDR). (n.d.). *History*. Available at: www.unisdr.org/who-we-are/history

United Nations Office for Disaster Risk Reduction (UNISDR). (1994). *Yokohama Strategy and Plan of Action for a Safer World*. Available at: www.unisdr.org/we/inform/publications/8241

United Nations Office for Disaster Risk Reduction (UNISDR). (2005). *Hyogo Framework for Action 2005–2015: Building the Resilience of Nations and Communities to Disasters*. Available at: www.unisdr.org/2005/wcdr/intergover/official-doc/L-docs/Hyogoframework-for-action-english.pdf

United Nations Office for Disaster Risk Reduction (UNISDR). (2015). *Sendai Framework for Disaster Risk Reduction 2015–2030*. Available at: www.unisdr.org/files/43291_sendaiframeworkfordrren.pdf

3

THE IMPACT OF DISASTERS ON ANIMAL WELFARE

In the last chapter we explored the key concepts of disaster management and the current community and how it works as a way of setting the scene within which a disaster response for animals would sit. This is critical because the welfare of animals during disasters is fundamentally linked to the welfare of their caretakers and owners. Thus any animal based response needs to consider the humanitarian effort. Without a consideration of this, it is very difficult to ensure and protect good welfare in animal populations. Once we have ensured alignment, however, we need to understand the needs of animals in disasters and begin to think about how we might meet these needs. This chapter will aim to detail basic animal welfare principles and how these are compromised by disasters generally, and then through different types of disasters.

The impact of disasters on the welfare of animals is, in most cases, the result of the initial (or baseline) welfare of these animals being exposed to the initial impact of the hazard itself, sometimes compounded by secondary impacts, courtesy of the stressful conditions left behind. Basic animal needs in the aftermath of the disaster are very similar to those of humans, namely water, food, shelter, evacuation and medical care. In principle therefore post disaster interventions for animals should aim to meet at least one of these needs. In order to adequately meet these needs, a process of rapid assessment is required to identify the impact of the disaster, the correct needs of the beneficiary and the provision of the right aid at the right time to the right animals. Without such methodology, resources can be deployed unwisely or inefficiently, leading to duplication of effort and ultimately the beneficiary (the animal) suffers. While the following chapters deal with the issue of needs assessment, it is important to note that any operation for animal needs should be based on a sound welfare assessment, preferably with synergy to those processes undertaken by humanitarians at the same time.

Contrary to common belief, humanitarian agencies do undertake work helping animals as a part of their mission to secure livelihoods, thus the better aligned mission data gathering and reporting is with their systems, the better chance of expanding the usability and influence of your findings. In this case a disaster needs assessment for animals becomes more than administration, rather, it is a piece of aid in itself.

Understanding animal welfare criteria

The most universally accepted criteria for assessment of animals are the Five Freedoms and these are critical as baseline criteria for assessing the effect of disasters on animals.

The Five Freedoms

The Five Freedoms are the most widely recognised attempt to assess animal welfare. By utilising five important aspects of the welfare of animals under human control, they offer a measure of the welfare of animals at any given time or in any circumstances. The concept of the Five Freedoms was developed in response to a 1965 report by the UK government on livestock husbandry, and was formalised into the present 5-point format approximately 12 years later by the UK Farm Animal Welfare Council (FAWC, 1979). This was also referred to as the measurement of 'A Life Worth Living'.

The Five Freedoms have since been adopted by professional groups and NGOs worldwide and are currently accepted as:

1   Freedom from hunger and thirst
2   Freedom from discomfort
3   Freedom from pain, injury and disease
4   Freedom to behave normally
5   Freedom from fear and distress.

Some consider the Five Freedoms the equivalent of rights for animals (merely without the right or freedom from exploitation), while others consider them redundant and outdated. Objections to their use pinpoint the lack of guidance when, for instance, in the example of the requirement to ensure freedom from hunger and thirst there is little or no guidance about the amount of time animals should be granted access to feed or water. Another such limitation is the lack of ranking of these five principles by order of priority, in the event of contradictions. This suggests the Five Freedoms may be regarded as broad principles and not as an exact measuring tool or checklist. The SPHERE standards (Sphere Project, 2011) apply minimum standards of duration and care to humans and are widely accepted as the standards agencies should aim to achieve (although they remain difficult to consistently deliver). While the Livestock Emergency Guidelines and Standards (LEGS, 2015) work as a companion document to SPHERE, they do not specify the minimum standards to deliver for animals; rather they offer a valuable tool to the assessment of need and effective guidance on how to decide on the correct interventions. Considering the need to provide a simple, commonly understood and accepted method of defining welfare, the Five Freedoms are the most useful in underpinning disaster needs assessment for animals. Experience with rapid disaster management assessments has proven that each freedom still serves as the basis for documenting the different types of impacts animals suffer during and in the aftermath of disasters, and therefore provide a firm basis for the recommendations of action to address these impacts. The Five Freedoms may not be able to help us with the quantification of the level of animal welfare compromise during disasters, but they can be useful when establishing the initial baseline needs of those animals.

While the concept of needs analysis will be discussed in more detail in later chapters, any disaster needs analysis for animals should consider:

- type of impact;
- priority of need;
- likely duration of suffering;
- likely duration of required support;
- required action.

In the case of more pernicious, chronic disaster types such as droughts, many of these 'freedoms' and needs may be compromised to begin with and continue to be so in the long term. Thus, aside from providing shelter from the sun's radiation and water, most other actions to improve the welfare of animals living in these conditions are systemic in nature, implying the need for significant investment, and are often unsustainable in nature and the timescale required. When we consider such chronic events we must also consider how we might change the root causes of the problem in how they interact with the emerging emergency.

Affect and impact for animals

Freedom from hunger and thirst

Domesticated animals are, by design, completely dependent on their caretakers and owners to survive. When disaster strikes, the means their owners and caretakers may have to keep them alive may be seriously compromised, to the point of often initiating secondary hazards and animal victims.

Farm animals

The way farm animal breeds have been selected and raised for generations implies that their level of domestication means most small farm animals and many pets are kept confined to small enclosures or restrained. Thus, avoiding danger (self-rescue) by the animal needs to be ruled out as a possibility here. Their conditions of dependency, the link with human livelihoods and more importantly, the likely suffering they would endure during a disaster, ought to make their protection a priority for action. When farm animals are raised under intensive conditions and in close confinement inside farms, their chances to move and seek water and food for themselves are very limited. Consequently, farm animal casualties may initially be large, with continued, significant mortality for days, or even weeks. Where grazing animals have access to natural pastures, they can maintain themselves, assuming adequate supplies of fodder or grass and water are accessible. Often however, disasters such as floods or volcanos degrade or destroy pastures and feed supplies, or contaminate water sources, leading to an inability to access the required sustenance.

For surviving animals, having to live in the rubble of their farms, often among other dead animals, with very little food and water, or being sold or slaughtered in haste as "cull" animals is the textbook example of unnecessary suffering. If death doesn't arrive quickly, it is an invitation to secondary, opportunistic infections, often of respiratory and/or digestive nature.

Poultry

In the case of poultry farms, bird density is the main vulnerability, as power shortages produced by hurricanes, floods or quakes downing power lines, and damaged ventilation systems and water pumps can suffocate and kill an entire farm population in minutes. Poultry are at real risk of dehydration and heat stress at these points in time, especially in hot countries. Every time we visit poultry farms after cyclones and hurricanes in Asia, Central America or the Caribbean have struck, the scenario is very similar. We find a significant number of surviving birds, barely alive among the partially fallen roofs and structures, walking among the corpses of dead birds, with little or no food available, and probably doomed to die of thirst, lack of food and care. The problems their caretakers face when trying to rescue surviving birds to reconstruct their farms are complex. The poultry farms are often damaged and cannot be rebuilt soon and the surviving birds are so stressed that laying hens lay no eggs. Broilers do not get access to water until they die and weak birds are simply left to die or sold as 'culled' birds, all in the most appalling conditions imaginable. Often feed supplies are contaminated or destroyed or their supply is disrupted and water is either contaminated or not available.

Swine

Swine are very intelligent animals but also some of the most adapted to their domestic environment. In some parts of the world such as the Pacific, species less physically adapted to domesticity are still used, but on the whole, pigs in intensive farming systems are much more susceptible to a breakdown in their care during disasters. Pigs suffer from high levels of stress during disaster and are much less resilient to the removal of food and water than other species. Starving or thirsty animals may increase their aggression to nearby animals further compounding individual welfare conditions. Surviving pigs from pig farms are usually evacuated in haste after an emergency, often only to be taken to the market place for immediate slaughter.

Dairy cattle

Milking cows are the metabolic athletes of the livestock world. They are capable of converting large amounts of water and food, usually administered as concentrate, into large amounts of milk on a daily basis. This process needs incredibly intense metabolic rates and effort, thus the balance of nutrients needs to be readily available, and any lapses caused by an interruption in the supply or access may cause them to starve faster than other farm animals and, in addition, bring about serious consequences to the health of all the animals in the farm. This exact scenario happened to several small dairy farms during the earthquake in Cinchona, Costa Rica, 2009, when large mudslides blocked roads and weakened bridges to the point that made it nearly impossible to maintain contact and flows with these farms.

Beef cattle

For free grazing animals, isolation by large floods may create starvation and lead to the general weakening of their health. While breakdown in infrastructure may not necessarily cause health degradation, damage to pastures caused by volcanic ash or prolonged stagnant floodwater may very rapidly weaken an animal, bring foot rot and other complications. This scenario is somewhat common in Central America, Argentina and Bolivia in South America, where large floods cover vast extensions, leaving thousands of cattle in the water or isolated in small islands for months in a row, until the weakened animals succumb to hypothermia and respiratory diseases. Pervasive flood waters will destroy mature grasses leading to a loss of vital nutritional support. Even when new grass grows after floodwaters have subsided, it is normally low in key vitamins and minerals for the first month and cattle must be supported using other measures such as mineral licks.

Companion animals

Pet animals eventually starve or die of thirst when abandoned; often chained to the homes of their masters and caretakers who flee or evacuate without a contingency plan for their animals that may include extra water and food until they may be able to come back for them. Those let loose from the onset of the hazard may roam free, if the nature of the disaster allows them to, but many will not be accustomed to these new environs and get injured in territorial disputes with other animals or eat rotten leftovers or contaminated water and fall sick. During the Montserrat volcanic eruption in 1995, tons of ash eventually covered the island's capital, Plymouth. Many of the pet dogs in the city were left chained to their homes in a futile effort to avoid theft. Fearing certain death by thirst and starvation covered by ash, WSPA mounted a pet evacuation effort. First, animals were accommodated in a temporary animal shelter built in a safe area of the island. They were then ferried to nearby Antigua and then to mainland US to find them new homes elsewhere in the state of Florida, with the help of the local humane society in Broward County. A similar impact occurred during the Fogo volcano eruption in Cape Verde in 2014, where the forced evacuation of people living by and inside the old crater meant that their pets were left behind. Animals were injured in territorial disputes, ate poisonous plants and suffered acute dehydration.

Wild animals

Zoo animal collections are often abandoned, especially during armed conflict situations when food becomes scarce, especially for carnivores, and staff dwindle. Help in these cases is difficult, as access to some of these animals may be dangerous, in spite of the fact that they may be dying. The specialised and often diverse diets of so many different species can create a challenge to respond to, especially if food is in short supply for people. Many of the animals are specialist in terms of their environment and thus perish quickly from thirst or starvation. If escaped, most will end up in some kind of conflict with humans as they search for food.

Freedom from discomfort

Discomfort is an almost constant during disasters for animals. Caretakers and animal owners can, however, seek to diminish discomfort by preparing for emergencies in ways that may reduce discomfort in their animals. Discomfort can occur in many forms for animals, from hunger and thirst to a lack of shelter from the elements. In 2010 and 2016, a phenomenon known as a Dzud caused huge livestock mortality in Mongolia and significant suffering for animals. Disaster assessments highlighted that simple shielding of the entrances of animal shelters with tarpaulin dramatically reduced snow drifting and wind chill from the −40 degree Celsius conditions. Animals may also require shelter from the sun. Certain species, such as poultry and swine are especially susceptible to sustained, direct sun radiation and can die very quickly from heat stress. Animal shelters that are washed away, damaged or collapsed can lead to a significant degradation of an animal's existence. Often too little focus is placed by relief teams on sheltering issues for animals, favouring the perceived direct action of feeding and watering instead.

Evacuation must also be a consideration. Removing animals from harm can dramatically reduce discomfort. This may be more simple with companion animals, although finding a location to evacuate them to can be challenging. With large herds of livestock this process can be much more challenging. In all cases, the intense fear caused by a hurricane or a flash flood is unavoidable for most animals, but in the case of pets, it is a dangerous proposition due to their propensity to run away and into more danger. The perils and stress of evacuating large numbers of animals not-withstanding, discomfort may also be present if the wrong kind of transport or poor transportation ramps, enclosures, means (such as bedding, non segregation, time spent during transport) and poor methods (rushed, rough handling) are used prior, during or immediately after a disaster occurs.

Freedom from pain, injury and disease

This is probably the most important factor caretakers and animal owners can influence during and immediately after a disaster strike. Flying debris during typhoons and hurricanes can injure and often kill grazing farm animals in the open. Standing in stagnant water for long periods of time, contaminated with pathogens and chemicals can also cause significant hypothermia or infection. Cattle grazing on ash-laden grass will suffer intestinal distress, and poultry in a damaged chicken house can suffer heat exhaustion and die painful deaths. Stress caused by a disaster on the animal's immune system may also imbalance the natural parasite fauna in a ruminant's body and cause a range of health issues. Burns from fires or lava, smoke inhalation, intoxication injuries from evacuation, collapsed structures, or skin issues from exposure to the sun are merely a handful of the issues a disaster responder may find in an animal population exposed to the hazards.

Beef cattle

In the worst cases, the scenario of animals spending days and weeks in the flood waters with nothing to eat until weakness, hypothermia and pneumonia kills them is similar in its nature to dying of hunger and thirst during droughts. That was the case in Reconquista, Argentinean province of Santa Fe in 2008, where thousands of cattle died of pneumonia after weeks of starving and standing in the water and mud. While free roaming animals may be less susceptible to injury from building collapse they are at much higher risk of injury from flying or floating debris and contaminated pastures.

Working animals

Surviving horses, donkeys and oxen are often pushed to their limits after emergencies to earn money and compensate for the losses of their caretakers. In 2008 Cyclone Nargis in Myanmar led to increased pressure on surviving working animals to work the land and fields critical for the rice harvest. In Cuba during the same year, four hurricanes forced surviving working animals to be heavily overworked, to get the agricultural economy moving again (Figure 3.1). The animals were often pushed to work eight times as much land as they would under normal conditions. This overwork can lead to distress, heat stress, injury and exhaustion, all of which can be very discomforting for the animal, normally at a time when increasing food and water rations to compensate is impossible.

FIGURE 3.1 A farmer in Cuba pushes his oxen hard to recover his harvest in the aftermath of hurricanes in 2008

Source: James Sawyer for WAP.

Companion animals

The terror that dogs, cats and other pet animals may experience during high winds, an earthquake or a flash flood often provokes hysterical behaviour, including escape attempts, often leading them into more danger. By running through glass doors or windows, escaping outdoors during the high winds of a hurricane into intense traffic, or by falls or getting caught up in barbed wire, they will often get injured and sometimes lost. If none of these factors kill them, then lack of identification (tags, tattoos, microchips, marks) and the practical impossibilities of being reunited with their masters and the subsequent starvation and abandonment may do so. Abandonment per se or on its own does not kill animals, it is the behaviour they are forced into that does; eating contaminated leftovers, food and/or water that contribute to infections and diseases or weakened immune systems allowing new and numerous parasites in. The exposure to endemic diseases without proper immunisation available and/or the injuries obtained from walking on debris or the territorial fights picked with other animals, all augmented by weakened, hungry, thirsty, tired and stressed out animals, are often the cause of animal suffering. Thus the main culprits in the aftermath of an emergency are lack of baseline animal health and welfare, pet abandonment, lost pets and the lack of proper identification. The latter two can be remedied or prevented by properly identifying separated pet animals and by having a contingency plan to evacuate them, or alternative solutions to keep the animals safe. In the case of secondary infections, keeping prior immunisation levels up to date is paramount to keep this 'freedom' as intact as possible during disasters.

Wild animals

The original design and thus the relative exposure of a zoo facility to disasters, plus the pre-existence of contingency or emergency plans for evacuation and treatment is paramount, as the difficulties and obvious dangers for anyone trying to improve the welfare of a wild animal when it has been already compromised inside its cage by a disastrous event may be an important factor to consider, often to the detriment of the animal's welfare and destiny. During the post-war period of 2001 in Afghanistan, the Kabul zoo was left in a miserable state of disrepair, with many animals near-starved and most exposed to the inclemency of the harsh Afghan winter. Efforts to improve the welfare of the zoo animals were few in range and difficult logistically, given the difficulties of any post-war environment, and as the political and security climates were very volatile in Kabul, so the focus was put on treating main injuries and infections, and improving the food and shelter for all. Regardless of efforts, some of those animals did not survive to the next winter, due to the chronic problems with poor enclosure environments and living conditions they had endured for so many years.

Freedom to behave normally

During disasters, most animals would have no freedom to behave normally at all. In the aftermath, farm and pet animals alike have to live on with augmented stress levels, faced with living in the remains of their original quarters, cramped, in danger of further collapse and injuries, with less food and water. This may be caused by the general chaos left by the hazard and the event, or by the inability (financial or otherwise) of the animal caretakers and owners to provide better shelter and living conditions on a temporary basis. Normal animal behaviours may be more apparent during the post disaster phases of reconstruction and rehabilitation, and should be used as a measure of the success of disaster interventions for animal welfare.

Freedom from fear and distress

Finally, this form of 'freedom' is complementary to all the above elements of the Five Freedoms and almost an oxymoron during disasters. The level of resistance animal enclosures may be able to provide as shelter from the incoming hazard will no doubt contribute to levels of stress during an emergency event. This is how, for example, both fast and slow onset floods will leave little room for manoeuvre if the necessary precautions are not taken in advance. In these cases, the avoidance or reduction of the exposure of the facilities to the path of the water currents and the floating debris carried is a priority. This may be achieved at the onset by building on higher plains away from the path of water currents, or later on by building barriers and alternative ways or detours for the currents to avoid the animal enclosures. For cyclones and hurricanes, and where high winds are the primary hazard, reducing exposure may be attempted by location choice, or by building stronger animal holding structures such as poultry or pig farms, with accent on the roofs and gutters. In this case, and even at later stages in the business (and as late as prior to the arrival of the hazard), cleaning gutters and anchoring these roofs to the ground may help reduce a lot of casualties, especially in the case of poultry farms. The same can be said about the clearing of nearby fields from loose objects and materials, to avoid the chances of flying debris hitting and injuring free grazing animals.

Animal needs during different phases of disaster response

Relief phase

During this phase, humans and animals will still be living in emergency conditions. They will be stressed by the recent events, and sometimes will still be affected by aftershocks, weather conditions, injury and loss of shelter. Providing emergency food, water and shelter will depend on the ability of their owners and the support of their local and national governments to do so, but if these emergency relief–rehabilitation efforts do not happen at the right time, the risk will be to lose most of the surviving animals as well. In the Philippines, millions of laying hens were left to die after Cyclone Haiyan struck farms in 2013. Once the hens had stopped laying eggs, they were deemed by some unproductive and unworthy of investing in food and treatment and shelter for them. To add insult to the injury, the 'alternative' discussed locally was to starve them further until they lost most of their feathers and were on the brink of dying, at which moment providing them with food and water again led to the birds restarting laying eggs again. This is an extremely poor and cruel animal welfare husbandry practice that is still used in the egg business.

Animals may need to be evacuated from harm but may not have anywhere to be evacuated to. Most human shelters will not take animals but even the journey for animals can be traumatic if their welfare isn't considered. Many animals die in transit if not fed, watered and sheltered adequately and these needs are different by species type. Animals may also be already weakened (especially in the case of slow onset disasters) and may be moved out of danger too late to ensure their survival as productive assets.

Emergency veterinary care is critical during this early phase to ensure that injuries are treated and that supportive care is given to both production animals and companion animals to reduce the stress burden and improve their chances of survival. At this point their owners would be compromised in their resources to access this privately, indeed vet facilities may have been destroyed and government outreach for veterinary services may be ineffective or damaged in its capacity.

Sheltering is a critical and often forgotten consideration and should be focused on species most susceptible to the effects of their environment on them. Sheltering is often expensive and needs to be properly targeted and managed to be effective. Temporary measures are likely to be all that is affordable during these times.

Recovery phase

During this phase, farmers should be helped by governments and financing institutions to 'build back better' and thus avoid the reappearance of vulnerabilities entrenched in their systems. In this phase, life should come back to 'normal', and this is when animal welfare standards such as the Five Freedoms should be considered as guiding principles for reconstruction. This is the time to review and adopt the best standards possible on immunisation, identification, living conditions and as low an exposure to hazards of natural origin as possible, including the updating of risk assessment and emergency plans. This task may be difficult to achieve without the full participation of the academia and sector specific entities, as the main sources of information and the best targets for skill building to be made. This is also the time for local governments to improve access, bring back online vital infrastructure networks such as drainages and communication networks; and for financial institutions to provide soft loans for investment farmers to invest in to improve their resiliency and the welfare of their animals. It is important to consider that the recovery phase starts as soon as the disaster event is over. People do not wait to sort through rubble and try and rebuild their lives, this happens the day after a disaster strikes. This is often referred to as 'early recovery' but in essence it is still the same motivation that drives people. Animals are often forgotten at this early stage or they may be eaten to sustain human life, and yet early stage intervention in animal needs is the most successful form of aid for them.

Effects of specific disasters on animal welfare

Wind storms

Wind storms are known by different names, depending upon whether they start on land or on water and which geographical region they occur at. Hurricanes and cyclones are essentially the same and their land-based cousins are generally known as tornados. Some windstorms bring only powerful winds, some bring storm surges and others bring heavy rainfall as well. Some bring all of these at once, plus flooding and mudslides. Flying debris has an immediate impact for animals. They may be tethered and unable to move out of the way of falling structures or trees. Debris may strike them causing broken bones, cuts, lacerations, contusions and abrasions. Some of these cause discomfort, while a broken leg may lead to the slaughter of the animal. Water sources may be contaminated by storm surges, overflowing sewers or broken pipes and clean water may be in short supply. The spread of pathogens due to unclean water is a significant concern post disaster. The destruction of animal shelters is a more significant post-storm problem, exposing unaccustomed animals to the elements. Species such as poultry and swine are highly dependent on shelter in hot climates and without this they may succumb to the heat and radiation of the sun very quickly. Power is likely to be out for long periods after the storm and this can cause significant problems for chicken houses and other industrial farming facilities where backup generators haven't been fitted, leading to dehydration and heat exhaustion for the animals trapped inside. Sources of animal feed may have been destroyed during the storm; pastures, fruit trees and other key crops may be downed, damaged or destroyed and thus natural local food sources to maintain livestock populations may be compromised. During Cyclone Pam in Vanuatu in 2015, all viable food sources for animals in affected areas were destroyed and animals needed three months of emergency feed. In addition, commercial crops may also have been decimated, leading to a surge of pressure in rural economies dependant on animal draft power to drive oxen and horses harder in the aftermath of a disaster. Infrastructure may also be compromised, leading to feed suppliers being unable to meet demand. A priority for the relief phase is therefore to ensure that this feed pipeline gets up and running as soon as possible to ensure that local economies and their animals aren't compromised.

Flooding

Flooding can be fast or slow in onset, depending on the nature of the event. Fast onset flooding is often called flash flooding and is normally caused by a dam release/rupture or intense rainfall in a geographically localised and flood susceptible area. Slow onset flooding, sometimes known as cresting floods, builds more slowly in intensity but over a much larger scale and longer duration. Flash floods commonly involve the movement of large amounts of water very quickly and are very destructive to structures, dragging people and animals with them and causing drowning and near drowning. Debris carried by the water movement is a common cause of secondary injuries. Slow onset floods normally involve relatively slow rises in water, but they cover large areas, often affecting large animal populations that are commonly found on floodplains. Here the key effects relate to degradation of pastures, feed sources and secondary issues related to the still waters. After only a short period of time, the vegetation ruminants feed upon will start to die and it may take up to a month for regrowth once the waters recede (unless drainage isn't completed, in which case the roots of the grass will rot too). If pasture regrows, it will initially be very low in mineral content so supplementary mineral licks may be required. Feed stored in silos or barns may also be contaminated unless the silos or barns are above the height of the flooded waters. This can lead to the food rotting, being spoiled or becoming toxic, especially where the water is contaminated by sewage or chemicals. Animals standing in water for long periods will quickly begin to suffer degeneration of their health. Water is an excellent conductor of heat, thus hypothermia is a real concern. Water is also an excellent carrier for bacteria and viruses, and floods often lead to outbreaks of fatal diseases such as haemorrhagic septicaemia. Long-term exposure to flood waters can also produce respiratory challenges such as pneumonia. Foot rot is a common issue for cattle standing in water for long periods and ailments such as this can be debilitating. In reality the only solution is to remove the animals from the standing water.

Landslides

Landslides involve sudden movements of large amounts of earth, either loosened by previous tectonic activity or by heavy, sustained rains, or they can be caused by practices such as poor land management or deforestation. In some cases, mudflows can also occur where dams break, releasing toxic materials from mining as was the case in 2008 in Hungary, where many animals suffered chemical burns. In these situations, even dry matter can move down a slope, acting like a liquid in a tsunami-like motion, sweeping animals away and burying them. Trapped animals may be crushed or suffocate slowly. Debris in the flow may cause secondary injuries such as cuts, abrasions and contusions. The prevalence of corpses in the debris path (human and animal) also increases the chance of disease.

Volcanic activity

The slopes of volcanos are very popular places to farm and raise farm animals, as the soil is very fertile. This means that high populations of grazing animals may be found near seemingly dormant craters. Volcanos can have both immediate and chronic impacts on animals, dependant on the nature of the eruption. If an eruption is violent then lava flows, pyroclastic flows, poisonous gas and lahars can bury, burn, kill and injure animals. Often evacuation is very tricky due to the nature of the terrain and the number of animals present in these areas, combined with the limited options to accommodate them elsewhere. In the case of pet animals, as people evacuate, they would wish to take their pets with them. Some will even refuse to move out without their animals, while others may leave them behind and return or attempt to return to the danger zone many times, to care for them, causing further problems for authorities. With less violent eruptions, ash fall is a real problem. Ash is dense and when sustained falls combine with rainwater, a solid plaque of cement-like material, sometimes 20 centimetres thick can form, collapsing entire chicken farms and animal shelters under the weight and killing animals inside. Ash is made of silicates, which behave like ground up glass when settled on pastures, blanketing them in a snow-like form. Cattle will attempt to continue grazing and the abrasive ash will rapidly grind down their teeth, clog their digestive tracts and cause respiratory and eye problems. If it rains, the ash will start to form a more solid form of carpet, coating animals and their insides with a concrete-type substance, causing significant suffering and death.

Drought

Drought is normally a slow onset event, which offers time to prepare. At the same time its impact is incremental and initially slow, which means alerts are often required but the severity not always recognised. Declining levels of feed for livestock, coupled with reduced water access impacts less adapted breeds first and then all animal body condition reduces dramatically over time. As the drought continues, this reduced condition creates a reduced price at market and a tendency for herders or farmers to continue to hold on to their animals in the hope of changing conditions. This normally means animals suffer for extended periods rather than being sold or slaughtered early. As animal condition worsens, so susceptibility to disease grows and parasite burdens move out of balance, weakening the animal further.

Extreme cold weather

Extreme cold weather can also be exacerbated by preceding droughts, as is the case in Mongolia with the phenomenon of the frigid Dzud winds, where farmers are unable to store feed for the winter. Extreme weather can also be seen as a drought of sorts, negating pasture growth, restricting movement, covering pastures and depleting stored reserves of animal feed. These events weaken animals in other ways as well. Extreme cold depletes animal fat reserves (used up to stay warm) while suffering in harsh conditions. Pregnant animals may abort and nursing mothers may produce no milk or be so stressed that babies cannot suckle. Standing in snow for long periods of time can hinder circulation and render the animal unable to move and thus keep warm. Periodic melts may cause mud to flow into animal shelters and then refreeze, leading to appalling conditions for animals to stand in.

Earthquakes

Earthquakes come without warning as violent events. They create complex events to respond to as they may also lead to landslides, tsunami and technological accidents, broken dams and other flooding (including from diverted river courses). Largely, the issues for animals relate to injuries from falling structures or entrapment in the early phase of a disaster. Animals do, however, suffer greatly in the aftermath because of the abandonment of their owners, significant damage to the infrastructure used for their enclosures and the inability for effective evacuation. Surviving animals will find a new geography to their surroundings after a disaster and may be at risk from compromised building materials (glass, protruding metal, dust), chemicals and further collapses.

Tsunami and coastal surges

Tsunamis are caused by significant tectonic shifts (normally an earthquake, sometimes landslides) in such a pattern that leads to a series of waves, causing damage in coastal areas and inland (depending on size). These events carry large amounts of energy and debris and can cause impacts similar to large flash flooding and an earthquake combined, thus the impact for animals is often deadly. Coastal surges can occur from a combination of meteorological and lunar factors or can be caused by windstorms. These disasters have similar impacts to tsunamis but sometimes salt water levels can take longer to recede. Animals will suffer from injuries from debris and contamination, drowning and near drowning and salination of drinking water and pastures. Where devastation is widespread, feed supplies and veterinary care may be compromised and standing water may cause similar effects to slow onset flooding.

Nuclear

There are many technological factors that can cause harm to animals but nuclear disasters such as those seen at Fukushima, Japan in 2011, or in Chernobyl, Ukraine in 1986 impact over a very long period. Animals may perish, or in the case of Chernobyl, irradiated cattle were shipped away in trains and, due to their dangerous contamination levels, were left to die in the wagons. Many types of isotope irradiation have grave, long-lasting and widespread implications for people and animals. Mass evacuations occur here in a flash, which leads to abandonment, especially where exclusion zones are in place and people cannot remove their animals. Nuclear material can also travel on the wind and thus animal populations far away can be affected, with some isotopes requiring decontamination and others, euthanasia. Disposal of contaminated carcasses and animals is a complicated predicament handled only by experts.

For the discipline of disaster risk management for animals to be successful, it needs to include animal welfare as the core element. Without this consideration, many other considerations better suited for other types of assets may deviate the conversation and analysis in the wrong direction, such as risk transfer mechanisms or restocking. These can be considered blunt tools, too radical to be considered as primary utensils for a sustainable future to be possible and for live, sentient beings to be treated and replaced like inanimate assets.

Once animal welfare is prioritised and taken care of, the business continuity, health, prosperity and sustainability of animals, animal industry and owners can be secured. In the next chapter we explore the concept of the immediate rescue of animals for responders as the immediate response to a disaster.

Further reading

Heath, S. (1999). *Animal Management in Disasters*. St Louis, MO: Mosby-Elsevier.
Irvine, L. (2009). *Filling the Ark: Animal welfare in disasters*. Philadelphia, PA: Temple University Press.
Katz, J.M. (2013). *The Big Truck that Went by: How the world came to save Haiti and left behind a disaster*. Basingstoke, UK: Palgrave Macmillan.
Livestock Emergency Guidelines and Standards. (2015). *Livestock Emergency Guidelines and Standards*, 2nd edn. Rugby, UK: Practical Action.
The Sphere Project. (2011). *The Sphere Project*. Rugby, UK: Practical Action.

References

Farm Animal Welfare Council Press Statement. (1979). Available at: http://webarchive. nationalarchives.gov.uk/20121010012428/www.fawc.org.uk/pdf/fivefreedoms1979.pdf
Livestock Emergency Guidelines and Standards. (2015). *Livestock Emergency Guidelines and Standards*, 2nd edn. Rugby, UK: Practical Action.
The Sphere Project. (2011). *The Sphere Project*. Rugby, UK: Practical Action.

4

THE IMMEDIATE RESCUE OF ANIMALS

In the last chapter, we discussed the impact that disasters have on animals at different stages. The first stage of any kind of response is always the immediate rescue phase when needs are most acute and desperate and the most mortality occurs. In this chapter we explore the immediate rescue of animals in distress or danger.

We explore the skills and experience best suited for this situation with a focus on simplicity rather than a dependence on equipment that may not be available. To the untrained, animals can be unpredictable when in distress, when in fact, solid knowledge of animal behaviour can help greatly. As in all rescue scenarios, the priority of safety is always for the rescuer first and thus this will also be a focus of this chapter.

As with human rescue, this is a discipline and requires knowledge drawn from technical large animal rescue, animal handling and animal behaviour and requires some basic equipment very similar to human rescue. This chapter does not aim to teach these skills, rather direct the reader to the best practice they can access.

The difficulty of animal rescue

If technical rescue for humans is difficult, then the technical rescue of animals is even more so. Human psychology in rescue scenarios is relatively predictable and even the irrational can be anticipated. Animals are much more dangerous than humans. They don't respond well to rescuers dressed in bright rescue gear carrying all sorts of equipment.

Animals, unlike humans are not a single species and this poses its own problem as there isn't a single method across the species you may find.

As an example, dogs are predatory species by nature while cattle are prey animals and thus their behaviours and responses to danger are fundamentally different. Within these broad groupings, different species respond differently to stress dependent on a range of factors including intelligence, level of domesticity, and size. Often animals will be stronger than their rescuers; they can bite, kick, scratch, charge and attack, and pose significant risk to humans.

While animals will often solicit a response from people leading to a desire to rescue, the factors above mean that, unless simple and predictable, animal rescue should be left to trained individuals.

The human–animal bond

Humans tend to develop different levels of bond with different animals. This can be due to the level of exposure to the species or the level of empathy with them. The differences in empathy developed with particular animals of the same species are sometimes deep, sometimes completely the opposite and animal phobias may be apparent. Even when we consider the professionals involved in animal rescue, their experience can differ wildly.

A small animal vet, as an example, can have very limited experience with handling livestock while a firefighter may be at home with dog handling in a domestic environment but an aggressive stray dog or a scared horse may elicit fear. Fear is a deeply seated emotion that animals respond to and can make animal handling many times more difficult.

Thankfully, even with limited experience, a calm head and some basic principles can go a long way to reducing animal stress and thus rescuer safety.

When we consider the human–animal bond we need to consider the psychology of animal owners in a disaster, which is not always as predictable as one would wish. It is often the case that people will take unnecessary risks for their animals, including refusing to evacuate and returning to danger areas if they cannot make safe provisions for their animals.

When we factor in that in developed countries, where the line between animal owner and farmer have been blurred by horse ownership and 'hobby farming', the picture can become even more complex. An emergency responder or planner really needs to consider both the needs and the responses of the animal population and the motivations and psychology of the owner in order to effectively ensure safety and continuity for all.

Motives for immediate rescue

It is important for both the emergency planner and responder to consider the motives of the parties involved in the animal sphere as this will help define both the priorities and the pressures upon the individual and the team.

Ethical duty

Many believe that we have a duty of care to the animals under our protection and this influences our actions. This duty is often picked up by mainstream media and can apply additional pressures on rescuing agencies. Most, however, would agree that the needs of the animal come secondary to the needs of the human in the prioritisation of rescue. As ultimate guardians of animals, our responsibility should be, where practical, to rescue animals in distress.

Financial value

Livestock as well as companion animals have a value. Aside from their social value they are often likely to have a monetary value as well, either as a productive asset or merely as an asset. Different owners will see the relative value of their animals differently.

For some, insurance may lead to less concern for animals, while for others, animals may represent their own survival. Here, the welfare of the animal and even its life is secondary to their expected output. That is how we have witnessed tens of thousands of cattle and poultry being left to die at one given time, because their market value would have dropped under the tipping point where insurance would consider them valuable.

That said, often the productive and social value of these animals is currently only measured by the remuneration at the point of sale. With livestock, the contribution that they can make to local economies beyond their individual head value and the social value of companion animals is often yet to be quantified by market systems.

When evaluating the Demaji District response to floods in India during 2012, Ecolarge (2014) found a benefit–cost ratio to local economies of $7 for every dollar spent on early stage intervention to save livestock. More work is required to understand the contribution of livestock to direct and indirect inputs into local economies to better understand local populations' needs and wants in the aftermath of an emergency.

Wild animal rescue

Often in disasters wild animals can seize the headlines. This was seen to be the case in the recent Australian bushfires where images of firefighters providing water to rescued koalas circled the globe. Certainly disasters involving charismatic species of wildlife will capture the imagination. Often images of oiled seabirds highlight the destruction of an oil-spill and when the media pick up on these stories, pressure will build to act.

Safety considerations

The dangers of dealing with animals in distress can be inherent to their behaviours and instinct and these need to be carefully considered. Aside from this, however, are the practical considerations. Loads of larger animals such as livestock or horses can be much larger and the risks of injury from the equipment and the techniques can multiply accordingly.

Rescuers should always employ the same principles for rescue as those for people. Self-rescue and that of other potential victims should come before the consideration for the casualty and careful consideration of the working environment has to be undertaken before engagement is considered.

Personal protective equipment is crucial to the delivery of effective rescue, often protecting both the rescuer and the rescued animal. This should form a core part of the provision for rescuers and the training of individuals, for in rescue without correct instruction and practice personal equipment can be as much of a danger as the animal itself.

Finally, and most important is training and practice. With the best will and equipment in the world, little will be achieved without coordination, good technique and correct use of equipment. These cannot be simply learned from a book but rather need to be learned practically and then rehearsed to a level of competence where the rescuer and their team become part of the solution. Currency in training is everything when it comes to the success of an objective in animal rescue.

Core rescue principles

It is unlikely that animals will cooperate with rescuers; indeed, extra measures will be needed, to avoid getting bitten, kicked, scratched, stabbed, punched, trampled or drowned by the victims. While this may not seem to be a large problem, many people are killed annually by horse kicks, stampedes by cattle and by rabies bites from dogs and cats. Animal rescue is a specific emerging discipline, requiring specific knowledge and skills. In the developed world this responsibility will fall to the emergency services although often they remain poorly equipped and poorly sensitised to the issue. Just like human rescue drills, familiarisation with techniques and equipment needs to be constantly refreshed.

It is commonly the case in both the developed and developing world that animal welfare organisations may choose to get involved in animal rescue, whereas in the developing world they may be the only able bodies to do so. In addition, where neither exist, the responsibility may fall to either private veterinarians or professionals in government services. It is a common error to assume that animal groups and veterinarians are automatically experts in animal handling, rescue techniques or even self-rescue. Often, they will want to step in, but their role in a rescue should be agreed and determined based on their experience, their training and the requirements of the operation.

Scene assessment and control

The first step of any responder, regardless of the desire to get involved, is to assess the scene. Asking oneself how the animal got into its situation allows for a rapid dynamic risk assessment to protect the team. This initial first step can define the difference between success and tragedy and should never be underestimated.

Understanding the situation from the flow of a river, to the potential for live wires or the risk of further landslides will help you plan for the rescue and protect yourself and your team.

Once assessed, working zones should be employed. Different technical rescue fields (water, collapsed structures, road accidents) will employ different variations on the theme of an active (or hot) zone and buffer zones for specific types of activity and kit storage around the rescue area. Competence, training, experience and personal equipment will define participation and individual action within these zones and these should be adhered to (Figure 4.1).

Priorities of rescue

Regardless of urgency the priority for a rescuer or team is to prevent more casualties, human or animal, regardless of the risk to the individual in distress. This can often be a very difficult prioritisation when urgency is apparent. In most rescue scenarios and training, the following hierarchy is taught:

1　Rescue of oneself
2　Rescue of the team
3　Rescue of equipment

FIGURE 4.1 UK firefighters rescue a trapped horse

Source: British Animal Rescue and Trauma Care Association (2017).

4   The safety of bystanders
5   Rescue of the victim.

This may seem counterintuitive to instinct, but without the first three, rescue of the individual is impossible and without securing the first four, further casualties can be expected. These principles need to be considered sacrosanct.

Self-rescue

Any rescue operation or technique to rescue an animal inherently involves risk and thus avoiding this factor is not possible. No human life however should (or needs to) be lost for the sake of saving animals. Self-rescue is the first responsibility and skill any animal rescuer should master. It involves the assessment of risk, control of environments and preparation of equipment to prevent peril. Should a rescue environment emerge, the combination of assessment, preparation, equipping and accessing of skills and experience will ensure the rescuer can regroup to complete the mission.

Good self-rescue training should include the following scenarios, techniques and skills:

* first aid including CPR;
* correct equipment provision for team members and instruction on safe use;
* evacuation from environment (i.e. Swift water training).

Key training competencies for the animal rescuer

This chapter does not aim to provide the information on animal handling or technical rescue required for a responder as these are specific disciplines in themselves. The following should be a minimum for rescuers involved with animals and some best practice options are offered.

Animal handling and behaviour – Good books are available on animal behaviour, the best in the opinion of the authors are those by Temple Grandin (Grandin, 2014, 2017). Practice in these methods is importance to maintain currency.

Technical large animal emergency rescue (TLAER) – These should be taught courses. The authors would recommend those run by British Animal Rescue and Trauma Care Association (BARTA) (http://bartacic.org). Giminez *et al.* (2008) offers one of the few texts on the matter.

In addition to the above, animal rescue training should include the following skills and knowledge:

* logistics;
* incident command system training;
* swimming and apnea technique;

- water rescue in rapid flows or stagnant water;
- inclined angle rescue, knots, gear: ropes, webbing, anchor systems, edge rollers, makeshift animal harnesses, etc.;
- collapsed structures awareness and rescue;
- effective use of communication and communication technology;
- mechanical advantages of using cables and machinery;
- animal anatomy with accent on pressure points for different species;
- basic veterinary first aid for various species.

Rescue steps

Activation and deployment

There are several key stages to an activation for an animal rescue that are required in order to ensure the safety of rescuers and the public and to ensure the success of the mission.

Deployment

Getting 5–25 or more people together and ready to deploy in the middle of the night, on a weekend or during a holiday, and at different distances from each other is a challenge. Cascade call-out systems are useful tools to ensure that everyone gets the message but some redundancy in teams is required to ensure that vacation leave or unavailability for reasons of sickness doesn't compromise the operation. Where rescue is part of one's job description, permissions to activate are more simple. Where part-time, voluntary or retained relationships exist for rescue then the team need to think these through carefully and explore the implications of a refusal of permission to deploy by an employer.

Information gathering

Monitoring of incidents or events may be important (i.e. Developments with flooding alerts) to ensure readiness but once a team is alerted to an incident, an intense period of information gathering is required to ascertain the nature of the rescue. This may come from a range of sources that will allow the correct assembly of both human resources and physical resources as well as the team leader informing the correct authorities or stakeholders of their intentions. An important point to note is that secondary information such as this should be used to prepare and deploy but it should never supersede assessments and information gathering at the scene in decision making.

Maintaining currency

Being prepared makes all the difference in rescue scenarios. Ensuring that correct (and legally appropriate) protocols are either adopted or developed (dependent on availability and compliance requirements) is critical, but so is the team's familiarisation with them. Protocols are important for reference (for detail) but an emergency should not be when people refresh their currency in the knowledge of them; they should be as second nature as possible. Fire brigades and USAR teams may be a good source for information on organisational structure of rescue teams. Equipment should be appropriate to the potential scenarios the team may face both in terms of personal protective equipment, scene management and that required to affect the rescue.

This equipment should be maintained, checked, trained upon and stored correctly so it is ready and those who need to use it are ready too. Some equipment has a lifespan (i.e. ropes) which means that it will have a retirement point. Training is critical. Many militaries use the phrase 'train hard, fight easy' and this should be a mantra for rescue teams. Team roles, use of equipment, actions at the scene, knowledge of what happens next and crucially, action to be taken when things go wrong should all be as second nature as possible.

Training standards for roles should be developed and maintained, currency of training should be maintained and above all teams should not underestimate the importance of training the team rather than a singular focus on the mission. This more generic team building will be critical, especially when things don't go to plan.

Deployment

Knowing what and whom to take is critical and while as a general rule more is better prepared there are limits to this and operational viability. It is better to have units and equipment on stand-by rather than taking up space and resources at the scene. More often than not, however, and in spite of large volumes of rescue equipment, many scenarios end up demanding a lot more equipment than expected for safer, successful operations, so it is good practice to pack more, just in case. Teams should always plan for spending more time on the mission than they would wish for, preferably twice as much time, plus a contingency for emergencies.

Critical to this will be the need to ensure the maintenance of the team, allowing for food, watering, rest and contact with loved ones if on mission for extended periods. First aid, food, drinks, shelter, internal and external communications and rest facilities are all important if deployment is longer term. A team will rapidly lose its effectiveness without this provision. Remembering that operations can start in daylight and finish after dark (or vice versa) means adequate preparation for the risks of these changes to conditions is made.

Scene management

Scene assessment and management

Upon arrival the team leader will need to make an initial rapid assessment of the situation. This is to ensure no further harm to individuals or animals. Considering factors such as other active and passive individuals and agencies, emerging risk (environment or technological) and how management of the geography of the scene will affect rescue and safety are all critical immediate considerations in how the team engage.

The scene includes bystanders, the owners of the animals, local authorities, the parking lot where the equipment and vehicles will initially arrive and be displayed, the air space above, the river, the terrain, the weather, and the time of day. The scene will also need to include provision of communications, resting and feeding areas, bathrooms, and the safe areas for animals to be used once out of immediate danger, to get them ready to be evacuated.

Once this has been completed, the team should be briefed in the scene management, cordoning and management of other individuals in order to prepare the area for operations. Once safe, an in-depth assessment of the rescue needs and actions to be taken will be possible.

Liaison

Liaison is critical at the scene. There will likely be a range of interested parties from the animal owner to local authorities and bystanders. Scene management may involve the deployment of law enforcement for cordon management or the use of firefighters for technical access (cutting equipment etc.) that will require liaison, briefing and collaborative working. Interested parties cannot be ignored; as an example, if not managed and briefed, the press can become a hindrance.

Landowners and animal owners need to be handled for safety reasons but also to ensure the permissibility of the operation and equally important is how the general public are dealt with to ensure scene safety and the viability of the operations. Communication is critical to this and indeed in certain circumstances this liaison role may be specifically allocated within a team.

Briefing

Clear briefings should be given by the team leader and appointed individuals at key points in the operation to ensure viability. The periodic nature of these and the ability to review and adapt actions is critical as are they for sharing information and assessing the state of the individuals involved. They should, however, be at the right time and as regular as necessary. Getting busy people in the right place at the right time can be difficult, especially if the scene is geographically large and work occurs in multiple locations.

Ensuring every briefing ends with details of when the next one will be given is important for individuals preparing for their roles. Briefings will need to be formal in certain circumstances and involve individuals being drawn away from the team as particular actions are taken so all are aware of what their role is. Instruction should always be clear and confirmation that all have understood the instructions should be sought.

The team leader will develop the brief to provide his/her team members with the **Situation** (general overview, event, estimated number of human and animal victims, time available, etc.), **Mission** (estimated target of animals to be rescued), and **Implementation** (command and control, logistical details, techniques and equipment to be used, skills necessary, possible hazards, final destination for animals). At the end of every rescue operation, right after the cleaning and re-ordering process of the equipment, the team leader must hold a debriefing session to learn from mistakes and successes and document the event.

Planning

When a full assessment has been made, a clear plan should be communicated to all involved and roles allocated. These roles should be clearly briefed and the plan should include information on how to react and action to be taken should something not go to plan, an accident occurs or there is some kind of degradation of the situation, increasing risk.

Plans should be clear but actions from them should not become so task oriented that adaption to the situation doesn't occur. Dynamic adjustments to the plan based on experience and training will be necessary as will reviews of the plan at briefing points to adjust outcomes. Team leaders should ensure the reviewing element of the planning cycle is built into the operation in a manner that is useful but also in a way that doesn't paralyse decision making or progress.

The rescuers need to identify the exact number of animal victims, their age, size, approximate weight, current behaviour and any early signs of physiological problems they may be showing, with the help of their owner when possible, plus general and normal behaviour (whether the animals are tame or not). A map is advised.

LAST

Once the team leader decides to set the rescue operation in motion, one of the most common acronyms used for the steps to follow is LAST (Locate, Access, Secure & Transport).

Locate

The moment the rescue team lay eyes on the animal victim, the leader will convene his/her staff (veterinary, logistics and operations) to examine and analyse the situation, and propose possible solutions. In these cases, building a ramp or exit to facilitate walking rather than focusing on pure lifting should be considered as a first option; this will involve the best welfare for the animal and the least risk for all.

This may also be the last available moment for everybody (and the Safety Officer) to use the buddy check system: checking each other for gloves, kneepads, elbow pads, goggles, rescue helmet, boots, uniform (sturdy clothing not hanging around elements, especially around the neck), communications (radio, whistle, signals or agreed voice commands), command roles, checklists and plan (yes, one more time), lights, spare batteries, tools, harness, lines and climbing equipment if needed. Finally, and once the veterinary and operational assessment is completed, the decision needs to be made on whether to try to rescue or to euthanise the animal.

At this moment, two considerations must be held on top by the team leader, above all pressures from the animal owner, the public, the media, the context, etc. The safety of his team members and the future and continued welfare of the animal. Only then should logistical and financial considerations be weighed. While being dependent on the operation, often a safety officer will be tasked with overseeing the overall and specific safety elements of the plan at each step, and is supposed to stop the operation if the safety of the team members is at an increased risk at any given time.

Access

Here, securing safe access to an animal in trouble, especially large animals, needs experienced and fit handlers/rescuers, as scared and fractious animals trapped in mud, in water or under debris may still try to flee when in contact with rescuers, further injuring themselves and their rescuers.

Secure

The next step is to secure the animal for the safety of all. In most cases, covering their eyes and ears with a towel or a cloth is a good idea (especially if loud noises are going to be made or machinery is going to be used around them). Before that comes the assessment of the short areas they could reach with their horns, teeth and limbs. Then the possibility that the victim could escape and further injure themselves or others.

The veterinarian in the team needs to make sure the victim's breathing and pulse are not raised or compromised by the rescuers' actions and consider intervention with pharmaceuticals should they deem this appropriate. Next comes the diagnosis: examining the health, age, physical shape, possible wounds, as well as the circumstances of this particular case (entrapment, debris, obstacles) for an eventual extrication or rescue of the animal victim. The next step is the attention to identifying possible pressure points to hoist or pull an animal from danger.

Transport

Extrication – After all has been checked and rechecked, preferably with real checklists by a team member outside the theatre of operations, then the extrication takes place. Team member safety aside, extra equipment (cranes, 'A' frames, lifting devices, come-alongs, mechanical advantages set with a high anchor point, etc.), extra pieces of equipment or materials and extra hands may be needed and therefore need to be factored in as contingencies. If everything goes as planned, the last moments of the extrication may be awkward, as it often means going over an edge or the end of the pulley system, a small wall or fence to go over, or just the time when the animal's feet touch ground again and allows it to start struggling again.

A second, different team may be needed here to handle the victim and take it away from danger and to safety, as the first would be busy with equipment, getting out of danger around the animal victim or getting in position again for another rescue. Once everything has become calm and everybody is safely away from danger, the veterinarian needs to examine the animal, offer feed and water, and decide on any minor ambulatory treatments before transport, keeping in mind the victim about to be transported may be on the verge of exhaustion and shock.

Biosecurity: the golden rules

In the rescue of animals, biosecurity precautions are to be meticulously maintained and followed:

- always assume that disease is present when treating farm animals and act accordingly;
- always report disease, where appropriate, to the relevant authority;
- follow cleanliness rules to avoid being a vector for disease;
- report interaction with disease when you arrive back in your country of residence.
- if you cannot clean an item effectively, make sure it is destroyed.

Animal specific considerations

There are a legion of details that need attention when setting up a rescue, such as robust anchors, ten times (or more) stronger than those used for human rescues, if only because a horse rescue may imply the extra weight of 3–4 additional people weighing the same rescue lines next to the animal, anchors and knots during the extrication.

Special harnesses

All mechanical advantage systems and hardware are connected by special rescue ropes (static and over 12 mm in diameter for heavy load pulling, dynamic for rescuer safety) or by cable or chain to pull vectors through pulleys and points to reduce drag or to augment vector forces, and stopped or controlled by brakes. Using harnesses for large animal rescue needs knowledge, experience and expertise to correctly identify the pressure placement depending on the species, to be able to safely handle and extricate animal victims, and not to injure them and the rescuers in the process.

Lifting

The preference for lifting large animals should always be mechanical (with a preference for cranes or backhoes) but this needs to be weighed against the potential additional stress of the noise and vibration. Access or availability may however preclude this. In this case, a high point for anchoring and lifting may be necessary. 'A' frames made of long, 6 inch or more gauge metal pipes or solid wooden posts similar to electrical posts, firmly joined at the apex by metal plates or similar may be an alternative.

Aerial rescues

Helicopters are often seen in rescues in the movies, but costs will normally be prohibitive or safety and loads will be beyond the possibility of the pilot or the machine. Considering adverse weather conditions such as winds, low visibility,

FIGURE 4.2 An example of a correctly harnessed animal and the use of mechanical lifting

Source: British Animal Rescue and Trauma Care Association (2017).

proximity of obstacles such as foliage, electric posts, cliffs and small manoeuvring spaces, very few helicopters and even fewer pilots are equipped to handle technical rescues and to lift loads such as large horses or cattle plus the weight of rescue team members and guarantee a decent margin of safety.

The rescue craft must have rescue-specific features such as anchor points to the ceiling for the rescue team, a heavy duty winch or sling loading ability on the belly, and the rotor-engine capacity to move heavy loads in reduced spaces (Figure 4.2). Lastly, the small rotor is a big hazard to consider when manoeuvring a nervous tethered or untethered animal around before and after landing. There is also the static energy built by the large rotor and the friction of the rotor blades with dust particles in the air, that can produce nasty electrocutions to a person, an animal or to electronics (radios, etc.).

Species-specific rescue

Birds

Birds can injure themselves further when struggling to escape from their rescuers, so once in contact with them, wrapping their wings and covering their eyes with a small cloth or a hand towel is a good idea.

Cats

Felines should be wrapped in a towel and then placed into a laundry bag or pillow case to allow air inside. This will suffice to lift the animal out and away from danger, providing the bag is not dragged across debris or water; in the case of loose or falling debris, use a transport crate with a small towel inside to buffer eventual bumps. When lowering from height, two lines for control during manoeuvring are recommended. With multiple felines in close quarters, especially if they are scared, a net or a bed sheet may be useful to catch them safely. Outdoors, humane traps and open tuna or sardine cans as bait are the recommended method.

Dogs

Small breeds can be handled just like cats (above), with preference for transport crates. With larger breeds, especially if they cannot be led out of danger on their own, transport crates with towels as lining inside are recommended. For injured animals, immobilising the victim with towels or blankets before placing into the crate is the best course of action. If dog harnesses need to be used, avoid using a human harness on them as you may further injure the animal. Remember special harnesses are used on animals that have been trained to have them on. Sometimes, a larger net may be the answer. When catching dogs, small ones can be caught with nets if cornered, while large breeds are best handled with the help of humane traps and dog meat cans or sausages as bait. Ketch poles can be useful but should only be used if they have a quick release. In all instances, calming the animals after a small ordeal before transport is always a good idea.

Pigs, sheep, goats

Handling significant numbers of these animals will need coordination with their owners and marking them for easier identification, as well as not mixing groups to avoid aggression or unnecessary stress. Pigs can scream at the slightest provocation and at pitches difficult to handle, so proper protection for the rescuers' ears is advised.

Horses

Covering the victim's eyes when working around them is recommended to calm the animal down during the operation. Specialised harnesses, techniques and lifting structures such as 'A' frames and crane protocols have been developed for lifting horses (http://bartacic.org). The passing and placement of the straps over the appropriate pressure points under the bodies of large animals collapsed or trapped in mud or debris, or in deep waters is a dangerous and tricky challenge, and one that can be facilitated by the use of large, two-metre curb 'needles' made out of half an inch of metallic pipe to help pass the initial rope or webbing under the trapped animal.

One way of going without specialised harnesses for large animals is the careful examination of pressure point locations for individual animal victims and the building of makeshift harnesses by passing rescue lines or cables inside and through cut-off sections of old fire hoses (real discarded ones from fire departments) to be used as padding on those pressure points.

Cattle

Similar to horses, covering their eyes would allow rescue workers to deal with a calmer animal. Makeshift harnesses should be avoided as, if the animal victim moves and the weight shifts, these pressure points may vary or shift, causing more harm than good. The best advice is to purchase specialised harnesses for each species, or to develop them at the local veterinary faculty, keeping in mind dairy cattle are morphologically different from beef cattle, goats are different from sheep, males are different from females, etc.

Blood circulation, breathing and bowel movement must be under the close supervision of the veterinarian during a lifting or pulling effort, and it should be possible to stop the procedure, release the pressure and allow blood to flow before the rescue effort starts again. The tail and the head should never be used for weighing and lifting, although they can be gently secured to steer the animal's longitudinal axis in the air (the head with a hoist), especially before setting it back on safe ground. This is especially true during HELO operations (helicopter lifting).

Flight zones

As for moving, luring and herding cattle to safety, knowledge of their flight zones and escape mechanisms is a must, and the work of Dr Temple Grandin on livestock behaviour and psychology is highly recommended here (Grandin, n.d.).

Types of technical animal rescue

Inclined angle

For animals fallen into holes, sinkholes, off cliffs or into swimming pools and generally in need of exiting vertically, the first consideration is the animal prognosis. In the case of large animals and if the trauma is large, the decision needs to be made between their likely future and euthanasia. Also, if the high angle scenario is compounded by fire or heavy rain, flooding, thundering, or loose rocks and rock fall, it may be that any rescue efforts need to be postponed or abandoned altogether. Before deciding on action, rescue teams must exhaust any possibility that the animal victims could walk out of danger, even if this means digging a way out such as a passage or a ledge with heavy machinery, in which case the job and challenge will be to keep the animals still and calm during the effort, in spite of the loud noises and tremors in the terrain.

Mechanical advantages

If the technical rescue is decided upon, then hardware and mechanical advantages and species-specific harnesses ought to be considered first. For larger animals, to withstand heavy and repeated weights, steel cables would seem to be advisable, but the use of machines and engines such as electric-powered winches may actually put them in more danger, as the sensitivity of when to stop to readjust or avoid an obstacle or any issue is lost, and the pulling or lifting forces could end up crushing bones and organs, not to mention what would happen to anyone if one of these cables were to snap under tension.

There are, however, manual winches and manually operated lifting systems such as the 'come alongs' and cable grip clamps that can compensate these problems and that are the tool of choice when dealing with very heavy animal victims, if only because of the weights they can handle and the limited-motion range manual mechanism that allows for careful processes.

Stretchers

When moving a large animal, the amount of loose soil, rocks and debris resulting from such a large body and 'dead' weight moving away from the bottom can be a safety consideration for the animal and for the rescue team. In fact, a scared animal may end up kicking and struggling, thus causing more falling debris than may have originally been estimated. For such scenario, special kinds of 'stretchers' have been developed by large animal rescue specialists to allow for the strapped and immobilised victims to slide easily to safety. This works well when having to deal with the natural drag of heavy loads or with complicated features in the terrain and obstacles such as stumps, branches, roots and rocks getting in the way of a large body in a harness going against an inclined angle or a wall of any kind on its way up.

Water rescue

The rescue of animals in water is a far more serious proposition than it may initially seem (Walsh and Gannon, 1967). The force of moving water needs to be carefully considered, influenced by the gradient and the nature of the surface (features and resistance coefficient) of the substrate, the initial speed of the stream (total gradients) and the volume of the body of water. As an example, water flowing at an easy walking speed (less than 5 km an hour) can start knocking crossing cattle off their hooves at slightly less than three feet in depth. Flooding can start rapidly and forcefully and with little warning, sweeping away everything and everyone on its path, then expanding sideways out of the riverbanks onto floodplains. Several international companies offer training on swift water rescue techniques, such as Rescue 3 International,[1] and all rescue teams should be of swiftwater responder level if operating in water with animals.

Water rescue can be divided into two different categories: rescue in moving and still waters (flash versus expansion stages of flooding), plus a sub-division on residual mud entrapment. Moving waters are riskier, given the powers that water carries. Laminar water currents can also carry suspended logs and sinking cyclonic or barbed wire fences and vehicles, while at the bottom (and depending on the force of the current) they may carry boulders rolling down the stream. Finally, there is also the hidden danger of dissolved chemicals and pathogens, with the potential to seriously harm animal victims and rescue teams alike long after the flood would have receded.

When possible, rescuers should aim to lead the animal to safety and out of the water rather than trying to physically handle it. In fact, animal rescuers should never jump in the water to try to make physical contact with an animal victim, as chances are both of them could end up in the same rescue scenario. When leading is not possible, either because the animal is tired or injured or the current is too strong, the alternative is making contact with the animal from the boat to try and secure it to the side of the boat with ropes (head, abdomen and tail) or to attach floatation devices to it, but in a way that to secure its breathing. In past situations, spending an hour or more in the water, hanging by the side of a boat made cattle numb and unable to walk once secure landing was reached.

This difficulty was overcome by patience and a slower and calmer transition from the river to the shore, until the animals regained control of their limbs. Once out of the water, and past the initial veterinary check-up, hypothermia should be the next consideration for rescued animals.

Mud entrapments

Mud entrapment is a complicated form of rescue, as there may be no solid footing for team members and the equipment to work with, let alone the high anchor point that may be needed for the rescue. To resolve the lack of solid footing, wooden boards or inflatable platforms are used to allow the teams to approach the victim. In many cases, and once certain about the relative good health of the animal victim, clearing the debris and the mud in front and out to safety while providing secure footing for the animal using sand, gravel, wooden boards or smaller stones may be all large animals need to get to safety by their own means.

Negative pressure can form in mud entrapments which creates a suction effect making the removal of the animal much more difficult. To resolve this issue, devices called 'octopus' have been developed to pump water or/and compressed air underneath the body of the animal victim until a layer between the body of the victim and the mud forms, releasing the negative pressure so the victim can more easily be pulled to safety.

Other entrapments

Animals of all kinds may fall into and get trapped in gutters, sinkholes, between apartment buildings, from trees or rocks, or into wells, structures or mud holes. In these cases, they may need careful manoeuvring, secure footing and gentle or even firm pulling or pressure from solid pressure points. Once again, the safety of rescuers is paramount and foremost here; the use of boards or plywood panels to secure footing around the entrapment point and safety tape to keep crowds away are necessary. Finally, foreseeing the likely flight pattern of a scared animal just rescued may help avoid injury.

Entrapment under collapsed structures

This is probably the most dangerous type of rescue, with tremendous skills and equipment needed for identifying the victim, reaching it, shoring the entrance and approach and then starting the painful and dangerous task of liberating and extricating it. In the case of animal victims, this challenging veterinary scenario brings crushing or traumatic rhabdomyolysis syndrome as the factor to watch for before attempting to free an entrapped animal that has been in that position and predicament for more than 20 minutes.

This can become a systemic condition characterised by major shock, renal failure and other neurological issues, once the crushing pressure on skeletal muscle is released by rescuers or otherwise. When possible, the recommended in situ field treatment is fluid, overloading the patient with added Dextran 4000 *iu* and controlled release of pressure, while watching for hypotension signs. In extreme limb trapped cases, a tourniquet may need to be applied in situ to control release by a veterinarian experienced in field trauma cases. It cannot be overemphasised how dangerous collapsed structures are to the rescuer and serious consideration should be given to engaging these rescues. As a minimum, close liaison with rescue services should be undertaken to ascertain the safety of the structure and the permissions to operate.

Collapsed animals

In this case, veterinary diagnoses and prognoses are paramount. Animals may collapse after a traffic accident, through poisoning, lightening, electrocution, drowning, heat stroke, hypothermia, disease, fights with other animals or a fall. The veterinarian needs to define the next course of action before activating technical rescue teams.

Fire rescue

During fires, smoke inhalation and burns are likely to happen, especially if the animals are trapped and cannot flee. If they can escape, locating and retrieving them to safety will be the task at hand.

Smoke inhalation and exposure to hot gases can lead to bad burns in the upper respiratory tracts, which in turn usually develop into respiratory infections. As for skin burns, field treatment depends on the degree of the burn, but it is usually slow, difficult and full of secondary infections.

Oil/fuel spills

Depending upon the nature of the spill and the relative 'heaviness' of the oil or fuel, the rate of success for clean-up efforts and survivability of rehabilitating animals is very low, and demands a lot of manpower and resources. Many oil companies task specialised teams whose mission is to develop protocols to treat oil spill animal victims, not necessarily allowing third parties and volunteers into these operations. Impromptu volunteers are seldom welcomed during oil spill clean-up operations, other than helping on very basic tasks.

There are a good number of protocols and instructional videos on the web that provide insight into the steps of oiled bird cleaning, of which the following knowledge is required (International Bird Rescue, 2017):

- training, team building, resources needed, logistics;
- setting up camp, team, facilities, equipment and roles/tasks, biosecurity;
- ID, adapted triage, search and rescue;
- vet assessment, transport, biosafety;
- stabilisation and vet treatment;
- cleaning, washing, rinsing, drying;
- observation: feeding, weight gain, blood values, behaviour;
- waterproofing, feather rebuilding and general recovering;

- banding and releasing;
- monitoring and evaluation (M&E).

Many of these steps may be applied to species other than birds, but the low success rates on bird recovery, however, will most probably be there anyway.

Wild animal rescues

With the technical rescue of wild animals there may be two main scenarios: zoo animals and wild species of animals in the wild. In most cases, extra precautions will need to be taken, as the levels of aggressiveness can surprise even the experienced.

Zoological parks

Zoo animals and wild animal collections threatened by hazards should always have pre-existing emergency evacuation plans that will allow the staff to evacuate, recapture or provide for alternate plans to shelter them in case of need, and it is up to the local governments to request such plans, training, equipment and drills, all in coordination with the local authorities, police, chief veterinary office and local veterinarians. Where the zoo has been abandoned, extra caution is advised. In the case of a natural disaster, cages may be damaged and insecure, animals may be desperate and inventories of what the area actually contains may not be present to plan for risks.

Animals in the wild

Wild animals affected by disastrous events may be affected in terms of their immediate survival or in the longer term through damage to their ecosystems. They may also be impacted by changes to their food sources, shelter or their population numbers (encroachment, new competitors or fragmentation of their genetics through isolation). In the past, large wildlife relocation programmes have been carried out during hydroelectric dam projects in which, in the case of Latin America, once the artificial flooding began, many wild animals were forced to the tops of trees and hills receding or turning into small islands.

Marine mammal rescues

This is a unique category that involves highly intelligent animals evolved to swim tens of kilometres a day. Experience shows that the requisites for the enclosures and the feeding of dolphins pale in front of the preparations for transporting them back to freedom, as their sensitive, complex skin needs to be protected. Marine mammal rescues should only be attempted by specialist teams with the right equipment, including flotation aids in case of stunned or traumatised animals.

Chemical immobilisation of wildlife: darting

With regard to remote chemical immobilisation of wild animals with darts, dart guns and blowpipes, these are tools that need the utmost care by experienced personnel, as the smallest shift, change or mistake may cause the dart to hit a bone or a joint and end up causing much more damage than good. With blowpipes at one end of the spectrum, dart guns and rifles can mount enough power to pierce through an animal clean or even kill it.

It is often hard to avoid muscle abscesses caused by the blowing up of an anaesthetic in a leg or the back, hence the need for experienced practitioners. If the animal is too old, too young, sick, weary, pregnant, or stressed enough by the chase; if the guessing of the weight by the operator of the gun misses by enough of a fraction of the safety margin, the target may metabolise the drug and render it useless, or it may collapse under it, compromising its breathing, temperature and life.

In the past, this lethal combination of darts, chasing and loud crowds around these captures have ended up with dead animals falling from trees, being drowned in ponds or plainly having died from stress and shock, their breathing and vital functions debilitated under the drugs.

Transport equipment for wild animals

Transport of wild animals requires much more expertise than that of domesticated animals. Sedation and specific enclosures for larger animals are in many cases a necessity and stress is a real issue. Cross-border paperwork and permits plus IATA live animal regulations in the case of air transport are the source of choice for building transport crates for wild animals.

Imprinting and domestication

In the case of baby animals born or caught at an early age, the process of imprinting means a wrong, filial, phase-sensitive, rapid learning in which newborns may believe their human captors are indeed their parents. Once consolidated, this is a very difficult process to reverse in order to return these individual animals to the wild, to be functional among their peers. Domestication is a term that goes beyond taming of an animal into a group of animals, sometimes using selective breeding, until their common traits (behaviour, size, litter size, hair colour, and even degree of dependency) are desirable to the tamer. During emergencies and disasters, wild animals held in prolonged captivity may become tamed and dependent on their human captors for food, thus rendering them unable to thrive in the wild again.

We have seen in this chapter that while the impulse to undertake immediate rescue may seem natural, the process, planning, equipping and delivery of animal rescue is highly specialised if we are to undertake it in the most humane way possible. Often formalised, technical animal rescue will only be found in developed countries where time and resources will allow. That said, informal animal rescue will occur outside of these spheres of knowledge on a regular basis;

thus this chapter aims to inform rescuers on the basic considerations and point them toward best practice. The next chapter covers the area where the animal responder can have the most immediate benefit through the provision of supportive aid to animals suffering in the aftermath of a disaster.

Note

1   http://rescue3.com/

Further reading

British Animal Rescue and Trauma Care Association (BARTA). (2017). *BARTA approved*. Available at: http://bartacic.org/barta-approval-scheme/

Giminez, R., Giminez, T. and May, K. (2008). *Technical Large Animal Rescue*. Ames, IA: Wiley-Blackwell.

Grandin, T. (1995). Restraint of livestock. In *Proceedings from The Animal Behaviour and the Design of Livestock and Poultry Systems International Conference, Indianapolis*, pp. 208–223.

Grandin, T. (ed.). (2014). *Livestock Handling and Transport*, 3rd edn. Wallingford, UK: CABI.

Grandin, T. (2017). *Behavioral Principles of Livestock Handling*. Professional Animal Scientist. American Registry of Professional Animal Scientists, Colorado. Available at: www. grandin.com/references/new.corral.html

International Bird Rescue. (2017). *Our Process for Helping Oiled Birds*. Available at: www.bird-rescue.org/our-work/aquatic-bird-rehabilitation/our-process-for-helping-oiled-birds.aspx

Wingfield, W. and Palmer, S. (2009). *Veterinary Disaster Response*. New York: Wiley-Blackwell.

References

British Animal Rescue and Trauma Care Association (BARTA). (2017). *BARTA approved*. Available at: http://bartacic.org/barta-approval-scheme/

Giminez, R., Giminez, T. and May, K. (2008). *Technical Large Animal Rescue*. New York: Wiley-Blackwell.

Grandin, T. (n.d.). Research Articles on Animal Behavior, Welfare, and Reducing Stress. A range of papers available at: www.grandin.com/references/research.html

Grandin, T. (ed.). (2014). *Livestock Handling and Transport*, 3rd edn. Wallingford, UK: CABI.

Grandin, T. (2017). *Behavioral Principles of Livestock Handling*. Professional Animal Scientist. American Registry of Professional Animal Scientists, Colorado. Available at: www. grandin.com/references/new.corral.html

International Air Transport Association. (2016). *Live Animals Regulation*. Available at: www. iata.org/publications/store/pages/live-animals-regulation.aspx

International Bird Rescue. (2017). *Our Process for Helping Oiled Birds*. Available at: www.bird-rescue.org/our-work/aquatic-bird-rehabilitation/our-process-for-helping-oiled-birds.aspx

Knowles, T. and Campbell, R. (2014). *A Benefit–Cost Analysis of WSPA's 2012 Intervention in the Dhemaji District of Assam, India*. Melbourne: Economists at Large.

Rescue 3 International. (2015). *Water Courses*. Available at: http://rescue3.com/water-courses/

Technical Large Animal Emergency Rescue. Available at: http://tlaer.org/

Walsh, J. and Gannon, R. (1967). *Time Is Short and the Water Rises*. London: Nelson.

5

IMMEDIATE RELIEF FOR ANIMALS

In the last chapter we explored methods that responders could use to rescue animals in distress but in reality this is rarely possible as travel times to disaster zones mean that teams arrive too late. In this chapter we take the needs of animals post disaster as described in Chapter 4 and explore how they can be adequately met, working within the confines of the event itself. When providing immediate relief, the starting animal welfare stage is the benchmark contextualised by the Five Freedoms (among other definitions). It is important to note that rarely in disaster-prone countries is the welfare of people or animals optimum prior to a disaster and the remit of the responder is to consider how to find the right balance between addressing acute needs and those relating to longer-term development issues.

Within animal welfare, some agencies will choose to meet only the needs of the animal caused by the disaster while some will aim to go further and attempt to improve conditions for animals using the disaster as an opportunity where a clean slate and political interest are on one's side. It could be argued that the latter should be an aspiration of any operation but the reality may well be related to resource availability.

Here it is also important to note that any support you may provide to an animal during normal times may be very different to that during the aftermath of a disaster. As an example, in order to help more animals with limited resources, one may choose to deliver 'survival' levels of feed as opposed to those found in a standard feed table. These are all considerations, and often a dilemma that a disaster response leader will have to take into account when planning their work.

As described earlier in the book, generally animals suffer in the same way as people and experience similar, basic needs. The following relief actions are the most common in emergency response for animals:

- evacuation
- shelter
- food and water
- emergency veterinary treatment.

We should also remember that the animal welfare imperative to attempt to prevent suffering and unnecessary death is important but disaster relief for animals also has an important role to play in the humanitarian response. Protecting the pet-owner bond or the capacity of the farm animal owner to recover after an emergency are the classic examples of resilience for communities. Studies are starting to show how early stage intervention for animals protects communities and economies (Knowles and Campbell, 2014) effectively in the aftermath of a disaster. Animals are not as easy to replace as a roof; often rebuilding stock levels can take years and yet they provide an important productive asset to communities that they cannot be without for extended periods.

Baseline animal welfare – what is normal?

In order to determine what an animal's immediate needs are, we first need to understand what normal behaviour would be. This allows us to compare with the animal/s we are assessing and make a judgement if their behaviour is abnormal and how to bring them back to the right place. Animal welfare is not possible without good health, and disasters are known to threaten the health and lives of both humans and animal victims. With animals, health may be assessed in similar ways to humans; by their output in the case of farm and working animals, and in the absence of clear communication to express feelings, by behavioural indicators. The generalised disruption of care and animal husbandry following a disaster may eventually catch up with the rest of unharmed survivors, but that comes at a later moment in time, and is considered to be the second wave of victims.

Depending on the species, age, group size and health, a 'normal' animal would:

- be alert and inquisitive about its environment;
- display a range of activities, play;
- interact with members of its species, especially its herd or flock;
- interact with humans but keep its flight distance;
- look healthy – bright eyes, look lean and muscular, be walking and moving normally.

Following the same criteria, an 'abnormal' animal would:

- limit its range of activity, show signs of lameness, alter its posture;
- display shyness, and not play;
- refuse to eat;
- show little or no response to external stimuli;

- show sickness or pain behaviours, increased respiratory rate;
- display abnormal fear or aggression towards humans;
- display irritability, abnormal aggression, fright;
- show stereotypes (biting, pacing, feather-pecking, over-licking).

In the case of animal survivors after a disaster, rapid disaster assessments in the field need to document the quality and the quantity of these behavioural observations and then undertake extrapolations to larger communities of animals and areas. This documenting process will no doubt highlight changes and will be important to draw conclusions that will influence the team's planned relief actions that may help reduce the stress and symptoms in the animal victims.

Assessing animal welfare and sentience

The notion of animal welfare is about how successful the life of animals may be and this is greatly influenced by the actions of humans. It is important to consider how the standards of 'good' animal welfare vary considerably between different contexts, geographies, beliefs and systems. These standards are influenced by our own experiences, by society's preconceptions and perceptions, by tradition, education, uses, economics and stability, by the industry of entertainment and the industry of farm animal production to cite but a few. Animal welfare standards are also under constant review and debate, contested by some religions, while supported by others; elaborated and revised by philosophers, animal lovers, animal welfare groups, scientists and legislators worldwide. They include indicators such as longevity (especially for companion animals), immune-suppression or proclivity to disease, behavioural traits per species, physiology and reproduction under what's expected to be normal for each species.

Body scoring

For those interested in practical, field-adapted tools to rapidly assess the health and welfare of an animal during a disaster situation, there are conventions in the animal science world to measure the physical wellness of different animal species by body measurements known as body condition scoring. These charts have been developed based on the amount of bone visible underneath the muscle structures, with preference on lumbar vertebrae, ribs, pelvic bones as well as any evident body prominences. The presence or lack of body fat, bone structures more or less apparent, muscle mass or lack thereof and/or protuberant abdomen is what will give away the condition, and hopefully the relative health and welfare of that animal. The score ranges from 1 to 5 or from 1 to 9, and from emaciated to obese. These charts are available for cattle of various types (dairy and beef), equines, pigs, dogs and cats, among other species, but are unavailable and of little or no use for birds, given their feathery cover. In assessing general health and making extrapolations from this, body condition scoring is the most useful tool to a disaster assessor. It must, however, be noted that disaster assessors may be moving quickly between groups of animals and not able to assess all, so a sample of animals would normally be reviewed across ages and sexes to ascertain a general health of the animals. It is also important to note that body condition scoring can be done by the lay-person with the correct photographic guides but is much quicker done by an experienced eye.

In the case of birds, palpation will be necessary to avoid the feather mirage. Breast musculature should be rounded, and on most species, reach the top end of the keel bone or leading edge of the breastbone. The rule of thumb for an emaciated bird is that the keel may be pinched and the bone felt with the pads of your fingers. The same goes for the lumbar area and the lower back. The lime-green droppings resulting from an empty gastro-intestinal tract producing bile on automatic can also help diagnose starvation in birds. Both extremes of the chart are signs of further metabolic problems, but in the case of disasters, starving animals will start to register as negatively scoring after only a few days of not eating, and will start showing one or several signs such as dehydration, weight loss, reduced output, fatigue and reduced mobility.

While the Five Freedoms are a useful framework to base any disaster assessment around, Professor Emeritus John Webster (2008), a specialist in animal husbandry at the University of Bristol, UK, defines this state as the existence of three positive conditions, which may be more poetic than the Five Freedoms, but are also more subjective to the eye of the beholder:

- living a natural life
- being fit and healthy
- being happy.

Living a 'natural' life may be very a different proposition for wild and domesticated animals, as the lives of domesticated animals revolve around humans. In the same manner, a dog chained to a post to guard his master's house is far from natural, just as farm animals living in intensive conditions aren't either. Being 'fit' is also not easy when an animal is tied on a chain or under intensive farming conditions, while being 'healthy' may be heavily influenced by the same conditions plus veterinary care. Finally, happiness or being 'happy' might be the hardest emotion or stage to demonstrate in animals, but most researchers associate that to 'normal' behaviour per species and to playing, or to the absence of fear and anguish.

Main welfare issues during disasters

With these basic notions in mind, it is important to recap on the mental 'picture' of the welfare of an animal being compromised by the extraordinary conditions of a disaster, and just barely having survived them (Figure 5.1). These would be the main missing essential components for their basic well-being:

FIGURE 5.1 Cattle stranded in floods in the north of England in 2015
Source: Russell Sach for BARTA.

1   Stress, discomfort, pain, fear, injury and risk of immediate death will be the first concerns and threats to their welfare and for any animal in a disastrous situation.
2   Thirst and hunger are usually the second concern.
3   The danger of disease and secondary infections, more discomfort, more fear, starvation, lack of natural behaviour displays and risk of eventual death (again) will follow.
4   These may not be all the factors to consider in the field, but during emergency conditions and pressed with time to provide emergency relief, it may be all rescue teams may be able to do.

Immediate relief

To cope with and manage these risks, five distinct events in time and space can be identified. The immediate relief and attention to animals during and right after disasters of shorter onset nature includes offering animal victims or animals in danger the following services:

•   **evacuation** for domestic animals, including pre-existing or emergency ramps for farm animals and control measures such as transport cages and leashes for pets;

- safe **shelter** for farm animals, including corrals and barns, while for pets it is usually alternative accommodation with friends and family, or temporary shelters;
- **water and food** (pet food or fodder) to domestic and zoo animals, to help them survive a stressful, disastrous situation and for all kinds of disasters that may disrupt access and care for them;
- **first veterinary aid** for wounds and traumas, plus prophylactic treatments to prevent prevalent pathogens and first infections in all kinds of disasters;
- securing the **animal–human bond**; emergency sheltering should include reassurances in the later stages for reuniting pets with their owners, to keep the bond intact.

Evacuation

Pets

The welfare and destiny of companion animals in need of evacuation during disasters depends initially and in no small measure upon their owners and the preparedness plans they may or may not have created ahead of time. An ideal pet owner would train his/her pet to walk down the stairs from an apartment building; train them to jump inside a carrier; socialise with other animals and get used to staying with friends or family in case their owners may not be able to take them with them during an emergency evacuation. The same pet owner would have his pet properly identified with a tag or a microchip in case it runs away and will have everything handy to evacuate with his/her pet, such as vaccination registries, as well as photos, all kept in waterproof containers, just in case. Whether leaving the pet behind or evacuating with one, different logistical considerations are created for authorities.

The relative importance animal lives may have is completely dependent upon their owners' views. The decision to rescue and help them during emergencies will, in part, relate to their owners, but also to the priorities (and limitations) of emergency crews and other civil functions. This is clearly influenced by customs, social conventions, laws, the economy of the market in the case of farm animals and the means of animal owners. These factors will always be more decisive in the decision-making process to start an animal rescue mission, than the rescue team skills and training.

In many disasters such as Hurricane Katrina in 2006 and the Japanese Tsunami of 2013, owners went to great lengths to protect their pets, often to the hindrance of human rescue efforts, but this isn't always the case. In Venezuela in the Vargas state in 1999, rescue teams found many pets left behind in apartment buildings after a flash mudslide, and most need new families to adopt them, a rehoming effort put together by the local municipality and local and international NGOs and with the help of local radio stations. A similar situation happened in post-conflict Kosovo in 1999 and 2000, where hundreds of dogs were left behind roaming the main cities after the inhabitants were forced out based on their ethnic origins. Apart from saving an animal life, the main mission of pet rescue is to maintain the integrity of the animal–owner bond, especially in the context of the family unit and of pets being part of that unit. Studies show how important this bond is to pet owners in recovering from loss.

Livestock

Large animal evacuation involves personnel, ramps, bedding, trucks, experienced handlers, veterinary certificates, IDs, and alternate pastures and corrals for destination. Probably as important, however, is the eventuality of having to use the same routes of exit as the human population would; an issue that poses serious security and logistical problems. Considering this, livestock should be evacuated earlier than the evacuation of people, not to complicate, hamper or endanger human evacuation in any way. If this isn't possible (and this is likely) livestock have to take a lesser priority and be evacuated after human evacuations have occurred, or take different routes. Depending on the nature of the disaster, its location and resources at hand, the right decision should be made. It is clear from experience, however, that undertaking this task at the same time as human evacuation should be avoided.

During the 2008 eruption of the Chaiten volcano in Chile, a layer of over 20 cm of solid volcanic ash turned into a thick cement-like paste by the constant rains that completely covered the fields, forcing thousands of head of cattle and sheep to evacuate. The government sent dozens of cattle transport trucks, but once in place, they found themselves not equipped with enough bedding for the long journey to safety. When that was taken care of, the truckers and the farmers realised there were not enough loading ramps available to safely load the animals. When both issues were taken care of, the lack of veterinary certificates needed to cross borders became an issue and by the time everything was in place, only the cattle were able to be evacuated.

Sometimes local economics or even the market economy can hamper evacuation plans due to low prices for farm animal by-products (meat, milk, wool, fibre, eggs), high transport costs and lack of alternative pastures, which ends up forcing owners to abandon the animals to their fate. Often insurance for livestock, not adequately linked to risk reduction and preparedness can also lead to the abandonment of livestock with a belief from farmers that their loss will be covered regardless. In other instances, evacuation is simply not a reality because of geography or lack of logistical resources. In the Beni region of Bolivia, year after year, tens of thousands of animals would be trapped by floods covering thousands of square kilometres, making the provision and transport of emergency fodder or evacuation a daunting task. Soon enough, weakness, starvation and respiratory infections finished most survivors.

A disaster responder should not underestimate the logistical considerations of the movement of large numbers of livestock. Considerations such as feed and water and the method of transport need to be carefully planned. If herding as a form of movement, permissions may be required across private land, feed and water stations may be required en route and there may be national or regional requirements relating to the registration of movement of animals off farm that need consideration. Often responders will forget about the location, such is the focus required on the journey, and may find the end location of the journey poorly equipped or requiring mixing of herds, surfacing a host of new veterinary challenges. Evacuation thus should be considered a last resort where populations cannot be made more resilient to the effects of the disaster but at the same time shouldn't be left so late as to be either counterproductive or compromising to animal welfare.

Zoo animals

Most zoos and zoological collections have a modest inventory of transport crates according to IATA live animal regulations (IATA, 2017), or CITES specifications (CITES, 1981), animal handling equipment and trained personnel but seldom enough to evacuate their entire animal collection or in haste. Without pre-existing protocols and staff trained and experienced in animal evacuation, it may be virtually impossible to successfully move an entire zoo collection away from danger. Problems also occur when one considers where these animals might go in this eventuality. Many animals may not be suited to standardised enclosures, may be too dangerous to move quickly or may not survive outside the very specialised environments found in the zoo.

Wild animals

Only a few successful documented examples of mass evacuations of wildlife exist in this field, and these were mainly undertaken to evacuate wild populations away from extensive flooding caused by hydroelectric dam projects. In 1964 ISPA sent a young John Walsh to Suriname to rescue wild animals from land being flooded by the Brokopondo dam. In 18 months and with a team of locals, Walsh rescued over 10,000 animals in Operation Gwamba, which captured the imagination of the press. His book *Time is Short and the Water Rises* (Walsh and Gannon, 1967) details the difficulties of operating in such environments. Animals were captured with darting and cage traps and relocated to higher ground once they had passed through observation and quarantine camps. Subsequent operations (Noah and Noah 2) saw similar efforts. In recent years no large-scale wild animal relocations have been attempted.

It is important to note than reintroductions of wild animals are difficult and often unsuccessful, more so, the longer the animal is out of its natural habitat. These new areas for relocated wildlife must have been monitored in advance, to assess whether the environmental impact of newly arrived animals may be absorbed without negative consequences to the ecosystem or without exceeding the natural carrying capacity. Ideally, relocated animals should be monitored post release to ensure success of the operation. The best land for a wildlife reintroduction may be recovering secondary forest areas in which previous hunting and human encroachment may have thinned the wild animal population in the past, but that may now be protected by a change in legislation or similar, to become home for the new wild animals. This new population may in fact help the recovery of the forest, if able to stay undisturbed and protected.

Shelter

Pets

Pet animals are often not allowed entry into human shelters, normally on sanitation and human health grounds, and this often drives human behaviour contrary to the wider rescue effort. This can include refusing to evacuate, leaving animals behind to fend for themselves and people returning to high risk areas to tend for their animals. None of these actions should be considered desirable by a local authority. In the case of family pets, authorities need to consider the building of temporary shelters near the human shelters. When possible, cleaning, feeding and exercise should be the responsibility of the same pet owners, to maintain the bond and the peace of mind of both. Keeping the pet–human bond intact is difficult during emergencies, and where emergency dog shelters are built near human shelters during forced evacuations, the secret to maintaining this bond and avoiding proliferation of unwanted animals at the end of the emergency is to assign the maintenance and animal care duties to the animal owners themselves.

Virtual dog shelters

After an earthquake hit the Cinchona region in Costa Rica in 2009, a dog shelter built near ground zero was soon deemed unfit to hold rescued pets for longer periods of time, as conditions of humidity and low temperature would have taken a toll on the surviving pet dogs sheltered there. The alternative chosen was to dismantle the shelter (all animals had been through registration, quarantine, first aid and feeding), and to organise a media push to find temporary volunteers willing to hold one dog each for a few weeks, right in the middle of the capital city. Pet food and regular veterinary care visits were organised and distributed, together with another public push to find the original owners of those animals, or to put the rest for adoption. With proper organisation and publicity, this was cheaper, more effective and a much more pleasant and humane experience for the animal guests than the original one. This is a model that should be considered more often where a willing donor population is available and local animal groups are willing but lack the physical capacity to house animals.

Sheltering of companion animals is a distinct area of knowledge and while conditions in disasters may preclude responders from creating idyllic shelters, accessing some expertise on the set up, management and day to day running of shelters will undoubtedly add value to a sheltering effort, improve security, increase chances of rehoming, be more cost efficient and (most importantly) be better for the residents/welfare.

Livestock

In the case of considerable numbers of livestock in need of shelter, ministries of agriculture, municipal governments and livestock chambers are closer to the animal victims and their owners than the central government to organise alternative, temporary shelter and fodder for farm animals during a disaster. Livestock auctions may be a good alternative point to start. Segregation of animals by origin and age is crucial during temporary sheltering, to avoid aggression and fighting, and there should also be quarantine and treatment areas. Due to the size of potential herds and the needs of the animals, the authors would always propose that provision of sheltering materials for individual farmers or communities for livestock remains more productive than mass evacuations and sheltering of livestock in alternative locations. This has the secondary benefit of not forcing farmers to relocate with their animals away from centres of existing livelihoods and local economies.

Wildlife

The most treatment-intensive temporary shelter for wild animals occurs during oiled bird and marine mammal rehabilitation projects, controlled and handled by specialised groups. In the case of wildlife rehabilitation centres for animals caught in forest fires, affected by trauma due to hurricanes, or just starving during droughts, avoidance of human contact is paramount to in turn avoid domestication of the young and imprinting of the adult individuals, as well as biosecurity measures to avoid outbreaks and zoonosis. Designs do exist for dolphin rehabilitation and release projects, built in the proximity of other dolphin pods, away from oil spilling areas and heavy boat traffic, with as much depth as possible, good currents and if available, good marine life nearby.

Food and water

Providing food and water in situ versus after evacuation brings in different logistical considerations. When in situ, it is important to cover bowls, water and food receptacles from contamination such as in the case of volcanic ash fall. Emergency pet food (normally of concentrated dried kind) if different from usual diets often causes digestive problems such as diarrhoea, as they may not be accustomed to the specific make, flavour and consistency of the new rations. Solving this is difficult, as they may be several brands on the local market at one given time. Protection of feed is also key as subsequent events (further ash fall, further floods, aftershocks) may damage storage areas or contaminate feed. Consideration needs to be placed on water rations for dried concentrated food which will need to be increased to take account of this.

Once one has considered that emergency feeding is the right choice, a key decision needs to be made on the quantities and length of feed. While in optimum conditions, the availability of feed would allow for normal feeding regimes for indefinite periods, a disaster will compromise these factors. In order to keep animals alive, survival rations, or merely mineral support may be the only option. Where possible any feed operation should last for the time it takes to restore normal feeding. For floods this would be a minimum of a month, but as was the case in the 2015 Cyclone Pam in Vanuatu, severe damage to all vegetation meant an emergency feed period of three months was required. Too often feed operations extend to a few days of supplies rather than a meaningful attempt to sustain life beyond the acute phase of the aftermath.

Livestock

Livestock also cannot be automatically assumed to be comfortable with processed feed if they have fed for all of their lives on natural pasture. Consideration of normal diets and the impact of a change to this should form a key part of any feeding intervention. Equally, animals in feed lots may have only ever experienced concentrated feed and as such could react to more natural food in a similar

FIGURE 5.2 A WSPA disaster responder assesses a goat on Malalison Island, Philippines after Cyclone Haiyan in 2013

Source: James Sawyer for WAP.

manner. Obtaining emergency feed and water in large quantities and amounts for large numbers of farm animals such as in the case of extended droughts has proven very difficult in many situations in America and Africa. This often involves trucking in large quantities at great cost over long distances, thus where possible local alternatives should be sought. In 2013 in Vanuatu, the island's Copra production had temporarily halted and this material was available at reasonable price and quantity to provide emergency livestock feed. Where local people perceive their animals may die, some cultures will slaughter and consume the meat while others will hang on to the animal even when its condition deteriorates terribly. These social factors need to be considered in designing a disaster intervention that works for animal populations. Equally important are the decisions made around quantities of feed; where there are limited resources and large numbers, the authors would always advocate for survival rations rather than those detailed in conventional feed tables as a way of improving the well-being and survival rates of more animals.

Wild animals

Rescued wild animals may need fruit, vegetables or meat, depending on their diet. It is important to consider that some wild animals' diets are highly specialised, and more generalised offerings of food for them can lead to either refusal to eat or significant gastro-intestinal distress.

Emergency veterinary treatment

Unlike other normal treatments, emergency veterinary treatment focuses on veterinary first aid, and ensuring the immediate survival of the animals in case of shock, injury, intoxication, suffocation, or cardiac or respiratory arrest (Figure 5.2). It may also include elements of supportive care for animals under stress such as vitamin injections. When considering these measures for farm animals often a cost–benefit analysis may come into play and it may be necessary to employ an adapted version of triage such as VMAT or VSTART.

Veterinary treatment can be delivered in a range of different ways. In terms of professional competence, treatment may be delivered by veterinarians, zoo technicians, para-vets or vet-nurses. In some parts of the world treatment may also be administered by community animal health workers and sometimes by animal control officers or even unskilled volunteers. There is not necessarily any hierarchy in this list as experience in a disaster may be as equally valuable as professional knowledge and competence. Generally, however, the rule should be that vets, para-vets and vet nurses administer treatments appropriate to their skill level and other individuals provide a supportive function such as wound dressing and logistical support (filling syringes). Often, volunteers enrolling in disaster response operations assume the biggest challenge they may face will be the trip abroad, foreign food, and long, hot, humid hours, when in fact, translation, handling fractious animals, coordination, accommodation, security will be the first concerns, followed by secure transportation and drinkable water. Forse (1999) offers a very practical guide to emergency care for animals that all non-veterinarians involved in this field should be conversant with.

Most importantly however, is the fact that the veterinary skills needed are quite similar to war medicine, with field surgery and orthopaedics needed during the first week or so, quickly followed by field and internal medicine, soon followed by veterinary epidemiology. During large events such as the quake in Mexico City on 19 September 1985, the tsunami in Sri Lanka on 26 December 2004, or the earthquake in Port au Prince on 12 January 2010, volunteer veterinarians and veterinary technicians encountered challenges that overwhelmed regular skills and for which they were not prepared or trained for. This resulted in nasty complications such as sutures that came undone, compassion fatigue and animal attacks. Field skills and especially emergency veterinary First Aid need constant drilling and a lot of practice.

Treatment may be delivered from a range of locations depending on the nature of the disaster and the facilities available (Figure 5.3). At its most mobile it could be delivered from a backpack in a field location or from the back of a pickup truck as a temporary clinic. Community clinics set up in an agreed gathering point utilising folding tables is very appropriate for visiting damaged communities. At

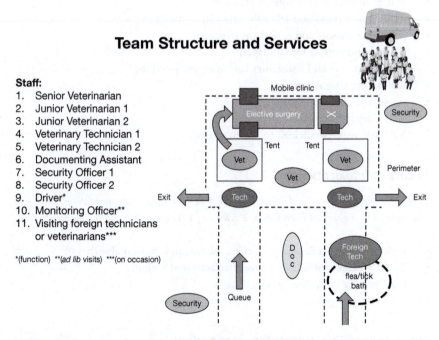

Team Structure and Services

Staff:
1. Senior Veterinarian
2. Junior Veterinarian 1
3. Junior Veterinarian 2
4. Veterinary Technician 1
5. Veterinary Technician 2
6. Documenting Assistant
7. Security Officer 1
8. Security Officer 2
9. Driver*
10. Monitoring Officer**
11. Visiting foreign technicians or veterinarians***

*(function) **(ad lib visits) ***(on occasion)

FIGURE 5.3 A suggested team structure and location plan for mobile clinics

Source: Gerardo Huertas.

the other end of the scale are the more resource-intensive mobile clinic vehicles and operations out of existing veterinary practices. All of these will have different operating needs but most will need some kind of awareness programme ahead of opening in order to ensure that people in the community know when and where to bring their animals. This can be achieved via loudhailer or through other community communication methods (usually SMS from the head of the community) these days.

First Aid kits for pet animals

For pet owners, an emergency First Aid kit for pet animals should include:

- your pet's prescription if under treatment and the contact info of your vet;
- veterinary records and control card (treatments, vaccines) and pet photos;
- phone numbers of the pet's vet, shelters, friends;
- water bottle, pet food;
- latex gloves, plastic bags, soap, towels and blanket (as a stretcher).
- leash, muzzle, pillow case for cat treatment;
- flashlight, batteries;
- digital thermometer and lubricant;
- eye drops;
- non-prescription antibiotic ointment;
- sterile gauze, tape and self-adhering elastic bandages;
- blunt end scissors and round tip tweezers;
- alcohol and cotton for bandages;
- wooden pallets and magazines for emergency splints;
- wound dressing materials;
- antiseptic: chlorhexidine;
- saline sterile solution;
- 5 ml syringes (needleless) to clean wounds.

In case of intoxications

From here on, medicines and instruments included in these recommendations should be administered by a qualified veterinarian, a veterinary technician, or under specific prescriptions:

- milk of magnesia & activated charcoal capsules (poison absorbent);
- 20 ml syringes (needle- less) to offer activated carbon;
- oral cannula with syringe adaptor;
- 3% hydrogen peroxide.

Small animal First Aid kits for veterinarians

(In addition to the above)

- resuscitation kit for acute haemorrhage, shock, circulatory insufficiency in small animals;
- phone list for Animal Health authorities;
- stethoscope;
- stretcher (blanket);
- sterile minor surgery kit (scalpels and blades, Kelly haemostats, bulldog clamps, Mayo scissors and rat-toothed thumb forceps);
- tracheal intubation kit;
- Atropine Sulfate, epinephrine HCL, Nor-epinephrine, xylocaine, calcium gluconate, potassium chloride, neostigmine sulfate, phenylephrine HCL, doxopram HCL, gallamine triethiodine, sodium bicarbonate.

Large animal First Aid kits for veterinarians

- stethoscope;
- harness for horses, dairy cattle, pigs;
- 'Z' system for mechanical advantage;
- lassos;
- documenting camera;
- surgical gloves, goggles, disposable masks;
- road signals and magic tape;
- heavy duty scissors;
- tracheal intubation kit for horses;
- antibacterial soap;
- antibacterial ointment;
- towels, disposable diapers;
- ice pack;
- rubbing alcohol;
- hydrogen peroxide;
- flashlights and spare batteries
- halter and ropes;
- needle-nosed pliers;
- wire cutters;
- disposable gloves;
- gauze sponges;
- skin cleanser;
- sterile saline (gallon);
- water soluble ointment;
- screw type bloat-torcher;
- disposable shaving blades;
- rolls of vet type wrap;
- duct tape;
- fly repellent;
- large syringes (35–60 cc);

- rolled cotton;
- antibiotic eye ointment;
- thermometers;
- calcium borogluconate or oral calcium gel (bottles);
- water based lubricant;
- epinephrine;
- needles and small sized syringes;
- mineral oil;
- knives;
- phone numbers for emergency transport and chief vet office.

Nature of impact and animal affectation

The nature of the impact and effects of various types of disasters on animals is in principle, more severe than on humans due to the exposure and vulnerability their owners subject them to. This can be seen in dogs chained to a post during hurricanes or floods, pets hit or crushed by falling furniture inside the house, horses locked inside barns during a fire, or cattle and farm animals in corrals with the gates locked up by chains and locks no one can find the keys to, and in the face of flash floods, bush fires, high winds, or mudflows.

This impact can range from unnecessary stress to unnecessary suffering and death. These effects can include:

- scared pets running through glass doors or windows or into heavy traffic;
- dairy cattle stopping milk production and then developing mastitis;
- farm animals losing weight or injuring themselves;
- starvation during isolation periods;
- dying underwater;
- getting crushed under falling debris;
- entrapment and suffocation in mudslides, lahars, landslips or avalanches;
- burns, smoke inhalation and dehydration from fires;
- trauma due to falling or flying objects;
- intoxication, radiation damage or burns by hazardous materials;
- dehydration and starvation.

Animal needs by disaster type

The following offers general advice on the kind of problems encountered for animals in specific types of disasters. While it isn't exclusive, it should offer a useful guide in terms of planning for entering into such events.

Earthquake

Immediate needs are first veterinary aid, shelter, and avoidance of further hazards such as walking on debris, eating contaminated food, staying near or under unstable structures during replicas, and restoration of care. Secondary concerns should be aftershocks, unstable buildings, fires and live electrics.

Tsunami

Immediate needs are first veterinary aid, shelter and avoidance of further hazards such as debris, contaminated pastures and restoration of care. Ingestion of chemicals and other contaminants is often seen.

Flood

Immediate needs are first veterinary aid, shelter and avoidance of further hazards such as unstable structures. Contaminated water and pasture is a common problem, which requires emergency or supplemental feed.

Drought

Immediate needs are water, food and veterinary aid.

Hurricane/typhoon

Immediate needs are first veterinary aid, avoidance of further hazards such as loose objects, and restoration of care. Common secondary issues are degradation of water and pasture.

Fire

Immediate needs are first veterinary aid including burn treatments and therapy, respiratory therapy, shelter and food.

Volcano

Immediate needs may be evacuation, veterinary aid, shelter, and avoidance of further hazards such as lahars, lava and then restoration of care.

Oil spill

Immediate needs are included in the cleansing, treatment, feeding and rehabilitation protocols developed by specially trained teams.

Hazardous materials (HAZMAT), chemical, biological, radiological, nuclear (CBRN)

Immediate needs are included in specific protocols developed and applied by specially trained teams, but only after strict veterinary triage, VSTART and contamination potential sorting, depending on the nature (long-term versus short-term irradiation) isotope. In the case of biological agents, the infectivity of an agent is the ability to enter, survive and multiply in the host, and may be shown as the percentage of animals exposed to a dose who become infected. Virulence is the relative severity of the disease. Lethality is the death rate produced in an infected animal population. Pathogenicity is the ability of a pathogen to cause illness, measured by the ratio of the number of cases versus the number of exposed animals. Incubation period is the time between exposure of an animal and the appearance of symptoms. Finally and for contagious infections or outbreaks, contagiousness may be measured by the number (over time) of secondary cases after exposure to a primary case.

Principles of aid delivery for animals

Building back better

In spite of their tragic nature, emergencies and disasters can also be an opportunity providing unique opportunities to build more resilient lives for the animals belonging to people who may depend on them. Build back better means that every action taken during emergency relief work must be designed to decrease the vulnerability, or at least the exposure, of the affected animal populations and of course, their owners.

Do no harm

Emergency relief for animals should be an opportunity-generating moment for the owners of those animals to improve conditions and output, instead of inadvertently hindering eventual reconstruction and recovery hopes. As an example, the use of internal de-wormers of residual effect such as ivermectine compounds in farm animals, may, when entering the ground as droppings, impact on soil biodiversity and other animals in the ecosystem, and eventually the grass and the pastures themselves. Advice that can be offered to owners through the trust you have built by helping their animals can impart vital risk reduction and preparedness ideas or even advice on more humane day to day practices. Careful consideration of factors such as aid dependency and exit strategies that don't compromise animal welfare are as important as the actual aid delivered itself.

Prioritise recovery of livelihoods and local economy

This is precisely the anthropocentric point behind protecting the welfare of farm and working animals, and one of the important new agendas for the UN ISDR. In another more complex example, the importation of free dried milk to Haiti as donated food after the quake meant the final blow or *puntilla* for small dairy farmers elsewhere in the island. Thinking hard about where your aid comes from, who benefits from receiving it but equally who benefits from its purchase makes all the difference. As a rule as much should be procured locally as possible, both from a practicality point of view and in order to support the recovery of the country and communities.

Prioritise animal survival and recovery over restocking plans

Very few restocking projects have resulted in less vulnerable or more resilient animal populations and owners, to name but the first of many concerns. This concept implies little concern or regard for those initial animals exposed to risk, their immune and climate adaptation history. Studies are beginning to show that there is far greater cost benefit in many situations through targeting early stage intervention for livestock than letting them die and then replacing them (Knight-Jones, 2012). This benefit goes far beyond the cost of the individual animal and includes indirect benefit to economies as well. There is again a practical benefit to this as the scale of restocking is generally always beyond the productive capacity of the affected country which means importation of animals that may involve disease concerns or even an inability to locate and transport that volume of animals humanely. During Cyclone Pam in 2013 more than four million animals are estimated to have perished in the aftermath of the storm, a figure that is simply unfeasible to replace within reasonable timescales. In the aftermath, much consideration was given to restocking animals while tens of thousands of surviving animals died due to lack of care. The loss to local economies of the mortality of surviving animals was avoidable but so much focus was placed on restocking programmes that this was missed as an opportunity and was only partly filled by NGO work. The practicality of shipping enough animals of the right breed to a small island nation in the Pacific made restocking both impractical and prohibitively expensive.

Reconstruction planning must factor future animal risks and hazards

Surviving animals should be raised in secure facilities to protect them from future hazards, but in practice debilitated owners often place them in more exposed, dangerous situations, thus increasing their vulnerability and the likelihood of becoming mortal victims next time a hazard occurs.

Conclusion

In this chapter we have explored the principles for consideration when engaging in an aid mission for post disaster affected animal populations. We have deliberately not been too prescriptive because the aid should match the animal need that is present at the time and caused by the disaster and this can only be defined by an accurate disaster assessment and needs analysis. Any operation itself needs to be undertaken by professionals with the right level of flexibility in their aid programme to adapt to changing conditions. In the next chapter we explore the recovery phase and the opportunities it offers for helping to build back better.

Further reading

Forse, B. (1999). *Where There Is No Vet*. Oxford: Macmillan.

Wingfield, W.E., Nash, S.L., Palmer, S.B. and Upp, J.J. (2009). *Veterinary Disaster Medicine: Working Animals*. Chichester and Oxford, UK: Wiley-Blackwell.

Wingfield, W.E. and Palmer, S.B. (2009). *Veterinary Disaster Response*. Chichester and Oxford, UK: Wiley-Blackwell.

References

Convention on International Trade in Endangered Species of Wild Fauna and Flora (CITES). (1981). *Guidelines for Transport and Preparation for Shipment of Live Wild Animals and Plants 1981*. Available at: https://cites.org/eng/resources/transport/E-Transp Guide.pdf

Forse, B. (1999). *Where There Is No Vet*. Oxford: Macmillan.

International Air Transport Association (IATA). (2017). *Container Requirements*, 43rd edn. Available at: www.iata.org/whatwedo/cargo/live-animals/Documents/pet-container-requirements.pdf

Knight-Jones, T. (2012). *Restocking and Animal Health: A review of livestock disease and mortality in post-disaster and development restocking programmes*. London: WSPA.

Knowles, T. and Campbell, R. (2014). *A Benefit–Cost Analysis of WSPA's 2012 Intervention in the Dhemaji District of Assam, India*. Melbourne: Economists at Large.

Walsh, J. and Gannon, R. (1967). *Time is Short and the Water Rises*. London: Nelson.

Webster, J. (2008). *Animal Welfare: Limping towards Eden*. New York: John Wiley & Sons.

6

SUPPORTING THE RECOVERY OF ANIMALS

In the last chapter we explored the measures and thinking required to deliver meaningful and impactful aid to animals in the aftermath of a disaster to meet acute needs. This phase and the longer term, however, don't reveal just acute needs but also those of the longer term. During this period, people will attempt to rebuild their lives. In some aspects this will begin as soon as the event has passed. People don't wait for help to fix roofs, rebuild walls or try and get their animals back into production. Traditionally, the recovery phase has been seen to happen after a month of acute need. This was merely a definition for planning and recently the concept of 'early recovery' has entered the discipline. In reality, recovery (also referred to as rebuilding or reconstruction) occurs throughout the post disaster phase and often for many years. Rather than getting stuck on timescales for intervening to help with recovery, this chapter will focus on the principles of recovery as they relate to animals. As already discussed, the role of the animal in relation to well-being and livelihoods is well established and they should figure in considerations during this phase. Often, however, the proportion of resources spent on their care is not proportionate to their importance or indeed their effectiveness in aiding human recovery.

It is during the recovery phase and with sensitised populations that longer-term thinking can occur. Aside from building back, one can begin to consider 'building back better', a phrase Bill Clinton coined during the recovery phase of the Haiti Earthquake in 2010. This means disaster managers must consider preparing people better for the next event. Supporting preparedness for those people and their animals implies supporting their recovery after impact from a disaster, if the concept is understood as part of a continuum, and not as an element waiting as the effect of a cause. Recovery for animals may then be regarded as a great opportunity to do right for what was originally done wrong, specifically when addressing the organic, endogenous and underlying causes of disaster at their origin in the shape of animal welfare, and in addition to just correcting the existing situation.

Recovery is, however, a more in-depth consideration. It may involve changes to structures or building codes as well as human behaviour change. There may be significant resourcing implications, regardless of how financially beneficial the initiative may be in the longer term. Thus this approach needs to be present in policymaking, planning and implementation, as well as in the minds of all stakeholders involved, from producers to consumers to academia to governments, and with animal welfare as a norm, for it to be truly-effective.

Farm animal recovery

There are two kinds of closely intertwined forms of recovery in the farm animal equation. The first is the recovery and continuity of the farm animal business, and the second is the recovery of the animal's health and welfare. Nearly a decade ago, recovery was merely conceptualised as the restoration of facilities to try and address the livelihoods based on animal farming within disaster-affected communities. The extra bonus to be sought would be any efforts carried to reduce future disaster risk factors through improvement to infrastructure. Largely, future resilience was considered a bonus rather than a core part of the consideration.

Years later, this bonus was translated as the concept of 'residual risk'. This was described as the remnant, unresolved and untreated risks of a various nature that should not be allowed to survive or come back into any recovery efforts. This marked a change in thinking by identifying underlying vulnerabilities as a core component of disaster risk and allowed for a more proactive thinking to develop how to address these. As an example, it may be a poor electricity system or risk to its supply that could lead to a fire in a disaster further exacerbating the situation, or the poor baseline welfare that animals face in disasters in the first place.

To understand this concept we could imagine a poultry farm impacted by flooding, killing one-fifth of all the birds. As soon as possible, the farm owner will try to put the business back on its feet by restarting production with the surviving birds after clean-up and repairs. In an even better world, however, poultry production should not start without first reducing the original vulnerability that caused the flood impact; and real recovery would only start when those vulnerabilities had been identified and dealt with. Ideally for all involved in this example, the surviving birds' welfare and health should revert back to their original stage (or ideally to a better one!) prior to the disaster, before any production can be reassumed. In all cases (farm and pet animals), the initial, baseline health and welfare of these animals will be paramount for any eventual recovery hopes and efforts.

Pet recovery

In this particular case, the psychological well-being of the pet owner and the integrity of the family nucleus, which includes their pet(s), is what needs to

FIGURE 6.1 The Humane Society of the United States rescuing companion animals in response to Hurricane Matthew in 2016

Source: Frank Loftus for the HSUS.

recover and return to its original stage; if not better. On the other hand, many pets, especially those living inside the households (and thus having high levels of attachment or even forming part of the family), tend to develop intense fears and even phobias when subjected to the extreme stress of disasters affecting their homes. Injury from falling debris in the midst of earthquakes, floods or hurricanes is as much of a risk for them as it is for humans. This can lead to the presentation of unwanted behaviours, accidents that result in injury and runaway animals at the smallest provocation. Therapy is slow but possible, and there are several animal behavioural approaches designed to help the recovery of these animals. Fundamentally, however, recovery for pet animals is intrinsically linked to matters of shelter for their human owners (Figure 6.1).

Rehabilitation and reconstruction

Rehabilitation and reconstruction are the main tasks during the recovery process, starting immediately after the rescue efforts; beginning when the emergency ends. Rehabilitation implies the recovery of pre-existing animal groups or populations and assets of the farm where they reside or within the farm animal business. This is achieved by restoring the original welfare of those animals as well as the quality of the enclosures and facilities in their farm, thus reducing or preventing the need for further assistance to ensure its normal function. Rehabilitation allows for the return of the original animals' health and welfare, while reconstruction may be less inclined to invest in the treatment of surviving animals, in favour of purchasing new animals or restocking.

During rehabilitation periods, the first priority for animals is to regain or maintain their health, followed by their welfare. When impact is significant enough however, rehabilitation is seldom achieved on their own means. To do so, and to apply the 'build back better' principle, rehabilitation efforts need to be aided by a multitude of fronts, including risk transfer mechanisms such as insurance policies. When we consider Government-aided rehabilitation efforts for the farm animal industry, there is a need to base these on pre-existing strategies and legal frameworks that facilitate institutional responsibilities for the rehabilitation of farm animals and the farms they live on.

In contrast with the above notions, reconstruction implies actions forced by an impact that has been so great (product of a large hazard or a big vulnerability) that there are no or few surviving animals. This may also include either the redevelopment of infrastructure or indeed abandonment of it in favour of a new site. Infrastructure may be critical for the survivability of animals or to replace mechanisms that protect future populations. In many cases this may be repairs to existing structures but in catastrophic events, this may mean complete redesign and rebuilding. Often the preference will be to build back as before but this instinct should be avoided until all factors relating to the failure of the infrastructure are considered first. The most effective way of doing so is to harness the sensitisation of disaster risk, caused by the event, to persuade people to consider ways of avoiding the same event in future. In this sense, it is proposed that the aspiration with regard to the rebuilding of structures relating to animals should always be to create resilient structures. Many considerations may come into play in this process.

Location

Considerations of how to reduce risk exposure should be paramount and a significant consideration relates to location. This may be the most immutable factor to change, however. Land ownership and the ability to purchase or acquire new land may prevent this as a consideration but the following questions should be asked:

1 Is it possible to reduce exposure by moving?
2 Within the site, are there less exposed locations (i.e. higher land to protect from floods)?
3 Are all the hazards relating to the locations realised and considered in planning?
4 Is there space for redundancy to help in an emergency (feed stores, equipment storage)?

Whether a commercial broiler facility or a herder's yurt in Mongolia, the same principles should apply to reducing risk from location.

Structures

At a location there may be structures to consider. These may be buildings, bird perching structures, animal sheds or even feeding troughs. Where these have been damaged they offer an opportunity to redevelop them in a more resilient manner. Suggested considerations may include:

1 Will these new structures be resilient to a future event of similar nature or even a different type of disaster the location is at risk from?
2 Do the structures need a different design to make them more resilient?
3 Can the structures be adapted to be more resilient? (i.e. tying down roofs, raising them above the height of flood waters, covering feed troughs to prevent contamination from ash-fall)?
4 How will evacuation routes potentially change the survivability of people and animals?

Utilities

The utilities that are supplied to the site may be critical to maintaining its viability. This could include a water supply for drinking or cooling, electricity for light or cooling, or other factors such as gas for heating. Considerations for rebuilding should include:

1 How reliable will the supply be in a disaster? Should alternative sources that don't rely on outside factors be considered (i.e. solar panels or back-up generators)?
2 How can the supply be better protected from a disaster? (i.e. raised plug sockets, armoured cabling etc.)?
3 What risks could occur from utilities in disaster and how can these be prepared for (i.e. preparing for fire, briefing staff on electrocution, ensuring shut-off valves, regular servicing and checks)?

Secondary impacts and secondary victims

When rehabilitation efforts fail, animals that may have survived the first, original impact, may suffer once again and fall victim to secondary impacts such as transmissible or opportunistic pathogens and infections, starvation or thirst, either due to isolation or neglect. All of these new, secondary hazards would compromise the health and welfare of the affected animals, but will in turn impact on the hopes of the farmer to recover and on the livelihoods of their owners. Government at all levels and the media can play a meaningful role during and right after a disaster strikes, to avoid secondary impacts on surviving animals, specially pets. Informing owners and groups involved in the process is critical to avoid suffering and death due to ignorance.

Restocking

Restocking is the introduction of livestock into an area that has seen a loss of its original population of animals. As a concept this is a reasonable measure to undertake in the recovery phase and examples of successful restocking exist. Because of the mass mortality of livestock related to disaster events, restocking has been favoured as a recovery activity by governments, UN agencies and NGOs alike. Sadly, however, this preference isn't always the most cost effective or humane choice for disaster situations. Often the preference for restocking overlooks the surviving animal population and its needs and can lead to a second wave of mortality as these animals are forgotten. The irony of this is that early stage intervention for surviving animals is often less expensive and more practical than letting animals die and replacing them. This ignorance of the surviving animal populations leads to greater mortality that then further justifies the need to restock in large numbers.

During Cyclone Pam in Vanuatu in 2015, damage assessments of affected islands highlighted an accurate picture of livestock mortality but offered little information about surviving populations or their needs. This led to mass mortality of animals which precipitated a requirement for another damage assessment that showed that at this point only restocking was an option. The problem of restocking was, however, also a practical one. No country has a huge spare stock of animals

FIGURE 6.2 Local knowledge is key to understanding future need. A WAP staff member interviews a local islander in Vanuatu

Source: James Sawyer for WAP.

at hand to replace those that are lost; they have to be bred. This meant that animals needed to be restocked from outside the country which was largely impossible due to the isolation of the islands. Thus a decision to restock at the outset drove animal mortality which required restocking that was not even possible in the first place. Vanuatu was not an isolated incident but rather part of a pattern in the last decade of poorly thought out responses to animal welfare needs and the securing of livelihoods. That is not to say that restocking is irrelevant, rather it has a place to play in the decision making during the longer term reconstruction. Where sources of animals are available, the conditions are correct for introducing them and the correct support to animal owners is given it can be a viable option.

Should restocking be a consideration, a useful guide on decision making to plan for it can be found in the LEGS guidelines (2015). Knight-Jones (2012) clearly points to the importance of the supporting requirements often missed to make restocking successful, measures such as animal husbandry training for owners and veterinary support can make a huge difference to the survivability of animals in the longer term. It is important, however, to create a hierarchy of preference when considering stocking options for animals:

1   intervention to secure the surviving animals as an effective productive and breeding capacity;
2   restocking of animals over an extended period of time by supporting breeding programmes within the country;
3   restocking from outside sources.

Restocking considerations

Choosing the correct breed/species

The aspiration should be to replace like with like. This helps as people are used to the animal husbandry requirements of the breed and normally had originally chosen it for a suitability trait. Local vets will be used to common problems with the animals and disease monitoring and control will already be in place.

Where new breeds are considered, there must be some consideration for their survivability in the environment. Darker breeds suffer more in the heat and need shelter and some breeds are more hardy to drought conditions or the cold. Culturally, sometimes certain breeds are more prized and this should be a consideration. Some breeds are used to much greater environmental protection and the systems they are bred in have bred out traits of resilience to disease and other factors in favour of productivity. Where different species are considered, there must be a significant focus on the benefit this will have to owners who may have no experience of handling the animals or caring for them and may not have the market access to sell the products from them.

Disease control

Movement of animals increases the risk of disease transmission and this can be significantly increased if this happens in concert with new breeds from areas where disease control may not be strong. During the aftermath of Cyclone Nargis in Myanmar in 2008, restocked water buffalo brought new and more virulent strains of foot and mouth into the Ayerwaddy delta because of a lack of focus on disease control and vaccination. All restocked animals should be disease checked, quarantined adequately and vaccinated as necessary.

Transport

The transport of livestock is a stressful experience for animals and needs to be a core consideration of restocking. In developing countries, the movement of large numbers of animals over long distances may not be the norm. This can mean that animals are moved in the wrong type of vehicles without adequate shade, feed, water or veterinary care. This has led to high levels of mortality of restocked livestock in transit or very poor condition of the animals when they arrive. Transportation of livestock in the restocking process has its own welfare and disease control concerns that need careful consideration in planning such an operation.

Animal husbandry

Especially when restocking with new breeds or species, a restocking programme should include information and training for animal owners on husbandry. This dramatically reduces the mortality of newly restocked species and allows for better provision for their welfare. Adequate animal husbandry training should include feed types, common ailments and illnesses, how to accommodate the animal and the safe limits of productive capacity of the animal.

Endemic and pre-existing welfare issues

It is sensible to assume that if the problems that caused the initial death of the animal are not removed then restocked animals will also struggle to survive. Mortality of restocked animals remains high and is often a large financial loss for donor agencies. Decision makers involved in restocking decisions need to be able to set one of the parameters of the decision to activate a restocking programme as the likelihood of survival. This parameter should relate to the disaster needs assessment and understand how much of the fatal drivers that created the situation in the initial disaster still exist and how these will impact on the new animals.

While the practice of restocking is established in disaster recovery, the decision making, planning and execution remains poor. This either leads to a lack of action for surviving animals, increasing restocking needs, or it can lead to animals being moved long distances to die in an inadequate environment.

Managing risk and addressing vulnerability

When a disaster of magnitude has hit farm animal interests or assets and the resulting destruction levels are so significant that there is nothing or very little to recover and rehabilitate, only building back or rebuilding remain as options. This is where 'building back better' comes in, as the imperative is to apply the lessons learned from the recent disaster and build with less vulnerability, addressing and tackling gaps in awareness, attitudes, knowledge, logistics and preparedness. But more often than not, post disaster recovery effort gets slowed by time-gaps and red tape, intermittent attention by donor and development partners, and declining government budgets. Attention and momentum from all fronts tends to slow down following post disaster assessments and emergency response efforts directed at saving human lives, making planning and implementation of subsequent stages of recovery and reconstruction harder and less common.

In the midst of a number of recovery and rebuilding efforts, governments face serious complications, in terms of planning during the fast pace of changing market conditions, in implementing recovery processes with less vulnerability as a guiding principle. Government efforts directed at the post disaster recovery of the farming industry for the protection of livelihoods or for food security, and specifically of local animal farms and their animals, should balance the first impulse and desire of farm owners to return to production at once with the longer-term goal of reducing vulnerability, and direct investment and efforts toward sustainable development. The results sought may be the reduction of exposure or other vulnerabilities, as well as the enhanced resilience of the system. This may be obtained by improving the baseline health and welfare of the animals themselves or increasing the resilience of the facilities they live in by better cooperation among animal owners, community drills, government programmes, risk transfer mechanisms, and better coordination between civil defence, government officials, etc. Common sense and experience dictate that a measure of each of the above proposals is necessary to achieve a degree of solid preparedness.

One of the main obstacles to this seemingly logical move may be time and money, or the lack of it. Reconstruction efforts are often undertaken in haste, attempting to return back to production and the status quo as soon as possible. This happens during the period when the economy is under stress, and scarce financial resources become even more scarce, especially when considering the costs of idle workers, debris removal, red tape for building permits, often on top of previous loans outstanding. If we include rebuilding for higher construction standards the result will be too large an effort to be able to cope with it under those circumstances.

If we were to imagine the scenario of a private veterinarian called to an animal farm after a disaster to check on the animals, whether pigs or broiler chickens, the cost–benefit argument of building back better will be the first question posed to him/her. How can the professional proposing such an investment justify and guarantee a return? Is the client even able to afford insurance? After all, how often do disasters hit the same target twice in a row? Judging from the way we humans

CASE STUDY: HAITI EARTHQUAKE 2010

On 12 January 2010, a devastating earthquake measuring 7.0 struck Haiti, causing catastrophic damage to Port Au Prince and the surrounding area. In the following 12 days another 52 aftershocks measuring 4.5 or greater were recorded. Due to the condition of the country prior to the disaster, human mortality figures remain hard to accurately define but estimates range between 100,000 and 316,000 (O'Connor, 2012). Haiti was without doubt a country on the edge of crisis before the earthquake struck with high levels of vulnerability and marginalisation of communities. Haiti is ranked one hundred and forty-ninth out of 182 countries on the human development index (UNDP, 2009) and was classified as economically vulnerable by the UN FAO. Prior to the earthquake the UN had been involved in emergency feeding programmes for the most vulnerable.

During the aftermath, significant problems were faced by the humanitarian effort. The port was blocked with debris and inoperable, mass escapes of prisoners had occurred, the UN headquarters was destroyed and many government departments no longer had facilities to work from. Security was a concern prior to the earthquake but in the aftermath, the country was very risky to operate in. This situation was improved significantly when US forces arrived to achieve basic infrastructure reconstruction to assure the logistics of the global aid programme.

The situation for animals was equally dire. The level of animal welfare infrastructure and provision of veterinary services was very low and government buildings involved in this were damaged or destroyed. Survivors were clearly suffering a humanitarian crisis but also had animals to consider. Pets were often the only surviving member of the family to provide comfort but equally important was the level of peri-urban livestock and its relation to livelihoods. These backyard animals formed the backbone of an informal economy that operated as an insurance policy for Haitians where animals such as goats may be sold for school fees or cows for hospital bills. Within Port Au Prince alone and, even considering the high mortality of people and animals, more than 100,000 production animals were thought to exist. Surveys of the dog population prior to the quake put the dog population alone at 500,000.

The challenge for responders was multifaceted. Dealing with a city where the rule of law at best hung by a thread (but was often non-existent) created an insecure environment but equally a fundamental change in the geography of the city itself and thus its populations created challenges. To address this, the Animal Relief Coalition for Haiti (ARCH) was formed and this group of animal welfare organisations set about undertaking a full assessment of the needs of animals. Emerging from this situation came an operation focused on the following areas of work:

1 Mobile veterinary care

In order to support surviving pets and production animals living in people's properties and in displaced locations, ARCH developed and delivered mobile veterinary services over a period of 18 months. This function served a key purpose of ensuring the health of these animals but was also used by the government as a useful tool to address focused vaccinations for disease outbreaks (such as rabies) which prevent mass culls of animals.

Delivering mobile clinics was a challenge, with a focus on organisation and security being key to this. The suggested designs found in Chapter 4 are those borne out of the experience of the authors running such facilities in a country. One of the key lessons learned from this was that sensitisation of the communities in advance of arrival led to much greater success rates for treatment. The employment of small teams to announce when and where the clinic would be for the following day dramatically increased the number of visitors.

In total, by April 2011 the mobile veterinary clinics had provided veterinary care to over 70,000 animals, some 20,000 more than the target and the budget planned.

2 Rebuilding veterinary infrastructure

Key to ongoing viability for veterinary services were the facilities they operated from. In a country where disease control relating to animals was a concern prior to the disaster, this was identified as a priority. Rabies was a significant concern for dogs and cats while diseases such as Newcastle and Teschen were common in livestock.

ARCH undertook a rebuilding programme of the main government animal disease monitoring and laboratory facilities which was completed within 8 months of the earthquake. These buildings were equipped with new diagnostic equipment to become functioning entities in the control of animal disease.

3 Building back a more resilient cold chain

In the aftermath of the disasters, government veterinary outreach buildings were destroyed and utilities cut off leading to a collapse of the cold chain used to transport vaccines out to more remote areas and keep them viable for use. This significantly compromised the ability of the government veterinary services to be able to respond to disease outbreaks and maintain vaccination outreach programmes.

ARCH chose to take a new approach to putting this cold chain back in place by looking at building resilience into the system. Solar panels and fridges replaced old tired units of refrigeration and old outposts were stocked with varying sizes of coolers to utilise to ensure that vaccines remained effective

> during field visits. This approach built a new cold chain more resilient to future disasters, offering a veterinary function more resistant to shocks.
>
> The ARCH programme of work was one of the largest delivered by animal welfare in response to a disaster and demonstrated how effective coordination, combined with solid disaster assessments and a willingness to think differently when providing aid, meant that the animals in the affected area undoubtedly experienced a more resilient future.

are accustomed to managing risk – when gambling, investing, or physically, many of us would be tempted to take the risk of not investing anything extra on preparedness if our capital and liquid cash do not allow us to take less risky decisions. The alternative of seeking yet another loan to invest in preparedness is a hard one, as preparedness seldom pays dividends in the short run. The professional would be hard pressed between recommending extra investments to his already financially strapped client. Balancing increased preparedness and lower vulnerability with the urgent need the farm may have to get back in production will be a dilemma.

Building back better, in short, needs outside support, especially government intervention through programmes that expedite and promote this sound, superior form of investment, with standards that contemplate sustainable development. When those supporting criteria are met, resilient reconstruction should be regarded as a unique opportunity to rebuild key blocks of the affected society in a more solid and prepared way. In the specific case of the welfare of animals, be it farm or companion, if the owner has the awareness and the financial possibilities to do so, the benefits for the animals will be abundant.

Development and prosperity

Sustainable development is an aspiration of the global community but there is no sustainable future in sight without resilient business models. Without these, disasters will continue to retard economic development but in the developing world are likely to create negative development. Farm animal businesses as the main source of protein, milk, eggs and meat, as well as an important source of livelihoods are arguably more at risk than many businesses. In business, risks are taken on a daily basis to compete in the market, when using market forces to obtain better prices, or when investing for opportunities. If resilient recovery is to be regarded as an opportunity for development and prosperity, results need to be apparent in real time, rather than waiting for the unknown to happen to demonstrate a cost/benefit logic.

Development priorities for animal related issues

1 **Publicly funded projects** should have an element of preparedness and resilience inbuilt from the design phase. This means government veterinary

services need to be more resilient to disasters, trained in the mindset of being more flexible, and be more mobile to deal with the aftermath of an extreme event.

2   **Private businesses** should be able to access incentives to ensure that investing in preparedness is economically viable. Veterinary practices need to understand that they will be at the forefront of community recovery; they need to consider how they may change their operating model in a post disaster environment and offer government services or at least maintain continuity. Livestock facilities need to consider how to ensure business continuity and plan for disruptions. Business continuity funds comparable to two months of operating costs need to be considered in high risk areas.

3   **Financial institutions** should carry out risk assessments before committing resources to animal related projects to ensure that the lending model is resilient to external shocks. Insurance companies should consider ensuring that within policy requirements, preparedness and risk reduction measures are made mandatory for farmers and pet owners.

4   **Animal professionals** have an important role to play by helping all stakeholders identify risks and develop strategies to cope with and manage them, be it before disaster strikes, or right after the emergency response stage ends and the recovery efforts start. This is the time when the animals and their owners are in most need of assistance.

5   **Academia** should prioritise the training of veterinarians and animal health workers in risk identification and reduction and the skills required to deal with disruption to normal services. A prioritisation in research seeking to further discipline of risk reduction and preparedness for veterinarians is necessary.

6   **Emergency services** should ensure they are adequately trained in the movement of animals during times of crisis. As modern emergency services undertake wide-scale preparedness messaging work, they may be a useful vehicle for informing owners (especially pet owners) of measures to take to build resilience.

Disasters must be seen as an opportunity because of the intense attention created that highlights to most elements of society the level of their vulnerabilities. This considered, not every preparedness or risk reduction initiative requires significant investment. Many of the measures required for resilience may well occur through ingenuity and creativity on the part of the owners, the community, professionals, governments and development agencies.

Building animal resilience

We can define animal resilience in disasters as the capacity of animals exposed to hazards of natural origin to anticipate and manage negative change (through the intervention of the owners), adapt to stress, shocks and adversity, recover from it and reach acceptable levels of welfare, health and outputs; all while keeping good quality of life and welfare expectancy.

There are two main elements that are crucial for animal resiliency:

- **baseline animal welfare** that includes health and the conditions of the facilities they are kept at;
- the **owner's capacity** to resist, adapt and respond to a disaster impact on the farm.

These elements may be manifested slightly differently in the case of farm or companion animals but they are core to all animals.

The parameters to consider for disaster resilience for animals may be further described as:

- the **subject** or types and numbers of animals exposed to hazards;
- the **type and intensity** of the disturbance and stresses threatening the animals;
- the animal's **capacity to respond** or adapt.

This is in turn dependent upon:

- the *exposure* of the animal(s) to the threat or hazard, dependent on where the enclosures to keep them were settled;
- the *sensitivity* of the animal(s) to the threat, dependent of breed, age, and baseline welfare;
- the *adaptive capacity*, or how well the animals can resist, adapt or adjust to the threat. This will of course, also depend on age, breed, baseline health and welfare, and the owners/handlers actions to assure the speedy recovery of their animals;
- the animal's *reaction* or the range of possible responses, also dependent on their human handlers, so much so that it is virtually impossible to consider them separately.

In short, animal resiliency is intrinsically dependent on their human handlers and owners; thus it may be impossible in practical terms to separate them both. To build animal resiliency then, the following concepts will be critical.

Using the Five Freedoms system for assessing animal welfare

Animal professionals and owners can measure baseline animal welfare and plan actions to improve it. This can then be measured post disaster. This kind of assessment and preparedness actions should include the following:

1 general and physical health of the animals;
2 nutrition;

FIGURE 6.3 A cat receives a vaccination in Tacloban as a survivor of Cyclone Haiyan in the Philippines in 2013

Source: Tonee Despojo for the HSI.

3   immunisation levels;
4   living conditions, with accent on animal density, ventilation (intensive versus free range production) and on structural aspects such as solidity of structures, wiring, drainages, structures, etc.;
5   ability to exercise and display normal behaviour;
6   identification in the case of eventual evacuations;
7   eventual training.

Measuring resistance

Critical to improving animals' resiliency is an understanding of how factors beyond their well-being might affect their vulnerability (Figure 6.3). Factors could include:

1   how the climate interacts with breeds;
2   availability of food and water and its resilience to disaster shocks. Understanding whether emergency stocks are required;
3   understanding the impact of the loss of utilities on animals (i.e. electricity and air conditioning);
4   how the geography of the area creates vulnerabilities;
5   how the local populous creates risks in times of crisis;

6   crime profile and likelihood of escalation in disasters;
7   disease profiles for country, region and locality and their likely change in disaster;
8   availability of medical care for animals;
9   sensitisation of responding agencies to animals' needs;
10 evacuation routes during periods of crisis.

For farm businesses a business continuity plan with accent on the following tasks is desirable:

1   map of vulnerabilities and threats plus measures taken to reduce them (roads, bridges, rivers, water sources);
2   emergency lists of veterinarians or important contacts to be kept available;
3   emergency response/evacuation plan with roles and responsibilities for each member of staff;
4   rapid access to savings, liquidity, disaster funds or soft loans to keep the farm running for 1–2 months;
5   stock piling or easy sourcing of emergency food and water;
6   previous planning and practice for animal caretakers;
7   previous coordination with civil defence authorities, fellow farmers and the community;
8   plans for the temporary and permanent repair of infrastructures including holding and systems supporting the animals;
9   emergency infrastructure such as loading ramps, transport crates or bedding and evacuation equipment lists;
10 periodical drills for validation and training of rapid, emergency response plans;
11 risk transfer mechanisms such as insurance policies.

Almost all of these actions towards the recovery of animals may be initiated and carried out without significant financial cost, merely requiring buy-in and commitment from the stakeholders. The generation of other, similar small initiatives should be encouraged, especially those aimed at improving the welfare and resilience of animals as part of a culture of prevention and preparedness that starts from within the academia, animal owners and the farm animal sector.

Therefore the recovery of animals after a disaster is intrinsically intertwined with the preparedness measures their owners take prior to the impact, and their capacity to recover by helping their animals resist and adapt to the impact of the disaster. The recovery of animals then, follows and supports the recovery of their masters and owners, and if seen holistically as it really is, they deserve protection, to protect the lives of their owners as well.

In the next chapter we will see how animal owners and animal professionals can expand these concepts to look at concepts of preparedness for animals facing the risk of disaster.

Further reading

American Red Cross. (n.d.). *Typhoon Haiyan Recovery*. Available at: www.redcross.org/about-us/our-work/international-services/haiyan-recovery#Overview

Food and Agriculture Organization of the United Nations, prepared by Emmanuel C. Torrente. (2012). *Guidance Note: Post disaster damage, loss and needs in assessment in agriculture*. Available at: www.fao.org/docrep/015/an544e/an544e00.pdf

Jayasuriya, S., Steele, P. and Weerakoon, D. (n.d.). *Post-Tsunami Recovery: Lessons from case study 1*. Sri Lanka. Available at: www.adb.org/sites/default/files/publication/1572 63/adbi-rpb20.pdf

Katz, J.M. (2013). *The Big Truck that Went by: How the world came to save Haiti and left behind a disaster*. Basingstoke, UK: Palgrave Macmillan.

Unicef (2008). *Ten years after Hurricane Mitch, Honduras is once again hit by natural disaster*. Available at: www.unicef.org/infobycountry/honduras_45850.html

References

Knight-Jones, T. (2012). *Restocking and Animal Health. A review of livestock disease and mortality in post-disaster and development restocking programmes*. London: WSPA.

Livestock Emergency Guidelines and Standards. (2015). *Livestock Emergency Guidelines and Standards*, 2nd edn. Rugby, UK: Rugby Practical Action.

O'Connor, M.R. (2012). *Two Years Later, Haitian Earthquake Death Toll in Dispute*. Available at: http://archives.cjr.org/behind_the_news/one_year_later_haitian_earthqu.php

United Nations Development Programme. (2009). *Human Development Report 2009, Overcoming barriers: Human mobility and development*. Basingstoke, UK: Palgrave Macmillan.

7

PREPARING PEOPLE AND ANIMALS FOR DISASTERS

In previous chapters we have explored how animals can be assisted in the early to long-term phases of the aftermath of a disaster. This however is akin to a sticking plaster over the wound. Disaster response and recovery have an important role to play but they are reactive and expensive and do little to address any reduction in the latent conditions that contributed toward the issues in the first place. It will be natural for people to ask 'what can we do to prepare better for the next one' and this is an approach to be encouraged. Dollars spent on preparedness are invariably better value and have a greater impact on reducing the impact of a disaster than response and recovery ever could. The farmer who removes his herd from the slopes of a volcano in advance of an eruption will invariably be better off after the eruption than the farmer who stayed, lost his herd or continues to farm in oppressive conditions. In this chapter, the concept of preparedness for animals is examined through the lens of its dependence on human activity and by comparing it to human preparedness.

Arguably preparedness can save more lives than any disaster responder can, regardless of resource. Awareness of risks for an individual or a community and the undertaking of measures to reduce vulnerabilities are critical factors in reducing both loss of assets and loss of life. Once this task has been completed, however, there is an element of residual risk that remains. As an example, it is impossible to reduce all of the risk from a community living close to a volcano and you cannot prevent the eruption of the mountain either. Even if you made the effort to move away from it, the direction of the seasonal winds could easily change the trajectory of the plume and catch up with you, to bury pastures and animals in a thick, solid layer of cement-like compound, especially during the rainy season. This was precisely the case of the Chaiten volcano eruption and the locality of Futaleufú, situated 156 kilometres apart.

One can, however, prepare for volcanic eruption and thus reduce the chance of experiencing undesired effects. As an individual this may be by planning an escape route, storing supplies, strengthening structures, monitoring radios and registering with the appropriate authorities. As an authority this may be setting up warning systems, preparing teams and equipment adequately, stockpiling emergency supplies and contracting for temporary sheltering.

Even the fastest international help will take 72 hours to arrive and in extreme situations local responders may be incapacitated or take more time to access the area. Yet most of the mortality in a disaster occurs in the first 72 hours; thus the more prepared a community is, the better its chance of reducing its losses and getting back to normality more quickly. We will examine all elements of preparedness (development and research, welfare and health, owners' perceptions, attitudes and behaviour, measures for preparing and responding, including coordination) up to the point when recovery begins. Special accent is paid to policies and strategies for animal preparedness, including recent and successful innovative solutions and mechanisms of risk transfer.

The good news is that it is virtually impossible to prepare animals for disasters without also fostering the odds of their owners, caretakers and in general, those depending on them. This should be seen as a great positive in the complementary nature of preparedness for animals with that of humans. Often human preparedness is more advanced and thus the animal element is easy to integrate.

Preparedness for animals – behavioural considerations

It may be impossible to be fully prepared for all eventualities or to prepare our animals with the same aim and to the same point, but we should always aim for as full as possible identification of hazard and mitigation measures.

Wild animals

Wild animals show various strategies to avoid hazards by fleeing, hiding, gathering in numbers, freezing or even attacking if cornered. In the case of natural hazards they seek shelter from floods, high winds, tsunamis or from wild fires and this is part of their natural survival instincts. The way some wild animals may be able to sense an impending earthquake, tsunami, or radical, extreme changes in weather have been studied in the past (Bressan, 2011), but with inconclusive results. During the Indian Ocean Tsunami of 2004, wild elephants and other wild animals in South West Sri Lanka were seen fleeing from the coast and seeking high ground, not to be seen for over a month. Anecdotal evidence shows birds and bats moving in large numbers before earthquakes but this phenomenon has neither been proven or disproven to have merit. A tsunami survivor the author met told the story of cats running up hill prior to the arrival of the waves, followed by rats! This is when the storyteller knew something very wrong was about to happen, and this sighting saved him. We have to consider that even if animals have this ability to foretell certain disasters, science is yet to prove it and animals are yet to be able to share this skill in any manner that would affect human life.

Domestic animals

Domestic animals on the other hand, are believed to have lost some of these wild survival faculties through selective breeding for docility and domestication, to the point that they can hardly improve their own preparedness to disasters by themselves, if at all. This is of course, due to being excessively bred for production purposes, thus reducing their flight zones and other natural instincts, to then be kept in large numbers, in captivity or/and under intensive conditions. Improving farm or companion animal preparedness is therefore a role and responsibility of animal owners.

Animal preparedness

Animal preparedness could be defined as the stage of readiness for people and their animals that allows them to contain and reduce the negative impact of a hazard; namely death, injury or affectation. The aim of this is to attempt to reduce impact, and downgrade a potential disaster to the category of an emergency. If this isn't possible then the principle is to reduce the effects to As Low As Reasonably Practical (the ALARP principle).

Preparedness for people and animals is meant to reduce the impact of potentially disastrous hazards. As a process, it includes the know-how, capacity and preparatory actions taken by animal owners, communities, all levels of government, and professionals involved in animal care, husbandry and production. All are meant to protect their animals by duty or they are dependent upon them for their livelihoods or for support and so are motivated to do so. This considered, the definition of preparedness for animals also needs to understand the baseline health and welfare of the very animals at risk, to ensure that decisions made and actions taken encompass all relevant factors.

Ideally we would aim to approach this using the following stages:

1   effectively identify and anticipate most important risks and vulnerabilities (with the aim to reduce impact);
2   take precautions to avoid impact where possible;
3   take mitigating action where possible;
4   respond and quickly recover those animals from the impacts of these hazards by reducing their exposure and vulnerability, and/or increasing their resiliency.

Preparedness for animals is largely based on the following:

1   information collection and analysis;
2   risk identification and prioritisation;
3   planning to prepare;
4   building protective measures for structures and animals;
5   training, drills and practice in advance of a disaster;

6 stockpiling necessary supplies;
7 fostering baseline animal health and welfare;
8 installing early warning systems and deciding evacuation measures;
9 preparing emergency veterinary attention;
10 agreeing coordination with people, agencies and authorities.

While this list may look like a useful checklist for an authority, it works just as well when adapted to the individual farmer, a community, a business or a non-governmental organisation.

Baseline vs real animal preparedness

Animal preparedness and vulnerability are difficult to assess independently from the actions of their human owners and caretakers, due to the strong dependence (and interdependence) domestic animals have on (and with) them. In general, the degree of vulnerability, exposure or preparedness humans have is often similar to or above that of their animals. Therefore, to try and define a clearer theoretical baseline for domestic animal risk, vulnerability and resilience we might explore the levels that similar wild animal species may have under normal conditions in the wild. This may be useful to allow researchers to measure the existing levels of exposure for similar species of animals now subject to domestication as pets or as farm animals, but now due to the decisions and actions of their owners.

A wild animal free in the forest would have different levels of welfare, health, exposure to or capacity to resist and recover from a hazard than another similar animal kept indoors as a farm animal and in intensive production conditions. The added factors affecting animal preparedness that domestication brings may be negative or positive in relation to a hazard and could include (but would not be limited to): confinement, handling, relative or even intense overcrowding, lack of exercise, relative exposure of the farm facilities to flooding, high winds, isolation from quakes, or other hazards, use of pre/probiotics and antibiotics in their food, food provision, disease, and even the results of market forces.

Human vs animal preparedness

There are, however, further differences; one of the more apparent contrasts between human and animal preparedness relates to the emergency rescue element. In the case of human rescue, no resources are spared and higher levels of risk are accepted for rescue teams during floods, earthquakes or volcanic eruptions. This may be different with animals, as human risk will hardly be tolerated, while resources will always be measured against the value the animals have for their specific owners, be it financial or sentimental. Additionally, humans may encounter difficulties when preparing for or reacting to a hazard, but it is important to consider that often they have more choice. Humans may be able to run away or be helped to run by others, while domestic animals are in many cases confined, and fully dependent on the actions of their human masters. Nowadays, and as per the new Sendai Framework for Disaster Risk Reduction of the UNISDR (UNISDR, 2015), farm and working animals are deemed and named essential assets for the protection of the livelihoods of their owners, as part of Priority #3: Investing in Disaster Risk Reduction (Item 30, sub-item P and Item 31, sub-item f). This shall eventually be supported and guided by community and sectorial structures and by institutional policy frameworks, both legal and budgetary. In practice, this new accent on animals may well include new approaches to animal evacuation and rescue.

Preparedness measures for animals

The primary elements needed to achieve or improve preparedness for animals are the following:

1   Baseline development and research:

- research history of disastrous events in the area;
- inventories of animals at risk;
- animal impact assessment and emergency needs assessment and capabilities for animals;
- pre-existing welfare and health level (baseline, prospective) of animal populations;
- better ID systems for animal herds;
- owners' perceptions, attitudes and behaviour research towards animal preparedness;
- early warning systems linked to forecasting, animal evacuation and transport, sheltering plans.

2   Policies and animal preparedness plans at every governance level.
3   Coordination:

- incorporation of animal risk into pre-existing risk maps;
- communication (ICS, LEGS).

4   Training and awareness:

- disaster preparedness awareness for the farm animal sector, communities and animal owners;
- Incident Command System (ICS), handling, technical animal rescue and evacuation training (TLAER);
- periodic validation pools, desk exercises and drills.

5   Measures:

- preparedness plans for big farms, small farms and backyard animals, pet owners;
- handling personnel, special equipment, materials.

Documenting impact

Most disaster animal impact databases are set to gather the numbers of animal victims at best, seldom in the field or for surviving animals in need, and usually only for livestock. These instruments, and the officials in charge often fail to document injured or affected animals in need of veterinary attention, vaccination schemes, or even nutrition requirements, as in the case of floods damaging pastures for grass fed animals and for months in a row. This often occurs due to lack of training, or even resources such as fuel and transport. The need to improve data collection and impact documentation on animals is one of the current challenges facing most countries during the development of the Indicators for the Sendai Framework. Initial enquiries on baseline information and assessment capacity conducted in Costa Rica during a local volcano drill in 2008, and in the Philippines after Typhoon Haiyan in 2013 revealed weaknesses in animal inventories for a series of reasons, such as the existence of rather old and simple procedures to position those herds geographically; rapid documenting of animal losses and needs after a disaster; and particularly, the real impact of these losses on their owners' livelihoods, as well as on the ways to rehabilitate animal populations and eventually reduce their vulnerabilities.

Perceptions

To give preparedness a chance, the understanding of animal risk, and the needs on commitment plus the availability of resources that animal owners and stakeholders have is paramount. A better understanding of animal behaviour in a crisis and that of humans, especially in relation to their animals, is required. This needs to be balanced with further work on understanding the human–animal bond in disasters and the full economic loss of animals in disasters. Critically, this understanding will help better define both human and animal evacuation and rescue. Limited research currently exists in this area and where it does much is not statistically relevant.

Some statistically relevant work does, however, exist. Investigations conducted on pet owner perceptions on disaster preparedness for their pets in 2011–2012 in three Latin American cities showed that 75 per cent of pet owners were willing to risk staying behind with their pets in an effort to save them, even if they only had a five-minute window to evacuate from immediate danger (Hesterberg, Huertas and Appleby, 2012). Glassey (2010) found similar statistics in studies in New Zealand and this research is backed up by the anecdotal evidence from rescuers in a range of disasters, most notably Hurricane Katrina in 2005 where rescuers struggled to evacuate residents without their animals (Hunt et al., 2015). Nevertheless, the research shows that only small numbers of these same pet owners are in reality prepared to evacuate with their pets. In Costa Rica for example, only 2 per cent of pet owners have in fact included their pets in their emergency family plans. In Mexico City, only 6 per cent of pet owners have taken the time to organise and prepare alternative shelters (and train their pets accordingly) with friends and family, and where to take their pet animals to in case of forced evacuation from their homes (More Market & Opinion Research, 2014).

When we consider that in the capital of Costa Rica, over 20 per cent of people own a dog as a pet (World Animal Protection, 2012), then one can assume that in cities with similar levels of pet ownership, emergency evacuation is likely to slow down or be complicated, should the need arise. If we were to assume that this is a fair estimate for most cities this means that 20 per cent of the inhabitants of any city are indeed a significant consideration for civil defence departments, logistical planners and rescue teams during the evacuation of humans, as time is always of the essence during the evacuation phase.

Lack of pet and farm animal preparedness, therefore, may end up enhancing the danger for their owners, as many show a clear intention and tendency to refuse to leave without their animals, or a tendency to come back for their animals, putting themselves and rescue teams in danger once again. This research strongly suggests that the combination of strong existing bonds between animals and their owners, coupled with their poor or misguided understanding of risk and of how to prepare or protect their animals for disasters, makes the efforts for improving animal owner perceptions and ultimately the measures taken to improve preparedness for their animals highly beneficial for both. The solution seems to be partly in the hands of the animal owners themselves by preparing ahead of time, and partly in the hands of government officials, by promoting awareness campaigns directed to animal owners and by factoring animals in emergency evacuations.

Very similar behaviour but with different motivations seem to be prevalent in the owners of farm or working animals, especially for small farms in rural environments and for backyard kept animals in peri-urban dwellings. In the case of backyard animals in cities such as in the neighbourhood of Xochimilco, Mexico, or around Port-au-Prince, Haiti, these animals are often of significant value and importance in the family's economy, or even a pillar in their owner's livelihoods, and the resistance to leave them behind or evacuate without them is marked, out of fear of losing them to the hazard itself, theft, secondary infections, disease or even starvation (Losada et al., 1998; Schiere and van der Hoek, 2001). When we consider the importance of these animals we also see them play a role as a secondary income or insurance scheme to soften the blow of living close to the poverty line. In the aftermath of Cyclone Haiyan in the Philippines in 2013 many fishermen lost their boats and thus their financial risk buffer of backyard animals immediately became a new primary income.

The same solution for preparedness may be cited for this sector, with the difference that, due to size and/or number, owners of farm or working animals may need outside support for transport and emergency sheltering of their animals. This, in the case of larger animal populations, means that market forces may often become a negative factor here. In both cases, pre-existing immunisation levels are paramount to avoid eventual secondary waves of outbreaks of prevalent pathogens after the disaster occurs.

Preparedness needs

When we consider needs we need to consider the scale and complexity of the systems that animals live in. They may find themselves living within the human household, or out on pasture. They may find themselves living alone or in large herds or indoors in intensive production. All these factors will impact upon the needs for preparedness. Large animal farms as an example may need their own detailed planning which will require coordination with animal health authorities to take account of:

- veterinary travel certificates;
- early evacuation time frames and specific routes;
- significant inventories of handling personnel, loading ramps, transport trucks, alternative corrals, pastures and emergency shelters;
- detailed ID systems for their farm animals;
- consideration of the market forces involved in the movement of large numbers of animals to new areas.

Small farms and owners of working or backyard animals have different needs and may find it difficult to transport and find alternative pastures and shelters for their animals. Local farmers should be encouraged to enter into 'emergency collectives' where they may work together during disasters to pool resources and expertise to prepare better. Much too often during emergency evacuation of livestock, identical tagging and identification systems for cattle are found to be weak. Often the same numeric sequences are duplicated on other farms, making it rather difficult to segregate evacuated animals when sheltered in larger numbers. This in turn tends to promote tension and conflicts among animal owners.

Pet owners on the other hand, need to keep their pets up to date with their immunisation schemes, and their animals should wear ID tags, a microchip or tattoo, plus a picture ID as a redundant system with their veterinary records at a safe place. These four measures are critical to ensuring that animals stand the best chance of staying healthy in a disaster and staying (or being reunited) with their owners. Critically these owners also need to keep carriers handy and train their pets into them, and if in doubt, consider including handling tools such as leashes and muzzles in the case of larger or nervous animals.

Experience shows that often emergency responders may not be keen to place a loose animal in a rescue vehicle for safety reasons. Equally when the animal arrives at an evacuation point, the transport box itself forms a useful temporary shelter for the animal itself and allows for easier management by authorities involved. Ideally, however, pet owners should identify and acclimatise their animals to alternate sheltering possibilities with friends and family, in case they need to evacuate without their animals. The placing of animals with another trusted household should always be preferable to evacuating with an animal. In the least ideal situation, preparedness for pet owners may also include the eventuality of leaving animals behind and at home. In this situation they should be left with enough food and water to last for several days, any potentially falling objects and furniture secured, and a warning on the door or windows that a live animal is inside. This is critical should the expected return of the owners be delayed or their ability to care for their animals reduced. For sources of information, many municipalities and humane societies have detailed checklists online of preparedness measures for pets available for the benefit of pet owners and governance levels elsewhere. It is important, however, to remember that pet animals are no longer simply cats and dogs but have expanded to include horses and donkeys as well as reptiles, amphibians, large felines, primates, insects and spiders. The needs of exotic species of animals are similar but deserve separate attention, given the logistical difficulties of handling, transporting and providing shelter to exotic species.

Communication and information

One crucial need is a common language for disaster management especially during preparedness and response operations, and thus the first rule of business for animal science professionals and the farm animal industry is to learn how to incorporate the farm animal 'layers' of animal risk analysis into pre-existing risk maps and emergency operation plans.

Smooth communications during emergency responses are critical, and thus a standardised field emergency management construct called Incident Command System (ICS) was designed to offer a common and integrated organisational structure that bypasses jurisdictional boundaries to respond to complex demands during a disaster. The ICS is the on-site coordination system that handles facilities, equipment, staff, tasks and communications to operate within a single organisational structure and for all kinds and sizes of emergencies.[1]

Hazards – animal exposure, vulnerability, risk and risk analysis

Of all the factors influencing our society, poverty is perhaps at the root of what makes most people and their animals more vulnerable than others to the impact of most hazards. This is true for the owners of backyard animals, small farm owners and for pet owners alike. As animal exposure is part of their vulnerability, and the *frequency* and *magnitude* these animals may be exposed to by the hazard are intrinsically part of it, animal preparedness needs to reduce all the above factors to protect animals from displacement, starvation, injuries, death, and with this, protect the livelihoods of their owners.

Animal risk analysis

Animal risk (AR) may be represented by the following formula: $AR=H+AV(AE)/AR$

$$AR = \frac{Hazard + Animal\ Vulnerability}{Animal\ Preparedness}$$

AR: Animal Risk
H: Probability of Hazard occurrence
AV: Animal Vulnerability
AP: Animal Preparedness

Planning

When planning preparedness for animals, efforts should start with the historical and present assessment, prioritisation and analysis of the risks animals and their owners may face, as well as the establishment of the ability to avoid, reduce, cope with and withstand the effects of those hazards.

This analysis should start by identifying and assessing:

*   historical data, characteristics, frequency and potential severity of hazards animals may face;
*   species, numbers, health, welfare, infrastructure (farms, shelters, corrals, barns, services), relative animal exposure (for pets), plus a resource-related characterisation of their owners;
*   geographical areas and vulnerable communities;
*   ability of the animal owners and related sectors (farm animal sector, governance levels) to withstand and cope with the effects of the hazard;
*   logistics involved (equipment, transport, sheltering, services);
*   cost/benefit of preparedness measures.

The result of this kind of analysis should feed directly into preparedness planning.

Preparedness plans often start with risk mapping, overlaid on pre-existing maps and representations of the communities, people and their animals involved. This will allow the interpretation of the location and visualisation of a specific area together with the vulnerabilities of the affected population, strengths and opportunities such as community cooperation, ways of access and evacuation, means and resources, etc. Once the risk map is ready, the process of planning involves identifying common resources and possible mechanisms of risk avoidance, reduction or transfer. This allows the determination of roles and responsibilities, as well as the development of policies, actions and measures aimed at ensuring preparation and business continuity during the recovery phase, leading to effective emergency response for the animals. Critical to this is the documentation of strengths and opportunities to balance against the vulnerabilities identified. This should occur initially during risk mapping and then with the aim to build the preparedness plan. This allows for the identification of coordination mechanisms in the community, infrastructure support from local governments, safe zones for animal shelters and alternative evacuation routes.

Planning can then be divided in Strategic, Operational and Tactical layers so as to discriminate between long-term policy planning; responsibilities, integration and tasks, and staff, equipment, resources and training needs, respectively.

Planning may also be split into Scenario-based, Function-based and Capability-based, or into Vertically integrated versus Horizontally integrated, mainly for implementation purposes, although the practical application often results in a mixture of all the above approaches.

Towards the end of the process, the financial consideration within any emergency response operation is important to factor. Money keeps the operation going and helps decide between evacuating farm animals to emergency corrals or to the auction market or it determines the building up of emergency shelters for pets versus keeping them in foster homes, transparency of process and continuity of business. In sharp contrast with preparedness plans for humans, the cost–benefit analysis of any actions to prepare animals for disasters will lie heavily on the result of this particular analysis. Finally, financial planning and analysis may feed lessons learned into reconstruction and future preparedness. The final objective of preparedness plans for animals will be to factor these animals as essential assets for the protection of the livelihoods of their owners, in any government and Civil Defence plans and work, and never to be separate or independent from it.

Animal preparedness policies, mechanisms and strategies

Legal frameworks and policies

Policies to promote preparedness for animals are expressed in legislation and protocols. These are systems of principles, rules and instructions set for individuals, institutions and governance levels to protect animal lives from the negative action of disasters and as essential assets for the livelihoods of their owners and those who may depend on them. In the last decade during the drafting of the Hyogo Framework for Action (UNISDR, 2005), the foundations were laid to protect human lives around the world and reduce the number of casualties due to disasters. The successor to HFA emerged in 2015 as the Sendai Framework (UNISDR, 2015) and is a global policy set to define how all actors involved in disaster planning will approach the issue to 2030. This was built as four main pillars:

1   understanding disaster risk;
2   strengthening disaster risk reduction governance;
3   investment in disaster risk reduction for resiliency;
4   augmentation of disaster preparedness for fast emergency response and to 'build back better'.

Pillar 4 focuses on preparedness, and farm and working animals are now considered essential assets, but all pillars have one or more elements of what disaster preparedness is supposed to be. Unlike other assets, however, animals are living beings, so in order to increase their protection from disasters, consideration will have to be given to their welfare. The 2005–2015 process provides valuable lessons on how to incorporate other sectors of society into the disaster risk reduction process. The new language including animals allows the targeting of the farm animal sector, animal owners and animal health departments for change in this area.

During late 2015, the UN started consultations with countries to discuss and adapt the UNISDR terminology and indicators to the new Sendai Framework, with the aim to include, adapt and define new concepts and new interpretations such as productive assets, both farm and working, as essential to their owners' livelihood protection, and thus worth protecting from disasters. By the time of publishing, indicators and targets should have been set that will drive the global community toward better protection for animals. Through this global body of policy, the UN will in turn promote similar policy manifestations at regional and national levels. The aim is to protect society from the effects of disasters, and within that, protect animals as essential assets for the livelihoods of those in society who depend on them for companionship, work, labour, income, food, services, etc.

Case studies

Costa Rica

On 6 April 2006, Law #8495 established the legal basis for the Ministry of Agriculture and Animal Husbandry to handle animal-related emergency responses (Leyes y Decretos, 2006, 2013). Title IV of the Act talks about emergencies, and Art. 95 foresaw the creation of an emergency fund. In 2010, the 'Performance of Veterinary Services' (PVS) audits carried out periodically by the World Animal Health (OIE) identified the providing of funding for emergency animal health care as a need. OIE recommended the National Animal Health Service (SENASA) to create an emergency veterinary fund in order to follow OIE standards, guidelines and recommendations. In 2011, the General Controller of Costa Rica conducted a study (period 2006–2010) to determine whether SENASA adequately ensured timely and efficient resources for the attention of animals at risk or in emergencies.

The results of the study highlighted the importance of regulating SENASA's law and responsibility for emergency animal health and welfare, and thus instructed the creation of a specific, cumulative fund for animal emergencies and to formalise the procedures governing the management of these resources. In April 2013, following OIE's recommendation, the Direction of the General Comptroller, and SENASA's law, the Director General of SENASA issued an official directive to establish the cumulative fund for sanitary emergencies, charged to the budget of SENASA.

By October 2013, a simulation exercise was co-organised with SENASA, CNE (National Commission for the Prevention of Risks and Disaster Attention) and facilitated by World Animal Protection, to test and validate the use of the new fund as well as SENASA's capacity to deal with an emergency. This simulation allowed stakeholders to identify areas for improvement and specific procedures needed to help expedite the activation and use of funding resources, in addition to flexible mechanisms of intra- and inter-agency coordination.

In March 2015, the fund was activated for the first time, and US$ 1.2m assigned to the attention of the drought generated by the ENOS phenomenon in the north-western region of the country. SENASA's emergency veterinary fund was formally presented and documented by the Inter American Institute for Cooperation in Agriculture (IICA) by mid 2015. It bases its financial resources on yearly budget under expenditures from the institution. Although conceptually and originally meant to replace lost animals, the tasks at hand quickly evolved to providing emergency fodder, treatment and transport.

During late 2015, the IICA presented the Costa Rican case documented in a comprehensive document to the Latin American Region. At the same time during 2015, the National Commission for Risk Prevention and Emergency Attention (CNE) initiated a 1.5-year long consultation period to prepare its 2016–2030 National Risk Management Policy, to be formally presented in the first quarter of 2016 (CNE, 2015). This Policy is based on five theme pillars and three cross-cutting approaches and seeks to include companion animals.

Within the human rights approach, the newly proposed text involving animal risk reads:

A. – . . .

– This implies the protection of animals, be it because animals form part of the livelihoods, or due to their status of companion animals, where the affective bond between people and their pets contributes to the peace of mind and emotional welfare.

Municipal level

Once global, national and state policies are aligned and ready, the next level of action is the municipality. This level of government is often, literally, metres away from hazards, possible animal victims and their owners; thus they could become the ideal champion of preparedness as well as the ideal first emergency response level supporting animal owners immediately. The first order of business for municipalities is an accurate animal inventory, followed by risk analysis, and then awareness work. The real challenge, however, is finding the continued will and funding to maintain effort, especially in locations where disaster frequency may be low and thus people become desensitised to risks. The key mechanisms to maintain preparedness include drills, stockpiling, training, equipment; all of these need political will and resources to realise. In the case of pet animals (although not specifically exclusive to them) identification and licensing may be the best allies of managing future risk.

Emergency veterinary response

When disaster strikes, preparedness may not have been enough to avoid having to respond. The time may come when animals may end up needing emergency help to survive, and it will be contingent upon owners and professionals to do so. Thus providing the knowledge, skills and equipment for disaster response can also be considered preparedness. Among the preparedness/response/reaction mechanisms that can strengthen and increase the effectiveness of an emergency veterinary response for animals are:

- animal impact and needs assessment capacity and procedures;
- stockpiling fodder, water, medicines;
- reinforcing infrastructures, ways of access;
- emergency veterinary first aid and treatment capability;
- emergency animal relief procedures and training;
- early warning and animal evacuation, sheltering and capacity:
  - farm animals should evacuate earlier and/or through different paths, not to jeopardise eventual human evacuation ways;
  - transport capacity for different species in place;
  - sheltering procedures for both farm and pet animals (this deserves a separate discussion);
- technical animal rescue (including training capacity);
- recovery planning (debris removal, transport, continuity of care/veterinary services, fodder).

Coordination

The effectiveness of any field preparedness plan requires in-depth coordination with key response agencies. While these actors differ depending on national settings they can include: civil defence, all levels of government, emergency services, the military and government ministries or departments. Coordination, however, needs mutual understanding, trust and coordination of efforts and resources among the stakeholders involved in the emergency, and thus the building of relationships, the understanding of agency remits, capacities and limitations and the practice for emergencies are all essential parts of preparedness.

Education tools

The arsenal of preparedness tools for animals ought to be built at every stakeholder level and this is thankfully growing by the year. These should be designed to appeal to the audience, focus on simple and memorable messaging, and delivered in a medium that has the highest chance of success. In a modern digital age, it may be assumed that digital forms of communication are most effective but in certain parts of the world radio, text messaging, DVDs and even written material can have an important role to play.

CASE STUDY: PREPAREDNESS IN THE AFTERMATH OF THE 2010 HAITI EARTHQUAKE

Preparedness posters were produced of the initial planning stages of a unique TV communication campaign originally thought of for Latin America but due to the 2010 Haiti earthquake adapted and produced in Creole for Port au Prince, featuring a local family preparing an emergency plan together with their pet dog that surprises them by talking and actively participating in the making of the plan. The campaign went on for over a year and it focused on including animals in emergency family plans, up to date vaccines, clean water, safe shelter for all of them, flashlights, batteries, etc. Performance was measured with the help of focus groups and TV ratings and was very well accepted by the local public, as the dog was the first animal to appear in local television talking in Creole.

Mexico City MX30

For the thirtieth anniversary of the Mexico City Earthquake, World Animal Protection developed a public awareness campaign called MX30, focused on preparedness for pet owners in highly urbanised areas of the city and based on social networks, Internet resources and eventually supported by field specific and demonstrative actions during 19 September 2015. The actions included awareness events at various public parks and a mobile veterinary clinic emulating emergency response for companion animals after a quake at the main city square El Zócalo, in cooperation with UNAM veterinary students and teachers (National Autonomous University of Mexico).

This effort sought to promote preparedness for pets in case of an earthquake, and also to strengthen the involvement of pet owners at the government's invitation to participate in the earthquake. The campaign reached over 2 million people on Facebook, and campaign videos had 290 thousand views.

Training, drills and innovative solutions

Simulation exercises and drills are without doubt excellent tools to evaluate preparedness and further develop disaster preparedness plans. They are also superior tools for training, evaluating strategies, procedures and tools, for vertical and horizontal coordination, decision making and developing teamwork. They can be used systematically by several agencies and a host of national and international organisations that may work in the emergency response field.

An animal disaster simulation is a table-top exercise that aims at recreating a theoretical disaster scenario involving pets or farm animals. Participants are assigned roles that match their real occupation or role in the community or sector (pet owners, farm animal owners, animal health officials, transporters), and make decisions based on information provided at different moments and by different mediums during the exercise. Events occur in 'simulated time' and represent hours, days or weeks. The event is based on a script of events involving animals at risk and seeks realistic reactions and responses, which in turn must be based on existing capabilities, procedures and resources. The aim is to evaluate reactions to particular circumstances and the effectiveness of coordination. Evaluation results and lessons learned may help improving pre-existing preparedness plans. Simulations usually last only a few hours.

A drill is a more advanced tool best described as a field exercise in managing emergency operations involving animals at risk, simulating deaths, damage and injuries to those animals in a false emergency situation. Participants face these scenarios, using the coordination skills, techniques and resources that would be applied in real situations. Unlike simulation exercises, field drills require the actual mobilisation of animals, use of handling personnel and material resources such as transport crates, trucks, etc. Drills allow the evaluation of coordination procedures, tools, skills, individual and institutional capacities. With regards to timing and roles, drills are similar to simulations, and human actors are to play their roles truthfully if the drill is to be successful. Drills can provide the most insightful lessons about pre-existing preparedness plans, and the lessons learned may well make the difference between success and failure during real emergencies. They can, however, be difficult and expensive to organise but form an effective tool in evaluating multiple elements at play in a disaster scenario. Normally the drill occurs in the field to offer realism and operates for an entire working day but can last as long as three. Community participation in drills can be the most effective teaching tool available for individuals to understand risk and how to integrate their response to emergencies.

Preparedness for veterinarians

The reality that most veterinarians face outside of government practice is that they will not have access to formalised networks they can join that discuss risk management for animals. They will be faced with a much more immediate priority of both securing their business facility and income at the same time as being expected to provide some support to communities. There will be an expectation from communities that supplies at a veterinary centre can be repurposed for aid when in fact most small clinics hold limited stock and in the developed world may have intermittent access to any pipelines of supply to replenish. Unless trained and equipped, local private veterinarians can end up misaligned with rescue efforts or indeed become a risk to themselves and others (Figure 7.1). It is recommended that private veterinarians in risk areas should familiarise themselves with emergency planning, inform local authorities what they are prepared to do and have the

FIGURE 7.1 Haitian vets being trained to better prepare themselves for future disasters
Source: Kathy Milani for the HSI.

capacity to deliver in a disaster and access any training or drills/exercises available to them. Outside of building capacity to agencies involved in coordination, there are other initiatives that can be useful to provide a resource for animal response during times of crisis.

Veterinary response units

In 2007 World Animal Protection piloted the first Veterinary Emergency Response Unit (VERU) at a local veterinary school in the National University of Costa Rica. This unit was designed as an emergency response tool to aid communities and animal owners after disaster strikes. Students are taught principles of emergency management and hazards of natural origin, first veterinary aid and relief, animal behaviour during disasters, animal handling, ICS, LEGS, principles of emergency logistics, security, biosecurity, coordination with civil defence and agriculture authorities, principles of technical animal rescue in inclined angles, water rescue and mud entrapments. The VERU concept subsequently spread to Mexico and South America, India, Asia and Africa, adapting to the conditions of each region. In Kenya the VERU project is now a mainstream part of veterinary teaching curriculums.

PrepVet

A new online training course for animal science professionals, endorsed by UNISDR and the Mexican Association of Veterinary Schools is in its pilot stages in Mexico, focusing on:

1   Animal Risk Management (risk maps, preparedness plans)
2   Climate Change Adaptation for Animals
3   Concepts of Emergency Veterinary Response.

The first strand discusses the making of risk maps and preparedness plans for animals, while the third strand focuses on the following topics:

- veterinary triage
- ICS
- LEGS
- security and biosecurity
- zoonoses
- animal evacuation and transport
- animal corpses management
- training needs on CPR and technical rescue.

Preparedness for animal owners and local governments

Innovative Solutions

Figure 7.2 shows an animal friendly emergency loading ramp, designed for large farm animals and particularly for the rapid evacuation of dairy cattle in volcano eruptions.

FIGURE 7.2 Example of portable cattle loading ramp
Source: James Sawyer.

CASE STUDY: INTEGRATED PROGRAM FOR RURAL DEVELOPMENT

In the case of Mexico, the Federal Government established the 'Integrated Program for Rural Development' for cases of hydro-meteorological and geological phenomena, called Component for Attention to Agriculture & Fisheries in Cases of Disasters (CADENA). Its objective is to support all animal producers, with accent on those with low incomes and without a public or private catastrophic insurance for their livestock. For producers with larger animal lots and access to insurance, CADENA recently added extra coverage for livestock:

1   Decease of livestock
2   Damage to livestock's productive infrastructure.

The producer covers 25 per cent of the cost of his/her insured animals as a premium, while local private insurance companies cover the rest, but in the second scenario of productive infrastructure, this would in fact support the future reduction of risk for the animals living inside those structures. With those additions, the Mexican Government is supporting producers, fostering integrated risk management at the three governmental levels (federal, state and municipal) with key actors such as the private and social sectors, the latest unfamiliar with insurance schemes. As these new concepts help strengthen the financial instruments for risk transfer and ultimately risk management, Mexico considers them as prevention actions to face disasters. Insurance schemes, however, seldom favour protecting the lives of the animals at risk or their welfare, as the aim here is to protect the face value of the asset, and the mechanism of choice is to replace a significant portion of that value once lost, be it by reimbursing a predetermined amount for the animals, or by restocking. Restocking, on the other hand, does not necessarily avoid or reduce pre-existing vulnerabilities, and thus cycle or risk is likely to perpetuate itself, with little or no regard for the welfare of the animals.

In 2015 World Animal Protection built demonstration shelters for small farm animals during and near the Calbuco volcano eruption in Chile, to show how to quickly build cheap and effective ways to protect livestock from chronic ash fall and acid rain.

Underground shelters to protect cattle and pigs and poultry from hurricanes and typhoons were also adapted for use in the Philippines and Vanuatu, and plans are underway to introduce the concept back to the Caribbean region as well.

Financial preparedness mechanisms

Animal insurance and reinsurance schemes

Some countries have insurance schemes meant to protect livestock in cases of disasters. These often have a range of rigid and flexible triggers, modified over time to increase the population coverage (livestock and producers) and to directly support livestock producers. In some locations this has a beneficial role to play and in others the lack of control of farmers through poorly planned mechanisms drives human behaviour, which means animals are left to die in expectation of automatic pay out.

As a concept, animal preparedness should be the cornerstone of effective disaster management for animals. Understanding how animal owners know, understand and perceive risk for their animals is paramount and foremost to begin attempting to reduce this risk. The reader does not have to start from scratch, as successful pilots and examples exist of how to tackle these attitudes towards risk for animals. Alternatives are out there to increase preparedness for animal owners and their animals and where to benchmark for guidance on how to construct strategy and public policy at all levels of governance. The veterinary and animal science profession is the final implementing expert for reference purposes in process, and the means are now ready and online to build this new capacity. In the next chapter we will explore disaster risk reduction and how this remains an important component in the aftermath of a disaster to harness the short-term willingness to invest in measures that will have a positive impact for the 'next one'.

Note

1   Full detail of how the ICS system works can be found here: www.fema.gov/incident-command-system-resources

Further reading

Federal Emergency Management Agency. (n.d.). Prepare for Emergencies Now: Information for Pet Owners. Available at: www.fema.gov/media-library-data/1390846777239-dc08e309debe561d866b05ac84daf1ee/pets_2014.pdf

Federal Emergency Management Agency. (2017). Incident Command Systems Resources. Available at: www.fema.gov/incident-command-system-resources

United Nations Office for Disaster Risk Reduction (UNISDR). (2005). Hyogo Framework for Action 2005–2015: Building the Resilience of Nations and Communities to Disasters. Available at: www.unisdr.org/2005/wcdr/intergover/official-doc/L-docs/Hyogo-framework-for-action-english.pdf

References

Bressan, D. (2011). Can Animals Sense Earthquakes? *Scientific American*. Available at: https://blogs.scientificamerican.com/history-of-geology/can-animals-sense-earthquakes

Comisión Nacional de Prevención de Riesgos y Atención de Emergencias (CNE). (2015). *Política Nacional de Gestión del Riesgo 2016–2030*. San José, CR: CNE.

Glassey, S. (2010). *Pet Owner Emergency Preparedness and Perceptions Survey Report: Taranaki and Wellington Regions*. Wellington: Mercalli Disaster Management Consulting. Available at: https://training.fema.gov/hiedu/docs/glassey%20-%20survey-pet%20owner%20emergency%20preparedness%20perceptions.pdf

Hesterberg, U., Huertas, G. and Appleby, M. (2012) Perceptions of pet owners in urban Latin America on protection of their animals during disasters. *Disaster Prevention and Management: An International Journal* 21(1): 37–50.

Hunt, M., Al-Awadi, H., and Johnson, M. (2015). Psychological sequelae of pet loss following Hurricane Katrina. *Anthrozoös* 21(2): 109–121.

Leyes y Decretos. (2006). *Ley General del Servicio Nacional de Salud Animal N° 8495*. San José, CR: La Gaceta N°150.

Leyes y Decretos. (2013). *Decreto N° 37828-MAG Reglamento al Título IV Dispositivo de Emergencias de la Ley General del Servicio Nacional de Salud Animal N° 8495 y Procesos de Contratación*. San José, CR: La Gaceta N° 150.

Losada, H., Cortés, J., Vieyra, J., Arias, L. and Bennett, R. (1998). *Suburban livestock rearing by smallholders in the backyards of Xochimilco in the south-east of Mexico City as an important strategy for sustainable urban agriculture*. City Farmer (Canada's Office of Urban Agriculture). Available at: www.cityfarmer.org/livestock.html

More Market and Opinion Research. (2014). *Estudio N° Preparación para Desastres en México. Estudio N° 738-2-3665*. México, DF: World Animal Protection.

Schiere, H. and van der Hoek, R. (2001). *Livestock Keeping in Urban Areas*. FAO Animal Production and Health Paper Series, Rome. Available at: www.fao.org/DOCREP/004/Y0500E/Y0500E00.htm

United Nations Office for Disaster Risk Reduction (UNISDR). (2015). *Sendai Framework for Disaster Risk Reduction 2015–2030*. Available at: www.unisdr.org/files/43291_sendaiframeworkfordrren.pdf

United Nations Office for Disaster Risk Reduction (UNISDR). (2005). *Hyogo Framework for Action 2005–2015: Building the Resilience of Nations and Communities to Disasters*. Available at: www.unisdr.org/2005/wcdr/intergover/official-doc/L-docs/Hyogo-framework-for-action-english.pdf

World Animal Protection (2012). *Situación de la Población Canina en la Gran Área Metropolitana*. Heredia: IDESP.

8

REDUCING RISK FOR ANIMALS VULNERABLE TO DISASTERS

Disaster Risk Reduction (DRR) is defined by the United Nations International Strategy on Disaster Reduction (2009) as:

> Disaster risk reduction is the concept and practice of reducing disaster risks through systematic efforts to analyse and reduce the causal factors of disasters. Reducing exposure to hazards, lessening vulnerability of people and property, wise management of land and the environment, and improving preparedness and early warning for adverse events are all examples of disaster risk reduction.

In the last chapter we explored the concept of preparedness and how people could identify risk and increase their readiness and response to its impact. In this chapter we explore the concept of DRR in relation to animals and the critical role that DRR measures can play in delivering reduced vulnerability of these populations.

Chapter 1 demonstrated the importance of animals to people and thus when one factors in the economic superiority of DRR over disaster response and how securing peoples' animals aids in reducing the impact of disasters and thus better prevents loss to livelihoods and food security, and economic loss, we can see that this is an important area of focus for future efforts.

We will now explore the concept of sustainable capital, essential animal assets and business continuity for farm animal owners presented within the context of risk reduction for animals. In addition we will look at current successful government level strategies, pilot projects and the elements needed to build a disaster risk reduction plan for vulnerable animals.

As a discipline, DRR arrived later into humanitarian practice once the disaster cycle had been defined and acknowledgement emerged that initiatives could be undertaken before and after disasters to ensure that following events are less severe in their impacts. DRR is fundamentally about reducing vulnerability and exposure, and this has meant progress in the discipline has often been slower than in disaster response. Many vulnerabilities relate indirectly to the event, but to underlying, long-term cultural, economic and environmental factors. Often the vulnerabilities that lead a community to be less resilient than they should be relate to development factors.

Disasters can be considered a social construct. As an example, a disease outbreak post disaster may trace its root cause to a range of factors but the main one may be poor original or baseline sanitation or access to clean water. The theoretical divide between humanitarian and development efforts has led to this complexity being laid stark and the challenges of moving these sectors forward in concert with government and industry have been very tricky. Often the debate has been about where the disaster starts and where it ends, what vulnerabilities were there to begin with and whose responsibility it is to pick up the underlying problems and deal with them.

Thankfully the Hyogo Framework for Action for the first time elevated governments to the highest level of responsibility and the subsequent Sendai Framework only further so. DRR is as much developing through the leadership of governments themselves as the international aid community. In reality this is the only way in which all the factors relating to vulnerability can be addressed and resources allocated but there is still a long way to go. The mutual distrust in many countries between the aid community and governments needs to soften before the most at-risk governments make significant inroads into DRR. These challenges aside, the cost–benefit of DRR is clear and now well proven, showing that DRR is many times more cost effective than disaster response. This should reinvigorate a reinvestment of funds away from disaster response to DRR and preparedness but in reality this is an initiative that is influenced by outside factors such as perceptions, donors and politics rather than pure economics. Over time, however, we are seeing this shift happen.

DRR for animals – concepts

This may be one of the hardest aspects of risk management, let alone animal risk management, if only because at the end of a lot of patient work and investment in human and financial resources, the end result is expected to be zero. For a DRR process to be perfectly successful, no impact will have occurred. In nature, wild animals have developed strategies to avoid becoming a prey to predators. The same principles are applied to the threat of forest fires, droughts, floods, winds, etc. They typically freeze, gather in large groups, flee, hide, seek shelter or high ground, or run away from perceived danger when possible, and if cornered and forced, attack. Domestic animals don't always display these behaviours or have that luxury, as they may be kept indoors or in captivity, conditioned to specific feeding conditions, or the environment they live in is highly urbanised.

Definition

Disaster risk reduction for animals can be defined in this context as the process and practice animal owners, private stakeholders and institutions in charge of animal health, welfare and production need to undertake to analyse and reduce vulnerabilities and exposure to disasters. This is achieved through systematic, periodical and cyclic review, in an effort to manage obvious and underlying disaster vulnerabilities for animals and their owners.

This review aims to reduce these in a systematic way, ultimately aiming for their insignificance to the welfare of these animals and that of their owners.

Disaster risk reduction for animals may be achieved by:

- reducing animal exposure and sensibility;
- increasing adaptive capacity to hazards, thus lessening their vulnerability and the owner's vulnerability on their livelihoods and capital assets;
- installing early warning systems;
- effective land planning;
- improving awareness and preparedness at all levels.

The concept of animal risk reduction includes animal preparedness, and this in turn, includes emergency animal response, as all and any action that may spare animal lives does in fact reduce their risk. These actions are located temporarily closer to the occurrence of the hazard than other 'pure' risk reduction actions. Outside of the preparedness and response elements, all actions taken should then be regarded as pure risk reduction elements.

They may be located further away in time from the disaster event and indeed some of them may at first glance seem distant from the welfare and health of the animals. These are dissimilar actions such as planting trees to reduce risk of soil erosion and landslides, planting resilient pastures that resist droughts or flooding, choosing sturdier or more adaptable species/breed of farm animals for certain conditions or vaccination schemes.

But there are also systemic-oriented actions that help reduce risk for animals at different levels, such as:

- building a dam to control the flow of a river or to irrigate an arid area or pastures;
- passing public policy to foster exposure in the farm animal sector;
- installing early warning/evacuation plans for animals;
- harnessing local market forces to help buy fodder for farms and their animals during difficult seasons;
- promoting public service announcements to reduce vulnerability of pet animals and increase resiliency for them and their owners.

Within the UNISDR Sendai Framework, farm and working animals were labelled as essential assets for the protection of the livelihoods of their owners.

New livestock-related indicators were developed to be implemented by countries, which include documenting animal mortality during disasters and the impact this has on the livelihoods of those who own them.

Implementing this new approach in particular will fall under the responsibility of animal owners, animal science professionals, communities, the farm animal sector and government institutions dedicated to animal health and welfare. Reducing the risk of disaster for animals will require the development of new preparedness, response and risk reduction skills, and when the time comes for rehabilitation and reconstruction after an event has passed, always aim for building back better. The good news is that it is virtually impossible to reduce the risk animals may face in disasters without also fostering the same positive stage for their owners, and also reducing financial and livelihood risks for their caretakers and in general, those depending on them.

Building DRR plans for animals

Much of the work needed to reduce the risk of disasters for animals needs to factor in the perceptions and attitudes of their owners. The previous chapter described research carried out in Latin America on animal owner's attitudes about preparedness for their animals. With this in mind, promoting risk reduction plans and measures for animals will need championing and awareness efforts to help create a culture of risk reduction for all. The initial element needed to address disaster risk reduction is the recognition of risk, moving to its factoring and quantification, vis-à-vis the animals at risk, identified, counted and geo-located. These allow the creation of risk maps, which are the diagnoses of animal vulnerability.

In the previous chapter we discussed risk maps as useful tools to seek, gather and document baseline information about the animals at risk and the environment and conditions provided by their owners, to then assess the levels of these risks. As opposed to the purist, classical conception of risk maps, the objective of building preparedness plans now also includes documenting all capital or assets, in order to help build the risk reduction plan. Emphasis was given to the historical behaviour of hazards, and although that is still significant, the periodicity and intensity of weather related hazards has been changing lately, to the point that previous records and benchmarks are no longer offering solid modelling or trending reference.

Preparedness plans

When developing preparedness plans, the success or failure of the plan itself is almost totally dependent on the research and thinking that has gone into it, in advance. Factors to consider should include:

* historic nature of disasters and hazards in the area;
* features of the terrain for bother urban and rural environments;

- farm animal business diagnosis;
- local economies and markets;
- inventory of animal owners, farms and animals at risk;
- historical disaster impact on animal databases and census;
- emergency response capabilities;
- welfare and health levels (baseline, prospective) of animal populations, including species, races or breeds and identification systems;
- state of animal related infrastructure, including drainages, electrical installations, roofs and access/location;
- owners' perceptions, attitudes and behaviour research towards animal preparedness;
- government capacity to foster preparedness, prepare and assist animal evacuations, carry emergency needs assessments, arrange for emergency sheltering, ability to document not only losses but needs and then deliver aid;
- early warning systems linked to forecasting, animal evacuation and transport, sheltering plans;
- policies and legal (animal risk management policies and laws, regulations and memos, capacities and plans at every governance level);
- animal risk transfer mechanisms (emergency funds, insurance schemes);
- stakeholder coordination mechanisms (governance levels, institutions, sector, stakeholders, community, owners);
- incorporation of information into pre-existing risk maps for humans (at Civil Defence);
- communication and assessment (ICS, LEGS), media;
- education, training and awareness for the farm animal sector, community and animal owners;
- technical animal rescue and evacuation capabilities and training needs;
- periodical validation pools, desk exercises and drills;
- academia, animal science profession;
- preparedness plans for big farms, small farms, backyard animals, pet owners;
- availability of emergency veterinary kits, handling personnel, personal equipment, transport trucks, ramps, emergency sheltering, subsistence (fodder, water) and other specialist equipment.

Large animal farms have a larger influence on local and national economies and may develop and use their own detailed planning and resources, in close coordination with animal health authorities, and may already have in place the following:

- veterinary travel certificates;
- early evacuation time frames;
- specific evacuation routes;
- significant inventories of handling personnel;
- loading ramps, transport trucks;

- alternative corrals, pastures;
- emergency shelters and detailed ID systems for their farm animals.

Small farms, owners of working or backyard animals and pet owners may benefit from studying and developing their own plans to reduce the risk for their animals. Seemingly small changes in climate are now important to factor; 1 Centigrade temperature increases globally are changing the behaviour and niches of pathogens, vectors and hosts, thus changing the impact of more recognisable hazards as well.

As is evident, the somewhat newer step in the planning process of including those positive factors that may be in *favour* of the animals and their owners (assets to the assets, in the context of development) will help counter or reduce the effects of hazards. As capital assets, the cost–benefit, return over investment analysis is equally important as a decision tool when the time comes to define a plan, a schedule and a budget, versus the estimated economic losses a hazard could bring upon a farmer owning livestock. At the end of the day, much of what may be done will depend upon this analysis. This should not, however, be made in isolation, as local governments can help tremendously with maintaining ways of access, communication and power lines, eventual debris removal, etc.

Finally a consideration for solidarity is an important positive factor at the community level. Neighbours will usually help each other with both preparedness measures such as gathering and setting sand bags before a flood, securing stable doors and chicken farm roofs before a hurricane hits. This kind of community-concerted effort should be high in the priority list of any preparedness plan and nurtured where possible through emergency collectives of smallholders. Once everything is valued and quantified, risk-reducing measures need to the prioritised matching the capacity of the stakeholders. This allows for the allocation of roles and responsibilities, final costing and time frames. Then the plan should be ready.

Animal impact assessment

Most national disaster animal impact databases attempt to gather total figures of animal victims and usually only for livestock. They often fail to document injured or affected animals in need of veterinary attention, vaccination schemes, or even nutrition requirements, as in the case of floods damaging pastures for grazing animals for months in a row. Another glaring weakness is the lack of documentation on the real impact of these animal losses on their owner's livelihoods, as well as their failure to recommend ways to rehabilitate animal populations and eventually reduce the sector's vulnerabilities.

Invisibility

This can only make animal impact and needs invisible to most people other than the owners, and in the case of governments, animal victims and their owners would be little more than ghosts, making future relief and help nearly impossible.

The need to improve data collection and impact documentation on animals is one of the current challenges facing most countries during the development of the Indicators for the Sendai Framework.

Initial enquiries on baseline information and assessment capacity conducted in Latin America also revealed weaknesses in initial animal inventories for a series of reasons including the lack of up-to-date tools, lack of real government motivation to update small animal inventories, lack of budget (vehicles, fuel) for officials to carry out or update animal censuses, or the intention to avoid taxes. As in the animal preparedness chapter, it is paramount and even *sine qua non* that any DRR plans for animals be merged smoothly as important elements of similar plans for humans.

Successful animal DRR pilots and innovative solutions

Argentina flooding

In the province of Santa Fe, the Parana riverbed gets several miles wide and engulfs high pasturelands on the margins and on large enough islands in the river. Small –sometimes itinerant – cattle producers owning between one and a few hundred head of cattle and not owning pasture lands originally used these common, state-owned lands to fatten their cattle, but lately, and due in part to the soy industry and other large cattle producers, the islands have also been used to keep and raise pregnant females and calves. The area has very few barges for cattle transport and in the past has suffered losses of up to 50,000 animals in one flood. After one of the largest flooding events of the Parana river in 2007, thousands of cattle drowned or starved to death, as was the case in the province of Santa Fe every 7 years or so.

A pilot project on risk reduction for beef cattle in the Parana basin was started at the locality of Reconquista, Santa Fe province, that lasted nearly 3 years. After diagnosis, letters of intent and memos of understanding were produced between the Argentinean Army, Ministry of Agriculture, Academia, Municipality of Reconquista, cattlemen associations (large and small), local media and most stakeholders.

This was followed by lengthy and interesting discussions about the elements of risk management and analysis, until a cost–benefit analysis and risk map were produced and specific measures recommended for small producers and the local municipality. The risk mapping process helped identify the timing needed between flooding season, lapse between early warning and occurrence (rise of waters), and time needed to evacuate and sell the animals. Then came the even more vulnerable uses of keeping pregnant females and young ones in the islands, the lack of alternative pastures for small producers, coupled with low market prices for beef cattle and not enough transport barges to bring all animals out of danger.

Eventually, awareness posters were produced to remind cattle producers of their time frame to evacuate, and more importantly, of the point of no return for their investment and their animals. During the next cycle of flooding in the Parana, no animal casualties were suffered, thanks in no small part to the realisation by their owners of the real dimension of risk for their animals and businesses. More importantly, and with the help of a watchful eye and small timely actions, they were able to plan ahead, take control and reduce the risk of disaster.

Mexico

Right after a long drought in the state of Chihuahua killed thousands of cattle in the state and nearly finished the business for small cattle producers, World Animal Protection started a DRR and CCA (Climate Change Adaptation) pilot in the locality of Aldama. The diagnosis included the drought conditions, the carrying capacity of the dried-up fields, human influence, local inhabitants and their perceptions and attitudes, local, state and national policies, plus possible solutions benchmarked elsewhere.

Work then focused on adaptive alternatives built as models under the form of small dams adapted from the African sand dams, larger dams, alternative pastures such as cacti, hybrid pastures (*Triticale sp.*) with enhanced resistance to harsh weather and increased levels of protein, wells, hydroponic systems to diversify income and food, etc. Local cattle producers and municipality officials supported the process of analysis of the return over investment of these actions, investments were carried by third parties and a risk map finally produced as a tool or annex to pre-existing risk atlases in Chihuahua. Results were presented at the UNISDR Global Platform in Geneva, 2013.

Animal hazards, exposure, vulnerability, risk, risk analysis and DRR

Animal vulnerability may be defined as the relative low capacity of an animal or a group of animals to withstand, cope with, resist and recover from the impact of a hazard, thus influencing (increasing or decreasing) the animal's susceptibility to the impact of or collision with the said hazard. It may include the degree of exposition, breed, immunisation, age, body/health condition, sensibility of the animal or pastures, and low adaptive capacity or resilience. Factors that affect domestic animal vulnerability to disasters include their baseline health and welfare levels, the level of knowledge of owners and caretakers of those animals about how to effectively resist the effects of disasters, the degree of resilience that intensive production conditions for farm animals may initially have, together with health, shelter and nutrition support systems after the event. Of all the factors influencing our society, poverty is perhaps at the root of what makes most people (and their animals) more vulnerable to the impact of most hazards.

Animal exposure is part of animal vulnerability and may be defined as the state or degree of subjection of an animal to exposure to an incoming hazard, and it can be measured by the *frequency* with which the animals may be exposed to the hazard, which erodes any resistance. This is the case for cattle exposed repeatedly to flooding that never have enough time to fully recover from previous events, thus getting weaker with every flood.

The *duration*, is a somewhat similar factor to frequency and is expressed in the uninterrupted duration of the impact (hours and days or more) that animals may be exposed to an event such as droughts, especially if confined in intensive rearing conditions such as poultry or pigs. The final factor would be the amount of *exposed surface* of the animal's body immersed in water and thus subject to hypothermia, or how much ash is in fact getting into their lungs.

A hazard occurrence (quake, flood, hurricane, drought) rapidly moves from present risk to the category of disaster when animal vulnerability is combined with the following factors:

- the baseline welfare of the animals (breed, age, immunisation, health/body shape);
- the owner's vulnerability and thus incapacity to respond, resist or recover;
- displacement;
- starvation;
- injuries;
- loss of animal lives;
- loss of the livelihoods of their owners;
- the animal sector and/or industry being overwhelmed beyond coping mechanisms.

According to current definitions, a hurricane passing over an uninhabited forest for example does not result in a disaster until it negatively affects humans beyond their capacity to cope. That means animal risk is intimately interlinked with and dependent on human risk.

The degree or severity of risk that farm and pet animals may be under in the face of a potentially disastrous hazard may also be defined by:

> *Probability of occurrence* × *bearable exposure to risk* = *the capacity or resiliency they and their owners possess*

Risk of disaster for animals is often underestimated or misconstrued by their owners, but more often than not it increases due to their owner's perception and the decisions they make. This is compounded by the fact that domestic animal populations around the globe live dependent on humans and in many cases in confinement, meaning their relative exposure, vulnerability and resilience relies heavily on humans. This suggests the main obstacles for preparing animals for disasters may lie in their owner's perceptions of what risk really is for their animals and their real capacity to handle it, including the crucial return over investment analysis criteria.

Assuming these factors, animal risk (AR) may be represented by the following formula:

$$AR = H + AV(AE)/AR$$

$$AR = \text{Probability of } \underline{\text{Hazard}^{(So,\ Mag)} + \text{Animal Vulnerability}^{(Exp,\ Sen,\ Ac)}}$$
$$\text{Animal Resiliency}^{(Ar\ +\ Or)}$$

AR: Animal Risk
H: Probability of Hazard occurrence
AV: Animal Vulnerability
AE: Animal Exposure
AP: Animal Preparedness
(Ar): Animal Resilience
(Or): Owner Resilience
        (So): Speed of Onset
        (Exp): Exposure to the hazard
        (Sen): Sensitivity to the hazard
        (Ac): Adaptive Capacity
        (Mag): Magnitude

Scale versus frequency

Another sub index or mathematical expression applicable to the hazard and worth considering may be the *speed of the onset*. This an important factor to consider for disastrous events involving animals. The development and intensity of this factor can dramatically influence the type and intensity of the response required. An earthquake, a flash flood, or a sudden volcanic eruption are examples of rapid onset disasters. These occur suddenly and violently, with little or no warning, taking the lives of many animals, and destroying the livelihoods and economic structures of their owners.

Disasters of slow onset, on the other hand, occur over time and tend to 'creep in', going initially unnoticed. Their slow, accumulating effects often 'numb' affected people and governments, preventing early reactions. These situations lead to the slow deterioration of the health and welfare of animals and a degraded capacity of owners and the community to withstand or even recover from the effects. The difference in these events is important to consider because human behaviour in relation to them is so different and as such adaptation levels to risk are different in nature and pace.

In reality, animal risk increases chronically by the erosive action of small, unidentified, under-the-radar events. These small emergencies slowly undermine the capacity of the animals to cope with stress to their health and welfare and that of the owners to cope with the financially stressful conditions. The sum of the effects of numerous events of negative nature on animals and their owners bear, at the end of the day, a far heavier weight on their capacity to cope and a far bigger add-on burden to their vulnerability than any large, media attention grabbing disaster. This process in itself may be enough to tip animals over the edge but often it is the larger event that does so, creating disproportionate suffering and mortality because of already weakened animals, people and systems.

Assets

We have seen how animal risk cannot be separated from the role they play for their human owners. For the sake of simplicity, this role may be divided in two main categories: as assets similar to material possessions or as capital items. Conventionally, sustainable capital is divided in five types or categories, as a tool for understanding sustainability in terms of economics and wealth generation, considering the activities of an organisation when maximising their value, and that of their capitals, but always keeping in mind its impact, in order to avoid 'trade-offs'. This framework can also serve as a starting point for the vulnerability analysis of livelihoods, assets, goods and services. This assumes that humans will always seek to improve the quality of their lives and farm, and working animals form part of those essential assets.

A capital *asset* is something of value that should produce a return or welfare in the future. The five types of capital are:

- human
- social
- manufactured
- financial
- natural.

Animal assets

Farm and working animals fall into the definition of capital assets, as they are bought or produced to yield future returns, either directly in the form of milk, eggs, meat, wool or hides, or indirectly through draught power or manure for crops. As investment is defined as the acquisition of capital assets plus the savings produced or obtained as new capital minus local consumption, this concept depicts perfectly the meaning of animal assets.

When assessing levels of vulnerability and preparedness for farm and working animals, all five types of capital need to be included in the analysis rather than simplistically including them in 'natural'. They may fall into the durable capital concept, and indeed connect in various degrees of intensity with each of the other types, such as in the case of livestock yield. Their return over investments as productive breeders, plus a role in financial capitals, or the role of gender in caring for backyard animals in social/human capitals should all be considered.

A fairly new concept emerging from Climate Change Adaptation thinking (especially for free range cattle) is that of sensitivity of pastures (or any system for that matter). This is the degree of affectation experienced after a disturbance occurs. This is especially important after droughts or longer lasting floods, as pastures may be vital in the survivability of free-range cattle. It may also be useful to differentiate how different species consume pastures. As an example, pastures contaminated with volcanic ash may have a greater negative impact on horses because they cut the grass closer to the ground and thus are likely to consume more of the ash. Thus, to reduce the risk of a negative effect on animals and/or their owners' livelihoods, the vulnerability and/or exposure of those animals needs to be reduced, while the preparedness and capacity of their owners or caretakers to respond increased. It is only through this process that one can achieve a heightened level of preparedness and resilience.

When we consider the development of any theoretical model of animal resilience we may experience difficulties. The difficulty of definition and the combination of intrinsic, biological attributes and the necessary resilience of the rearing conditions their human owners provide them with are not always complementary. That considered, possibly the most sensible definition is:

> The ability of an animal/s, owner/s and business including infrastructure and functions exposed to a hazard to recover, resist and absorb pernicious impact minimising impact to livelihoods and welfare preventing the permanent degradation of yielding functions. Learning from the event leading to adaptation, accommodation and readiness allows the development of a cycle of improvement.

One of the dangers of excessive focus on planning documents is the isolated planning or 'planning in the vacuum'. An example of this would be an expert that would write detailed risk reduction analysis and plans, but fail to involve all stakeholders, the community and the authorities in charge of both animal health and risk management. Often the desire to write a plan too quickly can actually hinder resilience. Many times they have plans without the identification of existing planning structures that could be integrated into creating a more efficient and effective process. Many governments around the globe have already prepared their own organisational structures to reduce the human risk in emergency disasters operations, thus the farm animal and veterinary sector needs to coordinate and merge their eventual animal risk reduction work under and within these conceptual systems and structures.

Public policies, strategies and mechanisms

Legal frameworks and policies

Risk reduction for animals could not be achieved without the leadership and championing, the active involvement and participation of all levels of governance. The past decade of disaster risk reduction efforts called by the UN the Hyogo Framework for Action (2005–2015) championed regional platforms and national frameworks and policies for disaster risk reduction and preparedness for humans. HFA's successor, the Sendai Framework is tasked with advancing risk management in the areas of integration with government at all levels. This new framework is positioned to champion risk reduction for animals and their owners at all levels and thus the next target should be the private sector.

Much is currently under development advancing the field and the concept of risk reduction for people and their animals but perhaps the newest and most important concepts to develop a culture of risk reduction for animals may be new public policies for the agriculture sector, new training and the use of innovative communications to break some of the existing hurdles in attitudes.

The UNISDR process involved in defining the Sendai Framework will offer valuable lessons on how to incorporate other sectors of society into the disaster risk reduction process, creating a culture of risk management, with accent on the farm animal sector: the farm animal industry, animal owners and animal health departments. While this book was being written, consultations with countries were starting to discuss and adapt the UNISDR terminology and indicators for the new framework in Sendai, with the aim of including, adapting and defining new concepts and new interpretations such as productive assets – animals, both farm and working – essential to their owners' livelihood protection, and thus worth protecting from disasters (UNISDR, 2009).

Country policy examples of DRR

Mexico

Center for Disaster Prevention (CENAPRED) – The dependency in charge of DRR at Mexico's Federal Civil Defense, co-organised with World Animal Protection two international important events in 2014 and 2015, where risk reduction for animals was first discussed and examined. On the second edition, a multidisciplinary group convened with members of several government institutions with the aim of developing and proposing public policy that includes animal risk management programmes, risk reduction policies, and legislation for Civil Defence and other institutions in Mexico involved in or tasked with animal health, with the final aim of strengthening national resilience and protecting the livelihoods of those Mexicans dependent on animals.

One of the conceptual differences between Sendai's global framework and national policies such as the Mexican one is that for the foreseeable future the country is currently seeking to include companion animals into Civil Defence's formal policies as well, for all the motives presented in previous chapters, making it the second Latin American country to do so formally. CENAPRED presented a federal manual on how to handle animals in disasters in October 2017.

Costa Rica

Ministry of Agriculture and Animal Husbandry (MAG) – on 6 April 2006, Law #8495 regulated the protection, health and welfare of animals and veterinary public health under the responsibility of SENASA (National Animal Health Service) within the Ministry of Agriculture of Costa Rica (Leyes y Decretos, 2006, 2013). Later in 2009, SENASA defined roles and responsibilities for farm and companion animal welfare.

In 2013 an emergency veterinary fund was created and in March 2015 the fund was activated for the first time. Plans are now under way to fund risk reduction measures such as family-size aquaponic systems to protect the livelihoods of small farmers in the drought affected areas of Costa Rica. The National Commission for Risk Prevention and Emergency Attention of Costa Rica (CNE) (Civil Defence) initiated in 2015 a 1.5-year long consultation period to prepare its 2016–2030 National Risk Management Policy, formally presented in the first quarter of 2016 (CNE, 2015).

This policy is based on five theme pillars and three cross-cutting approaches:

Pillars:

1 Resilience and social inclusion
2 Decentralisation
3 Education, knowledge and innovation
4 Sustainable financial investment, infrastructure and services
5 Planning, legal tools and DRR mechanisms.

Cross-cutting approaches:

1 Human rights
2 Sustainable development
3 Gender equity.

Within the human rights approach, the newly proposed text involving animal risk reads:

> A.– The human rights approach in the risk Management Policy must encourage the interest in protecting people and their essential assets: 'livelihoods, production assets, including livestock, working animals, tools and seeds' (Sendai Framework, 2015).
>
> This implies the protection of animals, be it because animals form part of the livelihoods, or due to their status of companion animals, where the affective bond between people and their pets contributes to the peace of mind and emotional welfare.

This may also be part of our cultural identity, and must be respected and affirmed. All the above, together with the criteria of solidarity and human compassion, according to the leading principles of this policy.

(UNISDR, 2015)

Climate change adaptation

Climate change is upon us, and having agreed to try and avoid global temperatures rising another 2°C, the implementation mechanisms are now being tested. All governments will in some way be affected. Aside from localised positive benefits in some countries, climate change is expected to unchain global events such as rising sea levels and the partial flooding of cities around the world, the desertification and soil erosion of vast agricultural areas, while in others flooding and harsh yet uncertain weather will cover and destroy crops and pastures, putting countless farm animals in peril.

The challenge for governments is that the changing conditions are hard to measure over time frames that they are mandated but the events this change cause offer great challenges. Over time these significant changes in the living conditions for humans will surely demand large behavioural changes from us and from the way we raise our animals but at single points in time disasters may be more severe in their impact.

What follows with changes in water and fodder availability and sources, temperatures and changed ecosystems, pernicious insects, protozoa, fungi, bacteria and viruses will no doubt change their behaviour and present new challenges to the health and survival of animals everywhere. We can see therefore that another dynamic element has been added to the challenge of a government planning for disasters and the impact that climate change will have on agricultural systems and the use of land will greatly impact upon that.

Adaptation to climate change is, thus, the new frontier. Breeds of animals may need to be more resistant to harsher temperatures, lack of water or conversely wet environments, and more resilient to new pathogen behaviours. It will be up to animal science specialists to breed, select and raise these new types of domestic animals. Types of adaptive mechanisms for raising cattle will be better use of water resources, the development of more shaded pastures, crops and pastures resistant to higher salinity levels, and better pasture rotations. In the case of pigs, poultry and zoo animals, building away from flood zones, better air circulation, air-cooling, water baths and ventilation designs and mechanisms for their enclosures will be the norm.

Pet animals, which usually live in or next to human settlings, may be exposed to new pathogen threats appearing in ecosystems, temperatures and altitudes previously clear of them. For wild animals little is known about their ability to adapt effectively either in location or through movement at the rates of warming predicted and with geographical barriers of human settlements and land-use. In all

FIGURE 8.1 Rescue teams transport stranded companion animals through the streets of New Orleans in 2005. This and the recent images from Houston after Hurricane Harvey maybe offer us a snapshot of what our cities may face as our climate changes

Source: Chad Sisneros for the HSUS.

cases and with all species, small controlled actions may have significant positive impact in the adaptation odds, comfort and welfare of animals, and it is up to animal science specialists to coach animal owners into a planned adaptation to the new conditions (Figure 8.1).

Other mechanisms for animal risk transfer

Animal insurance and reinsurance schemes

Mexico (and other countries) has insurance schemes based locally and internationally in the form of insurance and reinsurance schemes meant to protect livestock assets in cases of disasters. In the case of Mexico, the Federal Government established the 'Integrated Program for Rural Development' with a response element in cases of hydro meteorological and geological phenomena, CADENA. Its objective is to support all animal producers, with an accent on those with low incomes and without a public or private catastrophic insurance for their livestock. As these new concepts help strengthen the financial instruments for risk transfer and ultimately risk management, Mexico considers them as prevention actions to face disasters. Current animal insurance schemes seldom go in favour of protecting the lives of the animals at risk nor their welfare, as their real aim here is to protect the net value of the asset, and the mechanism of choice is to replace a significant portion of that value once lost, be it by reimbursing a predetermined amount for the animals, or by restocking.

The effectiveness of any risk reduction for animals requires fluid and constant communication and in-depth coordination between animal owners, academia, civil defence, the private sector, all levels of governance and police departments – all valuable during the risk reduction plan process. Also, many sizeable risk reduction measures may need capital investment, personnel or equipment beyond the grasp of individuals or small communities. The common objective for all will be to protect the livelihoods of the animal owners by reducing animal risk and the risk for those involved with them, their food security and the psychological well-being of pet owners.

Further reading

Livestock Emergency Guidelines and Standards. (2015). *Livestock Emergency Guidelines and Standards*. 2nd edn. Rugby, UK: Rugby Practical Action.

Losada, H., Cortés, J., Vieyra, J., Arias, L. and Bennett, R. (1998). *Suburban livestock rearing by smallholders in the backyards of Xochimilco in the south-east of Mexico City as an important strategy for sustainable urban agriculture*. City Farmer (Canada's Office of Urban Agriculture). Available at: www.cityfarmer.org/livestock.html

McClean, D. (2017). *Sendai Indicators 'only the beginning'*. United Nations Office for Disaster Risk Reduction. Available at: www.unisdr.org/archive/51777

More Market and Opinion Research. (2014). *Estudio N° Preparación para Desastres en México. Estudio N° 738-2-3665*. México DF: World Animal Protection.

World Animal Protection. (2012). *Situación de la Población Canina en la Gran Área Metropolitana*. Heredia: IDESPO.

World Animal Protection. (2016). *UN Recognises the Importance of Animal Protection in Disaster Risk Reduction*. Available at: www.worldanimalprotection.org/news/un-recognises-importance-animal-protection-disaster-risk-reduction

References

Comisión Nacional de Prevención de Riesgos y Atención de Emergencias (CNE). (2015). 'Política Nacional de Gestión del Riesgo 2016–2030'. San José, CR: CNE.

Leyes y Decretos. (2006, 11 de enero). *Ley Nacional de Emergencias y Prevención del Riesgo N° 8488*. San José, CR: La Gaceta N° 8.

Leyes y Decretos. (2006, 16 de mayo). *Ley General del Servicio Nacional de Salud Animal N° 8495*. San José, CR: La Gaceta N°150.

Leyes y Decretos. (2013, 7 de agosto). *Decreto N° 37828-MAG Reglamento al Título IV Dispositivo de Emergencias de la Ley General del Servicio Nacional de Salud Animal N° 8495 y Procesos de Contratación*. San José, CR: La Gaceta N° 150.

United Nations Office for Disaster Risk Reduction (UNISDR) (2009). *Terminology on Disaster Risk Reduction*. Geneva, Switzerland: UNISDR.

United Nations Office for Disaster Risk Reduction (UNISDR) (2015). *Sendai Framework for Disaster Risk Reduction 2015–2030*. Available at: www.wcdrr.org/uploads/Sendai FrameworkforDisasterRiskReduction2015-2030.pdf

9

THE ROLE OF ANIMAL PROFESSIONALS IN DISASTERS

In the last chapter we completed the exploration of the measures that can be undertaken within the disaster cycle for animals. We have already established the intrinsic relationship between the survival of animals and the presence of well informed, trained and equipped people. This chapter focuses on the key professions and roles involved in disaster management for animals and covers the key themes to consider for professions. It is important to consider this is an emerging field and as such few standards or guidelines exist and the beginnings of a veterinary discipline is occurring.

Working within this field, either full time or when exposed via presence in an event, requires a range of skills some of which overlap and many of which may not be the normal experience of the practitioner. The chapter is not exhaustive and indeed doesn't imply in any way that one has to be a professional to make a difference, rather focusing on those professions that will normally be involved and offering advice on how they can work both as an individual and together to ensure the most effective approach for animals.

On the other hand, these professionals should be and will be the quintessential reference points for animal owners to learn about animal risk management and about how to protect their own animals.

What does emerge very clearly is a hierarchy of responsibility for different groups within which professions may find themselves:

1 Animal owners should (and always will) be the first line of defence in the prevention and protection of animals from the effects of disasters. Their actions to prepare, and how they respond during and after a disaster has the most direct impact on the outcomes for animals in terms of their welfare.

2 Animal professionals should become the champions of preparedness and risk reduction, advising animal owners on how to improve resilience and then

having the skills and equipment to respond to the need during and after a disaster event. They will remain the vital interface between the needs of animals and people and the coordination or action for both.

3   Governments need to ensure the correct policy and legislation is in place to secure animals and provide the right resources to reduce risk, prepare owners and then respond to needs post disaster; but to do so they need well-trained professionals.

4   Where capacity gaps remain, the NGO sector should be present to respond. Where their work touches upon animal issues or where animals are critically important to people, they should be adequately briefed and resourced to consider these interrelations and develop aid interventions that meaningfully address the animal need.

Championing animal risk management

All stakeholders involved in the protection of animals from disaster risk have a role to play in championing and developing the concept of animal preparedness at all levels (family, private industry, municipal, state, national). In order to achieve this they need to consider *knowledge of risk*, by studying, identifying, recognising and measuring animal risk by its components of exposure, hazards and relative preparedness; and *management of risk*, by systematically reducing animal risk and improving their resiliency, and by repeating the process in an endless cycle.

This work may have several phases and approaches:

- Families need advice on preparing their pets to improve their resilience, and then their chances to evacuate and survive eventual stress, secondary infections, etc.
- Animal farms need risk assessments and risk reduction plans for the continuity of their businesses and the resiliency of their animals.
- The farm animal industry (farmers associations, federations) need disaster risk reduction policies and plans to pool their resources together for times such as when evacuation or emergency fodder is needed.
- Municipalities need to prepare risk maps of their territories, designate evacuation routes for livestock, pool transport lists, emergency corrals and emergency food sources for them, should the need arise.
- Financial entities (banks, insurance companies) need to include animal risk assessments in their MOs to invest in the farm animal industry.
- States and national governments need to document baselines for all species of animal, including numbers, health, production levels, and their relative worth in family and local economies. They can then develop the argumentation to push for the inclusion of animals in public policies in disaster risk management. Governments then need to create databases, develop or prepare risk atlases and develop emergency procedure protocols and policies to coordinate with Civil Defence and other relief and rescue groups during emergencies.

Channels of influence

Animal owners

Animal owners are the first line of defence for animal welfare in emergencies. Every action they take prior to, during and post disaster has an impact, on the well-being of the animals in their charge. As previously discussed, human behaviour and thus humanitarian action has a direct impact on animals which in turn can have a secondary impact upon humans again. Therefore, these individuals have a critical role to play and are important to influence. The problem posed with moving these individuals in the right direction is that there are many of them in any country. The task of directly engaging with millions of individuals is one simply not practical for any government or agency. Most citizens, however, respond in some manner or another to other measures they are exposed to or informed about. Examples of this include:

Legislation and policy

These measures have a strong influence on animal owners. In their most direct form they can force owners to take action by passing statutes (i.e. mandatory microchipping or licencing) through the threat of a fine or imprisonment; but laws can also protect rights of animals and people and many countries have animal welfare acts that affect the lives of animals positively. Policy and legislation, however, can also create a provision of resources that can impact upon the animal owner. This is certainly the case in Costa Rica, where legal provision for an emergency fund for animals and the operationalisation of that through the training of government vets will have a direct positive influence on the individual owner (World Animal Protection, 2016). They will be better advised and will have access to aid for their animals when they need it.

Economics

Hugely underplayed in this area, the power of economics should be better harnessed to exact change. This book has shown the economic benefit of considering animals within the disaster cycle because people depend upon them. Leveraging market forces for change is something that could be done more effectively and not simply for the animal industry but for pet owners as well. A greater awareness of the negative or positive consequences for the owner of not preparing (or preparing accordingly) would to some degree drive action in the individual. When we consider the impact that changes to insurance policy stipulations could have in changing farmers approaches or indeed those of pet owners in developed countries, the impacts could be huge. Farm animal owners consider the face value of their animals and their relative difficulty to replace those animals if lost, to assign a priority level to their well-being during disasters.

Communication

Individuals can be influenced at an individual level via effective communication that can in turn lead to behaviour change. Utilising messaging that activates the emotional connection with the animal, the risk of loss or the benefit of action can all have powerful impacts on human behaviour. In Costa Rica in 2012–14, a public engagement campaign run by the Animal Health Department and World Animal Protection based on a popular character dog called 'Thunder' in the case of domestic pets was aired to promote the four pillars of good pet ownership within family emergency plans. Evaluation studies showed at the lowest level of expectation of the researchers a 16 per cent change in human behaviour based on the consumption of a short TV commercial.

Active stakeholders

Communities

It is important to note that communities have a role to play in the equation. While they may be made up of individuals, they have a greater carrying capacity and resilience for changes in risk. Equally, in many parts of the world, pet ownership is pooled and becomes an important consideration. As an example, community owned dogs (as opposed to the Western approach of individually owned) pose different considerations. We must also consider farming collectives, increasingly in vogue again for smallholders in developing countries.

Often these collectives have far greater levels of resilience through working together and solidarity. This collective resilience can even be harnessed in disaster preparation in communities with no strong collective structure. Emergency/ temporary collectives are highly effective ways of reducing shocks and exposure for groups of farmers. In reality, communities are also one of the lowest levels of organisation in a country, only second to the family unit. Depending on their level of organisation, they can create their own risk maps and evacuation plans, provide shelter to other people's animals, loan resources, and mobilise people and assets into action. Finding effective ways to engage communities to undertake these critically important preparedness and risk reduction measures has to be a worthwhile challenge, to be addressed when designing better national resilience for animal populations.

Industry

Dependent on location, animals will always be found in commercial production as well as smallholder farming. Industry has an important role to play in building resilience in animal populations. Often this sector can be seen purely as those responsible for the husbandry of animals directly but this viewpoint should be broadened to a range of supportive functions from private vet practices and livestock markets to abattoirs and entertainment facilities. Many of the more 'production' focused businesses will have a greater interest in being proactive in building resilience as breaks in production can have a dramatic impact on business continuity.

Building resilience should see an accent on cooperation and strategic planning, protecting livelihoods and basic services such as water and ways of access, plus seeking larger partners at the national level; under clear protocols understood by all members of that society, these should be the missions of communities and municipal governments. The farm animal industry is most interested in preserving business continuity, and depending on the size and relative vulnerability of the producers that sometimes form the foundation of dairy industries, for example, this can provide for a sizeable challenge. Pooling resources and showing solidarity during times of need should be a natural starting point. Sometimes businesses will see the point of this but in situations where damage has not been uniform, other 'competitors' may choose to use the advantage and have a preference for operating alone. While protecting individual businesses may be an imperative, the powerful incentives of avoiding the worsening of conditions such as the dropping of market price, or general epidemiology, to the point when outbreaks may endanger entire animal populations, can drive more collaborative behaviour. Appropriate actions for the industry here would include preparing inventories of emergency fodder sources, veterinary medicines, transport trucks, alternative pastures, shelter in case of emergency evacuation, control of the market, and protocols on how to integrate and execute all the above elements.

On an individual farm level, risk assessment and management should be key. Measures should be considered in the following areas:

- History
  Has the location been affected in past history by natural hazards?
- Location
  Is the facility in a resilient or an exposed location when planning the build, i.e. not on a floodplain?
- The movement of animals out of harm in an emergency
  How will they be moved, where will they go, how will they be fed and their health maintained?
- Resilient structures
  Are roofs tied down, is the building flood proof or can handle floods etc.?
- Back-up systems and resilient utilities
  Can you assure water supply, are there back-up generators?
- Back-up downstream options
  Are there alternative options for the next stage in the supply chain to ensure continuity?
- Emergency organisation
  Are there local producers who can work together to plan and pool resources?
  Are there enough emergency funds available in case of need?
- Correct mitigation
  Is insurance adequate, does the facility and the operation meet the policy parameters?

- Adequate coordination
  Is the facility tied in with emergency functions so that aid is effective?
- Adequate monitoring
  Are the facilities adequately monitoring emerging risks and have early warning mechanisms?

Government

Without a doubt government has the greatest role to play in redefining national resilience for animals. Their functions exist and are present in the earliest stages of a disaster strike and, assuming that they are operational post-event, are there on the scene quicker than any external agency. They have access to resources at a scale other agencies don't and have the ability to move them and augment them with functions such as the military. They also generally have human focused emergency planning and resourcing already in place to some degree. They therefore have a priority to reform in terms of integrating animal welfare into their existing emergency planning and disaster response. Before we consider what a government can do in a disaster, they too need to prepare. Government buildings need to be resilient to disaster strike, responders need to be employed and mobile enough to deal with the conditions, and they need to have supplies capable of dealing both with the situation and any potential breakdown in the supply chain.

Critically, animal departments (such as the ministry of agriculture) need to foster this culture of preparedness, traditionally often missing. Because of the traditional view of the role of animal welfare in a disaster, these agencies normally have not been included in any culture of disaster planning or response and are equipped only for the day to day operation of their functions. Many may not even be aware that an emergency role may be required of them until a disaster strikes and they experience the different conditions. As an example, vets may not be able to access remote communities because their available vehicles don't take account of downed trees or bridges, they may not have a stock of veterinary supplies for the event, they may not have the equipment to survive in the field overnight or they may not be trained in emergency operations and the necessary inter-agency coordination. Consistently, government functions have little knowledge of how to engage with the humanitarian community when they inevitably turn up, leading to an inefficient and parallel response. This can often lead to disproportionate or ineffective response as seen in the 2015 Nepalese earthquake, where the government attempted to manage the NGO community through a slow method of registration that led to a long-term paralysis of the aid effort.

National governments need to enforce pre-existing policies to protect animals from disasters, control and protect the markets from racketeering and provide the necessary emergency elements to help animal owners save their livelihoods by saving their animals. These would include providing emergency fodder, veterinary care, evacuation shelter should the need arise. Governments also need to 'spread the word' on animal resiliency through the various communications channels available to them, to foster national preparedness and champion a culture of prevention both for farm animal owners and for pet owners. Governments should seal the 'construction' of sound and solid legal frameworks and policies that clearly include animals in their national emergency response and preparedness policies, with cross-cutting objectives to improve efficiency, sources of funding for all identified and agreed tasks, plus the building of the capacity to do so. Finally, Civil Defence, representing tactically the national government during a disaster, needs to foster the full integration of animal health and welfare, and animal production institutions and professionals to their emergency response structures and plans. This task may include facilitating training to develop capacity to carry out these plans.

Veterinary practice

Emergency veterinary treatment is fundamentally different from regular diagnoses and treatments at clinic or farm level. It has more in common with war medicine or humanitarian medical interventions in its nature and principles than it does with day to day veterinary practice. Vets will be dealing with fractious and scared, unknown animals, environments and terrains. They will be under stress themselves, possibly at risk of personal harm (from the environment or from people) and will be required to work in teams, taking on roles, managing people and involving themselves in inter-agency coordination or liaison. Many of the skills required for vets to respond adequately to disasters are not taught in veterinary schools and aren't experienced in veterinary practice. In addition, the type of personality required for the role isn't naturally commonplace in the vet community. This means that vets need to focus, plan and train where they may come into contact with emergencies. They need to develop dual roles and mindsets for how they may operate and see themselves as part of a bigger machine in an emergency where they may often be subordinate to other functions in terms of influence over their situation.

Most of the work required in disasters involving animals relates to larger volume work than the average vet may be used to but will include emergency feeding, providing water, shelter, evacuating. This means as much as veterinary skills are critical, so are the skills of logistics and animal management. Under normal conditions of veterinary practice, prioritisation of cases is limited but in an emergency environment triage of casualties and of actions even in the recovery period is a reality with limited resources and access to infrastructure being a reality where the number of patients outweighs the capacity of the vet.

The word triage is adapted from the French word *triagement* meaning 'to sort'. It was a technique used in the Napoleonic wars to identify the most urgent human cases for treatment and balance this priority against the likelihood of survival. Where limited resources or time is in play, its use is critical to success as a veterinarian. For animals, as with humans, a vet should assign the priority order of handling and treatment of surviving victims by deciding on the severity of their condition and the prognosis of their wounds or illnesses. Patients likely to fare or survive with little or no treatment are tagged green; patients likely to die with or without treatment are tagged black, and those that, with immediate care, would survive may be tagged red or yellow, depending on the priority of need and the scoring system. From this point, other systems and uses of this concept have sprung and in the case of farm animals and especially horses and cattle, the sorting criteria often need to include the ability to walk on their own, especially when large numbers of animals and difficult terrain are involved. This veterinary version of triage is called Triage Start.

When evacuating is not possible, animals are often sacrificed or left to die, given the logistical difficulties and the considerable resources needed to care for them in the middle of a disaster. In these emergency scenarios, however, the priority is to save the biggest number of farm animals, whereas when it's about pet animals, the degree of the pet–owner bond may determine the amount of rescue effort. Bearing in mind limited resources, veterinary professionals will be unlikely to be aiming for optimum levels of welfare; rather they will be seeking to ensure that the maximum number of animals survive until normal conditions return. This can create challenges for vets when they may have spent their career seeking optimum conditions for their patients in the delivery of treatment. As an example, the amount of food and water an animal needs to survive is significantly different from that it needs to maintain a good body condition score. This can

FIGURE 9.1 A vet rescues an orphaned goat from a damaged building caused by the Kathmandu Earthquake of 2015

Source: Jodi Hilton for the HSI.

pose challenges for vets where the decision may be about how many animals can be saved as opposed to how many animals can we make healthy (Figure 9.1). The moral dilemma of whether to save a larger number of animals, allowing them to hang on until conditions return to normal versus allowing a larger number to die to allow for the well-being of a few is tough for field vets to consider in emergencies.

What is not recommended is to allow scores of animals to die, as a prerequisite for restocking schemes, and for reasons that may be ethical, financial and immunological. It is certainly recommended that vets agree an approach with leaders of operations in advance of actual field operations, as the decision on resource allocation and target numbers and types of intervention may not be within the decision-making remit of the vet which can be very frustrating.

Emergency responders

Emergency responders are invariably the first professionals on scene in an emergency. Their involvement with individual animals and dealing with the issues animals can cause is both clear and documented. Currently most emergency service personnel have either limited or no animal handling experience and invariably zero experience of managing large animal numbers in incidents. While in the developed world there is an increased move to skilling firefighters to undertake paramedic duties and firefighters are often called to technical animal rescues of individuals, they are not vets and thus other than providing basic care and rescue, their role in the welfare of animals is largely limited. Other emergency service personnel may only have first aid training and very limited experience of animal management or handling. This should be borne in mind with regard to the roles that may be allocated in an animal operation or in discussions relating to inter-agency coordination. The exception to this is with dog handling specialists. These may be police dogs or urban search and rescue dogs. Handlers have a much enhanced level of knowledge of welfare and may even be trained in animal first aid.

As previous chapters have shown, however, animal presence can have an impact on responder's ability to undertake their tasking. In some countries emergency responders are not able to enter buildings if certain unrestrained animals are inside (i.e. dogs). A range of issues can be caused for responders when they find themselves in evacuation or rescue situations in disasters; owners can refuse to leave their homes because of a lack of provision for animals at a point of shelter or because they aren't allowed to take their animals with them, a lack of provision of adequate transport conditions can mean animals (and people) are left behind and in some cases people leave animals behind creating dangers to search teams or leading to owners returning to risk prone areas to care for their animals.

When we consider livestock, the significant financial capital tied up in animals can drive behaviour that is counter-intuitive to safe practice. Again, refusals to evacuate can occur but equally people in displacement situations have been known to return to dangerous locations as the provision of animals at a point of shelter isn't provided. Certainly some preparation at the local level would be useful to advise people on matters of how to prepare and equip their pets for evacuation (vet vaccination certificates up to date, the provision of ID tags and transport boxes being simple solutions) but any response by emergency services needs to consider the animal element if present in order to ensure an adequate response to people. Certainly within a developed world setting (but also in other countries) emergency responders will find themselves involved in inter-agency coordination that over time is likely to include representation of the animal issue at differing levels; thus, developing knowledge of the management issues, the problems and the response required within emergency services ought to be a priority of authorities.

Emergency planning

Emergency planners have a critical role prior to disasters in considering the impact of potential animal issues and developing capacity to cope with this. Adequate population and risk mapping is important to this as is understanding the stakeholders involved at all levels and how they will react and respond to disaster events. Dependent on location, emergency planners may find themselves considering the temporary sheltering of pet animals in an urban disaster and working with NGOs and private shelters to discuss and plan capacity, or seeking out larger temporary options. In a rural setting they may find themselves involved with mass movement of cattle and the rather intense logistics required, from loading to transit, to relocation, health, separation, feeding, watering and veterinary care. During times of emergency, the planner still has a role, often representing municipalities or government in inter-agency coordination and response and as such needs to be well versed in animal management issues, well prepared in terms of planned actions and able to manage the multiple stakeholders involved.

Academia

Academia has different levels of influence depending on the national situation. On the whole they are an important stakeholder to consider. Academia trains new vets, it researches new techniques and can provide a surge of support for emergencies (as seen in the 2001 UK FMD outbreak) (Figure 9.2). The part of science that concerns itself with zoonosis and human–animal health interactions is usually well developed in most countries and normally has a level of monitoring and response to these issues. The focus will be on epidemiology and veterinary epidemiology relating to the incidence, causes, patterns, distribution, effects and possible control alternatives of diseases and other factors relating to the health of both human and animal populations. As epidemiology is a cornerstone of public health, it helps shape policy decisions, while the veterinary side of it may also be used to research animal welfare and animal productivity issues.

Academic development on the issue of animals in disasters has been somewhat slower and certainly is currently given less attention and funding. Academia does, however, have an important role in driving this discipline forward in three key areas:

1 **Skills development** – Veterinarians going through their training need to be better equipped where they may encounter disasters. Currently very few universities offer any disaster management training within their curriculum. An understanding of how to form, manage and lead teams, operate safely in challenging environments, how to engage with inter-agency issues and the differences in disaster care for animals compared to day to day requirements are critical. Equally important is an understanding of how to ensure their own veterinary practices or roles are resilient to the shock of disaster to ensure continuity of services. As important as this, however, is fostering an under-standing and culture of risk reduction and preparedness in new vets. It is the individual vet while working in practice, or the government vet working on outreach who are most effective in working with individuals or companies to advise on resilience. Understanding risk mapping, planning evacuation routes, needs for animals under stress, as well as resilience options for structures and practices and advising individual farm or pet owners on the correct actions to be taken should all be part of the day to day role of vets in their practice.

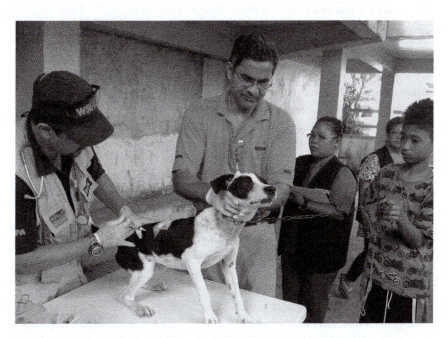

FIGURE 9.2 Veterinary training for university staff occurring concurrently with disaster response in the Philippines in 2013

Source: James Sawyer for WAP.

2. **Research and development of new approaches** – Academia has long been involved with advancing both theory and practice, and veterinary and disaster management academics are no exception. There is a clear need for the development of a disaster discipline for animals that addresses the different conditions and develops different veterinary interventions or management techniques to deal with the situations communities face.
3. **Surge support** – Some universities have developed a disaster training curriculum for their vets and develop them to form surge support in domestic disasters. Bearing in mind the natural decay of expertise as students graduate and the limitations of their stage of training to their capability in the field, this remains a useful resource in localised emergencies. The provision offers pride and status to universities and offers a way for students to experience wholly different types of field work, while authorities have an extra resource to draw upon as needs arise. Often these teams demonstrate a need to government that is then resourced directly rather than from academic funds.

Humanitarian NGOs

Humanitarian NGOs arrive en masse in disasters and emergencies to deliver much needed aid to people where government capacity has been exceeded. The sums of money disseminated can be huge; in the Haiti earthquake of 2010 alone, over $9bn was provided in aid funding (Ramachandran and Walz, 2012). Humanitarian workers come across animals, the problems they face and the issues a lack of attention to them causes on a daily basis. Animals remain the cornerstone of many people's lives in the most disaster prone parts of the world and yet humanitarian aid is yet to fully realise the benefit of their mission of including them in their programming. This picture is however not geographically homogeneous. Aid interventions in sub-Saharan Africa have long considered livestock, especially in pastoralist areas, but often at the wrong stage of the disaster cycle or with the wrong interventions. Elsewhere, funding for animal related work is limited compared to the disproportionate role they play in economies and people's lives. Smallholder farmers and pastoralists absorb 22 per cent of the economic costs of natural disasters, yet receive less than 5 per cent of post disaster aid. Livestock mortality costs the sector USD 11bn annually (FAO 2015). Studies show the benefit of early stage intervention for livestock in disasters and the benefit it creates in terms of helping people recover, although there are many issues of sheltering people without provision for their pets.

The benefit to aid effectiveness of working with animal related projects post disaster are starting to emerge but needs assessments rarely take into account the interplay between people and animals. The development of the Livestock and Emergency Guidelines and Standards (LEGS, 2015) has undoubtedly helped but they are a tool that can only be effectively adopted with a change to mindsets. Key to this is developing an understanding that the only way to get the best from animal related programming is to approach it from this angle. Restocking programmes often fail because they don't take account of animal welfare and epidemiology vis-à-vis local conditions, and a lack of understanding of animal needs hampers any attempts to address the problem adequately. There are, however, positive developments, the most important of which is the global attention the IFRC have placed on training their national society staff in best practices in animal management, which focuses not just on the emergency phase but also the development programming work in the country. With the continued scrutiny on aid dollars spent and the desire to look at cost effectiveness in humanitarian delivery, developing work that benefits animals will come to the fore as a strong option. Currently, capacity remains low and a strong need exists for animal protection to be seen as a cross-cutting issue in humanitarian aid.

Development sector

The development sector of the NGO community works on a multidisciplinary approach to human development. Its spending is in the billions, of which a large proportion is bilateral aid from national governments. Its reach is global and its work with some of the world's poorest comes into contact with animals. Increasing acknowledged is the concept that many, if not all, of the vulnerabilities that communities have to the effects of an event that would cause a disaster are development issues. For example, a community that suffers a cholera outbreak in the aftermath of a disaster could trace the reason back to poor sanitation provision. It stands logically therefore that animal vulnerabilities will also be the same in nature and thus it is a priority that the development community focuses on animal welfare as a cross-cutting issue in its programming. Additionally, often development personnel are the first NGO agency staff available in the aftermath of the disaster and their roles are repurposed accordingly; thus, understanding the principles and benefits of good animal welfare to their work is critical. Again the IFRC leads the way with the integration of best practice in this area into its national society training structure.

International organisations

International organisations such as UN institutions currently play a key role in all stages of the disaster cycle. They have an important facilitative role to play in undertaking approved sector-wide disaster assessments, coordinating humanitarian and development effort, requesting funds from government and disseminating these monies to field implementation bodies from the NGO sector, or setting standards for governments to follow as best practice. Their role is often pivotal in a disaster and often decisions they make define the sector-wide response. When their roles are overlaid on the animal protection issue we see a patchwork of approaches, some positive and some negative. On the whole international organisations are yet to fully realise the benefit of animal welfare to their work and in some cases their lack of engagement leads to significant loss of animal life. Recent developments include:

Sendai Framework for Disaster Risk Reduction

This framework, agreed in 2015 and currently in its implementation phase recognised the need for 'protection of livelihoods and productive assets, including livestock, working animals, tools and seeds'. This framework will run for the next 15 years and the first major piece of global policy to recognise the need to protect animals from the effects of disaster. Its impact on governments and humanitarian and development sectors is yet to be realised but it will be influential (World Animal Protection, 2016).

OIE guidelines for animals in disasters

Published in early 2016, these standards by the body responsible for animal health globally provide guidance to Chief Veterinary Officers on how to integrate animal welfare into their national plans for animals. While stopping short of standards, it is another significant push toward governments adopting responsibility for animal protection (World Organisation for Animal Health, 2016).

UN cluster system

The UN cluster system was developed after the Indian Ocean Tsunami of 2004 as a way of reducing duplication of effort and improving coordination. A global cluster meets several times a year while clusters are activated in a country in emergency situations. While several clusters have relevance for animals, the real focus should be on the Food Security Cluster which is co-chaired by the UN Food and Agriculture Organisation and the World Food Programme. This cluster has specific responsibility for the coordination of matter relating to agriculture, is responsible for disaster assessments for the UN CERF and flash appeal funding processes and the dissemination of government donations to the responsible areas. The cluster system remains a work in progress, struggles to integrate with government level liaison and often undertakes the wrong assessments for animals, but its existence is certainly progress on the issue (Humanitarian Response, n.d.).

CASE STUDY: TRAINING FOR PROFESSIONALS – PREPVET

In 2007, World Animal Protection piloted a training tool for the first time called Veterinary Emergency Response Units (VERU), designed as an emergency response tool for animals to help their owners and support the role of rescue teams and agriculture officials in the rapid assessment process. This involved a teaching curriculum, field training and equipping of teams for operation in the field. The teams were activated many times and were active in national disasters in Costa Rica and worked with emergency response agencies on a range of deployments and operations. The concept spread to other countries, being successfully realised and developed in Mexico, Nicaragua, Colombia, India, Thailand, Myanmar and Kenya. In Kenya in 2014, the University of Nairobi integrated the VERU teaching modules permanently into their teaching curriculum for veterinarians.

Primarily, however, the ultimate responsibility for animal health, welfare and the production of farm and working animals threatened by disasters lies with the owners first. Second, the responsibility falls to government through the use of laws, control of animal health, veterinary public health regarding foodstuffs such as milk, cheese, meat, animal by-products and the spread of zoonosis. As the sovereignty of the State may not be transferred to third parties outside the Government, the overall responsibility for the health, welfare and veterinary health of animal populations and production in each country should always be under the control of official veterinary departments, or the Chief Veterinary Office, especially for animals under risk of disasters. While convenient in specific locations, training veterinary students to help during emergency response operations could only have a temporary, supporting function, and could not be a durable, sustainable solution, especially when these students could only function within a team format and once graduated would move on to their respective jobs and thus the capacity would be lost. With the increase in the intensity and number of disastrous weather-related events, training in emergency response for animals alone cannot be enough anymore, especially in the light of the new approaches championed by UNISDR.

Thus, a new global priority was set on developing preparedness and risk reduction for sustainable progress including the protection of livelihoods that depend on farm and draft animals. PrepVet was the product of this priority which would meet the changing conditions in approach, society and climate around the world, requiring not only veterinary emergency response, but also rapid assessments of the urgent needs of surviving animals in disaster needs. More importantly, the needs to develop veterinarians competent in the diagnostics of the underlying causes of disasters for animals, as well as on more direct vulnerabilities to hazards of natural origin also had to play a key role. When animal production and welfare was considered, a clear need for leaders with the knowledge of disaster risk reduction and climate change adaptation to ultimately tackle and transform the causes that reduce preparedness, resiliency and adaptive capacity, and to champion the avoidance of hazards and vulnerabilities triggering animal emergencies was highlighted.

In 2015, the PrepVet online course piloted in Mexico, and composed by 11 rapid learning modules set on a Moodle online platform. Upon completion, attendants will be able to protect animals by analysing and reducing their vulnerabilities and eventually their risk, all by teaching animal owners what to do in different disastrous situations, such as floods, hurricanes, earthquakes, volcano eruptions, droughts and wild fires. The new skills will allow professionals to help tens of thousands of animals at a time in their communities, by assisting their public or private employers in the design, development and implementation of emergency management strategies and public policies. This will ensure protection of millions of animals and thousands of farmers and their families from the uncertainty of the weather and other hazards in the future. PrepVet will integrate concepts of wildlife protection and public policy in future editions and will extend its reach to academia, governments and private industry over time.

Eleven rapid learning modules originally comprised the course:

1 Terminology and concepts of disaster risk management
2 Vulnerabilities of animals at risk of disasters
3 Management and pet care in the context of disasters
4 Climate change adaptation for animals
5 Security, biosecurity and zoonosis during emergencies
6 Incident Command System (ICS)
7 Veterinary triage process
8 Animal evacuation
9 Livestock Emergency Guidelines and Standards (LEGS)
10 Role of the veterinarian and academia in DRR
11 Concepts of animal welfare in the context of science, ethics and law.

It is expected that graduated students with this training will be able to obtain and generate new income for themselves through private enterprise. The professional will be equally skilled to assist companion animal owners to be prepared and prevent the loss of or injury to their pets, by recognising the importance of animals and their emotional significance for the owners' psychological well-being and their families.

Further reading

Humanitarian Response (n.d.). *What is the Cluster Approach?* Available at: www.human itarianresponse.info/en/about-clusters/what-is-the-cluster-approach

Livestock Emergency Guidelines and Standards (LEGS). (2015). *Livestock Emergency Guidelines and Standards*, 2nd edn. Rugby, UK: Rugby Practical Action.

World Organisation for Animal Health. (2016). *Guidelines on Disaster Management and Risk Reduction in Relation to Animal Health and Welfare and Veterinary Public Health*. Available at: www.oie.int/fileadmin/Home/eng/Animal_Welfare/docs/pdf/Others/Disasterman agement-ANG.pdf

References

Food and Agriculture Organisation of the United Nations. (2015). *The Impact of Natural Hazards and Disasters on Agriculture and Food Security and Nutrition: A call to action to build resilient livelihoods.* Available at: www.fao.org/3/a-i4434e.pdf

Humanitarian Response (n.d.). *What is the Cluster Approach?* Available at: www.human itarianresponse.info/en/about-clusters/what-is-the-cluster-approach

Livestock Emergency Guidelines and Standards (LEGS). (2015). *Livestock Emergency Guidelines and Standards*, 2nd edn. Rugby, UK: Rugby Practical Action Publishing.

Ramachandran, V. and Walz, J. (2012). *Haiti: Where Has All the Money Gone?* Centre for Global Development, Washington, DC. Available at: www.cgdev.org/files/1426185_ file_Ramachandran_Walz_haiti_FINAL.pdf

World Animal Protection Latinoamérica. (2016). *Towards the Resilience and Prosperity of the Livestock Sector.* [Online Video]. 8 March 2016. Available at: www.youtube.com/watch? v=-lfB5iz4sPE&feature=youtu.uk.

World Animal Protection. (2016). *UN Recognises the Importance of Animal Protection in Disaster Risk Reduction.* Available at: www.worldanimalprotection.org/news/un-recognises-importance-animal-protection-disaster-risk-reduction

World Organisation for Animal Health. (2016). *Guidelines on Disaster Management and Risk Reduction in Relation to Animal Health and Welfare and Veterinary Public Health.* Available at: www.oie.int/fileadmin/Home/eng/Animal_Welfare/docs/pdf/Others/Disastermana gement-ANG.pdf

10

THE FUTURE FOR ANIMAL WELFARE IN DISASTERS

Without a focus on the systemic issues relating to disasters, little change can be predicted. We have seen significant effort put on effective early warning, preparedness and risk reduction systems, reducing human mortality. This has however been against a backdrop of rising loss to assets. Within the classification of 'assets' sits the animal issue. Losses grow year on year and events, at least to the lay person, seem increasingly devastating. Placing animals within the assets category is both advantageous and disadvantageous when looking to address animal mortality and well-being in a disaster. Being classed (as is the case in the Sendai Framework) as a 'productive asset' is advantageous as at least animals find an important place; yet we know that this classification doesn't encompass companion animals in any way.

Urban Disaster Risk is quickly becoming the next frontier, both because scores of humans around the world are gathering in urban centres for good or bad, and because pets tend to have a different, enhanced status and significance in big cities and also pose extra considerations from the general population's safety and health points of view. The role and place of companion animals will be in this worldwide discussion whether we want it or not, not as productive assets, but as elements of the family or the individual's micro cosmos, essential to their peace of mind and well-being, and a significant factor to quantify and include when planning to protect and move numbers of folk out of harm's way.

Equally, we also know that animals are sentient beings and as such classifying them in the same manner as inanimate items (buildings, infrastructure, vehicles) in the asset category is problematic. If we are to maintain life, assure well-being and maintain productivity, then we need to consider the intrinsic link these aims have with the nature of how an animal feels or what it needs to achieve this. Thus the major long-term solution we should seek for animals is a much broader understanding of animals within this sphere and how to meet their needs to achieve the goals of any disaster effort. This change in mindset and the change in approaches that follow will take time and in the interim measures are required to demonstrate this but also to offer solutions to decision makers that provide the best outcomes for both people and animals. The crux of the matter and the challenge is, however, whether or not animal owners, handlers and officials responsible for their welfare and production will choose to become champions of preparedness in their field and commit to real sustainable solutions rather than settling for short-term profits.

This chapter comments upon the changes required at national and international level to ensure the well-being of animals in disaster. It will then focus on concepts through the use of case studies focused on specific disaster events that offer possible solutions for sustainable futures at the local level. Here, we will analyse the array of possible scenarios in the future, the role of animal professionals and the way to provide for adaptive solutions and influence them for a better world for animals.

Future possibilities

If we were to envisage change in the future, we would have to consider the conditions for it and those who would be responsible for it. Until governments ensure the integration of animal welfare into existing disaster response and risk reduction functions, much of the responsibility for the well-being of animals will continue to fall wholly to owners. For domestic and wild animals, the future is, for all practical purposes, mostly dependant on the human beings who own them or that are in control of them. Disaster risk right now and for the immediate future for animals is in other words, in the hands of their owners and caretakers. This 'human' control is and will be influenced by a series of internal and external factors such as perceptions and attitudes towards risk of disasters, preparedness, the same risk of disaster on humans, economic capacity, external supporting systems at community and governance levels, and specific market forces.

We could, however, hypothesise that the ideal future for animals faced with disaster would be a world in which all animal owners and all governments have developed disaster risk reduction and built preparedness and resilience to include their farm, working, pet and wild animals (Figure 10.1). This would be a world where people and their governments are prepared and are ready to respond to animal need. In this world, all animals have good lives with good animal welfare and do not suffer or die as victims of disasters. If concerted efforts are started towards animal preparedness and resilience, the scenario will translate into less impact of disasters on animals, fewer losses in animal production and animal lives and better odds for their welfare, all with the beneficial impact on their owners' livelihoods.

Disasters, however, are the worst way possible of exposing failures and weaknesses in the development models of any given society or any given unit such as a national government, a state, a municipality, a community, a family or even a person. Until such time as poverty, ignorance about preparedness, prevention and the effect of climate change are addressed, people and their animals will have to face the odds of enhanced levels of exposure and vulnerability. The challenges are therefore big, but not impossible to tackle.

FIGURE 10.1 A community risk mapping exercise on the island of Panay in the Philippines in 2014. An example of mapping human and animal vulnerabilities together and showing how development NGOs and municipalities could work together to reduce risk

Source: James Sawyer for WAP.

Moving toward more sustainable governance

As discussed previously, governments are the only entities with the resources and the ability to put in place large sustainable solutions to help animal owners address the issue of animal vulnerability to disasters. Governments have disaster response and (often) disaster risk reduction mechanisms in place for humans with varying levels of capacity. As we have seen, the animal element is intrinsically linked to these efforts and as such great benefits can come from integrating these. It is acknowledged that developing this capacity at a national level is no small task, nor does it take a short period of time. Governments are unlikely to undertake these commitments without persuasion. Currently the socio-economic arguments of real strength are not well known within decision makers, unless they experience problems during a disaster on home soil but we can point to encouraging progress in some countries who are leading the way on this issue. Perhaps one of the main problems with disaster risk reduction work is that the desired result is difficult to visualise, thus difficult to champion and 'sell' to others. These difficulties must be overcome with solid metadata, baselines and impact indicators of all kinds, not just face value price tags.

Best practice

In order to foresee the benefits of a more integrated and long-term solution to the issue we must explore emerging best practices of which thankfully some are now emerging:

Costa Rica

In 2014, a legal directive was passed by the Costa Rican government to resource effective emergency response for animals in disasters at the Animal Health Department (SENASA) level of the Ministry of Agriculture (MAG). This included legal frameworks, assigning a Veterinary Risk Management function, developing financial content, capacity building by training SENASA officials on LEGS, CSI and Disaster Management.

Soon after, the National Emergency Commission (CNE) issued its own policy including the protection of pet animals as a legal human right, and hired the first veterinary officer with experience in disaster response within its ranks, making it the first country in the continent to take such progressive view and position.

Significant research has been carried out on animal owners' attitudes and perceptions towards preparedness of their animals for disasters, and the country needs now to consolidate these changes, always under pressure from a host of other development priorities, while animal owners slowly take responsibility for the fate of their animals in the face of disasters. The country is now poised to act as a successful example for the rest of the Central American region, so vulnerable to the whims of the weather transformed into simultaneous droughts and tropical storms year after year.

India

In 2013 the Indian government issued a directive that animals should be included in emergency planning and disaster response at all levels of government, and put in place a programme of resourcing to build capacity to achieve this. The National Disaster Management Authority and other government ministries working with NGO guidance partnered over a three-year period to create the correct foundation for full national integration of the issue. In 2016 the Prime Minister of India released India's National Disaster Management Plan. Within this, animals have been integrated in every stage of the disaster management cycle, mandating all government departments to consider and plan for their involvement in disasters (Modi, 2016; National Disaster Management Authority, 2016). The progress toward a fully integrated system may take some time but India has fully recognised the challenge that animals cause in disasters and the significant benefits that integrating them into the disaster cycle will have for the nation. It is hoped that analysis of the benefits of this approach will encourage other states to take similar steps.

Other government progress

Aside from whole model solutions, many other governments have made smaller steps toward improvement on this issue. In Kenya, veterinary emergency response training has been enshrined in national curriculums, and student vet teams are being used in proactive vaccination drives and to augment government functions during localised emergencies. In Colombia animal welfare is now included in civil defence guidelines and in Mexico the government has started promoting animal preparedness in advance of disasters through posters, social networks and radio messaging. Currently, Mexico is preparing to release the first federal manual for the management and handling of animal risk in disasters. On the other side of the world, New Zealand now has civil defence guidelines for both companion animals and livestock and Australia has started to develop state level emergency plans that include animals.

Looking forward and taking action

With the publishing of the Sendai Framework for Disaster Risk Reduction including animal protection within and the completion of the OIE guidelines for animals in disasters, we can see this issue rising up the agenda. This combined with the case studies and metrics that will start to emerge from the 'whole model' solutions are likely to cause a significant shift in attitudes, policy, legislation and resourcing for this issue over the next ten years.

Challenges will exist, however. Large numbers of the most vulnerable animals are found in the developing world under the governance of countries with extremely limited resources. While the economic arguments are clear for action, the investment to undertake this shift may not be available. In the developed world the mindset of believing disasters only happen in the developing world may render both people and their animals dangerously vulnerable to unpleasant surprises. This makes the role of those groups and organisations who 'bear witness' very important, to remind all of us to be ever vigilant and on the lookout for new vulnerabilities. Whether it be the climate change agenda or disaster risk reduction, the issue of who pays is a pertinent and very real one. Responsibility must be allocated and the following groups have an important role to play:

Academia and animal professionals

In an emerging field, new disciplines and techniques are required, existing approaches need to be evaluated and improved and information needs to be shared. This is undoubtedly a role that academia is well suited to. Academic professionals from those in animal health through to emergency planning need to embrace this topic as an exciting new frontier and as a viable and productive new area to contribute to. Equally, in order to achieve this, these studies and bodies of work need funding, and money needs to be driven to these areas. Some may argue that the need drives the funding which drives the research but this is an overly simplistic view as often academia can be the body that awakens the subject and creates the need for the new discipline. The issue of animal welfare in a disaster hides in plain sight; it is obvious when it is explained to you but isn't readily apparent to everyone until then. Academia has an important role to play in opening this issue up and improving the visibility of its importance.

Academia is also the birthplace of the professional. Whether a vet, an emergency planner or a humanitarian, all depart academia in search of a career and yet it is at the point of learning where the most efficient point of influence sits for individual professionals. Embedded with the right knowledge, the community vet can advise his/her clients on risk reduction and preparedness for pets or livestock alike. Enthused about the subject the government worker can influence national practices or policy and be aware of the implications, and the emergency planner can ensure that animals are included in the right place. Academia therefore has a huge role to play in influencing the future landscape for animals (Figure 10.2). There should be the following areas of priority drawn:

1   All animal professionals have access to training that equips them for a crisis in their community or role.
2   All animal professionals should have access to training on how to advise animal owners on how to prepare for disaster and reduce their risk.
3   Emergency planners should be aware of the impact of animal welfare issues in disasters and understand how these can be mitigated and the inter-agency coordination required to:

- buy-in to risk management (ID, analysis, preparedness and RR plans) to
  –champion it for humans and their animals;
- champion baseline animal welfare in all its facets;
- promote preparedness plans at all levels, with accent on coordination
  mechanisms;
- promote sustainable, resilient, long-term solutions to reduce animal risk.

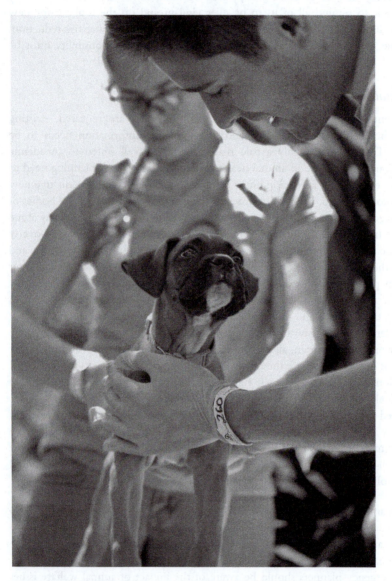

FIGURE 10.2 NGO staff and veterinary students train side by side in a drill in Costa Rica in 2015

Source: James Sawyer for WAP.

Animal owners

Animal owners will always be the first line of protection for animals, with the most control over the fate of individual animals. Often, however, owners have the motive to do something proactive but lack the awareness of what might be needed or haven't thought that animals may cause a problem for them or others in disasters. Research carried by the authors shows that animal owners see no distinction between their pets and their other family members and yet they often lack the knowledge to link this with needing to be prepared for disasters. Farm owners' livelihoods are fundamentally linked to the well-being of their animals and yet often they lack the means and the knowledge to prepare adequately for events they experience. Motivation to act does not seem to be a key barrier with animal owners. All when prompted will express a strong understanding of the need to prepare for their animals. It is the need to prompt, however, that is the issue; currently the need to think about this in disaster-prone areas is not yet intuitive. While the expression of the need to care for their animals is clear and often emergency plans exist for the human element (the family or farm), this doesn't yet translate to adequate preparedness for animals (Figure 10.3). In order to create awareness pet owners should:

FIGURE 10.3 A livestock owner in the Philippines with a newly constructed cyclone proof swine house

Source: James Sawyer.

- have a plan for themselves and their animals;
- be able to transport their animals safely away from harm if needed;
- in the event of an evacuation, ensure that there is adequate shelter (family and friends or in situ) for their animals;
- ensure that their animals are identifiable and can be reunited with their owner;
- ensure that their animals are healthy and vaccinated prior to a disaster and documentation is safely put away.

The NGO and IGO sectors

These sectors have an important role to play in the future plight of animals affected by disasters. The NGO sector comes into contact with a large number of the most vulnerable people and their animals on an annual basis but currently lacks the skills and the knowledge to deal with situations they come across or to leverage the benefit of animal welfare to better achieve their goals. There is currently very little funding available for welfare based work within the humanitarian and development sectors and what is available is heavily focused on sub-Saharan African issues. We do see restocking of animals in the aftermath of disasters, which demonstrates a clear understanding by these sectors of the importance of animals, but currently little is done to focus on the well-being of these animals meaning that their benefit is reduced (and their suffering is unnecessary). Looking forward, the development and humanitarian community need to recognise that:

- animal welfare offers the opportunity to reduce disaster vulnerability and economic shocks within communities if included as a cross-cutting issue in development programming;
- humanitarian programmes can benefit greatly from a stronger focus on supporting animals in the aftermath of disasters as a core component of sustainable recovery and protection of livelihoods;
- animal welfare improves aid effectiveness when included as a cross-cutting issue in programming;
- early stage intervention for animals in the aftermath of a disaster is a considerably more cost-effective method of securing economies and animal livelihoods than replacement through restocking programmes;
- only by including the welfare of animals as a key consideration of restocking programmes is the investment in the animals adequately returned.

The IGO sector is one that has an important influencing role on both governments and NGO sectors alike. Equally important is the amount of influence they can exert on flows of money to where it is needed. Critically, current disaster assessments by key UN agencies don't adequately include livestock measurements and this hinders the ability for the correct money to be accessed during disaster.

This in turn compounds the ability of the NGO sector to find funding for projects with a strong animal welfare component. In addition, the role of animals in people's lives and the need to reduce risk is significantly under-realised. This is changing and we expect to see some significant progress made in this area over the next 10 years. Certainly the development of guidelines on animal health in disasters published in 2016 by the OIE has made an important step in this sector in the right direction of travel. In order to realise the right conditions for animals the IGO sector needs to consider that:

- the financial sector/stakeholders are included in the planning of resilient development plans at country level;
- livestock assessors are included in any agricultural focus on disaster assessment;
- livestock assessments in disasters don't focus and report just on loss but also on surviving animal need;
- restocking isn't the only solution and that early stage intervention for surviving animals is considerably more cost effective;
- funds are sought to support surviving animals rather than waiting to restock;
- animal welfare is included as a cross cutting theme for proposals considered for funding;
- animal welfare is a consideration in urban disaster planning, with specific focus placed on evacuation of people and animals and subsequent sheltering;
- risk reduction for animal populations is developed as a discipline with adequate investment to explore and research best practice.

The future – the end of the beginning?

In 50 years the approach to animal welfare in disasters has changed fundamentally. What was developed initially as an animal rescue approach for animal control and welfare agencies has blossomed in the last 15 years into something more significant and broadly relevant. It would have been hard to conceive even a decade ago that the protection of animals would be enshrined in UN frameworks relating to disasters, that humanitarian and development NGOs would be actively working on programmes that link the benefit of helping animals to that of humans, or that agencies actively would be providing support to over a million animals in disaster situations globally. This multifaceted growth has been helped greatly by the surge in interest in governments leading the way in protecting their animal populations, and as 'whole' models at national levels start to emerge we can expect to see wider uptake on the issue at national level.

It is the case, however, that much of this progress has been created through the efforts of a limited number of organisations and often by a limited number of individuals. While change at the scale of that of the Indian government or aid programmes numbering in the hundreds of thousands may be impressive, they are merely the start. The number of farm, companion and wild animals far outweighs the number of humans and the authors believe tens of millions in any average year (if there is such a thing as an 'average' disaster), at risk from disaster or suffering because of the consequences of these events, could be a conservative estimate. This poses a huge challenge for the international community and governments alike. Even at the scale of a single herd, the challenges remain for the animal owner concurrently. Much more action is clearly needed but so is a clearer understanding, research into appropriate aid and its benefits and much better inter-agency coordination. Much of this requires investment and thus an investment case.

This investment case comes from the momentum of the past and the increasing information being drawn from the present. Gradually, in urban centres planners are beginning to see the challenges that ignoring animal welfare in planning and emergency response will bring when disaster strikes. Increasingly, governments and international organisations are seeing that the loss of such a critical asset compounds their ability to recover communities from the worst effects of the disaster. Gradually, NGOs are understanding that the inclusion of animal welfare in their programmes is essential and academia is introducing these concepts into the teaching of veterinary students. Largely missing from the picture right now is the role of industry and commerce and this requires focus. The green shoots of a brighter future for animals are, however, there but the whole effort needs more grounding in research, better resourcing and far greater professionalism.

The next 50 years hold some considerable challenges for people and animals. Populations will grow, people will compete for land and move into more risk-prone areas as a consequence. Extreme weather events are likely to increase in intensity, frequency and duration and communities will already have started (they may have already) adapting to a changing global climate and the consequences of this locally. We can assume the focus on technological development and on the disaster topic will help further roll back the mortality of humans in disasters, but, while this should be celebrated, it should not shield us from the increasing loss of human assets and their long-term impacts.

All involved should of course think of the bigger picture in order to move this emerging discipline forward but we should not forget its impact locally because the welfare of animals, as it is with humans, is about the well-being of the individual. Virtually every day, farmers and animal owners around the world find themselves challenged in the aftermath of a disaster. Often silently and obediently their pets or livestock stand looking on in hunger, pain and discomfort, unable to express their needs. Often these individuals, already struggling to shelter and feed themselves, are unable to help their silent friends and they lose their emotional support and ability to recover from the event, often also losing their entire livelihood and well-being. The silent disaster continues, the inaudible need playing out as a sub-plot to the main human drama, storing further suffering for all as the days turn into weeks. It is clear we need to do more to be there for animals, because we are responsible for their welfare but also because without them ours is a poorer existence.

References

Modi, N. (2016). *PM releases National Disaster Plan.* Available at: www.narendramodi.in/pm-releases-national-disaster-management-plan-483880

National Disaster Management Authority. (2016). *National Disaster Management Plan.* Available at: http://ndma.gov.in/images/policyplan/dmplan/National%20Disaster%20Management%20Plan%20May%202016.pdf

INDEX